EMPTY VISION

Metaphor and Visionary Imagery in Mahāyāna Buddhism

The Curzon Critical Studies in Buddhism Series is a comprehensive study of the Buddhist tradition. The series explores this complex and extensive tradition from a variety of perspectives, using a range of different methodologies.

The Series is diverse in its focus, including historical studies, textual translations and commentaries, sociological investigations, bibliographic studies, and considerations of religious practice as an expression of Buddhism's integral religiosity. It also presents materials on modern intellectual historical studies, including the role of Buddhist thought and scholarship in a contemporary, critical context and in the light of current social issues. The series is expansive and imaginative in scope, spanning more than two and a half millennia of Buddhist history. It is receptive to all research works that inform and advance our knowledge and understanding of the Buddhist tradition.

THE REFLEXIVE NATURE OF AWARENESS
Paul Williams

BUDDHISM AND HUMAN RIGHTS
Edited by Damien Keown, Charles Prebish, Wayne Husted

ALTRUISM AND REALITY
Paul Williams

WOMEN IN THE FOOTSTEPS OF THE BUDDHA
Kathryn R. Blackstone

THE RESONANCE OF EMPTINESS
Gay Watson

IMAGING WISDOM
Jacob N. Kinnard

AMERICAN BUDDHISM
Edited by Duncan Ryuken Williams and Christopher Queen

PAIN AND ITS ENDING
Carol S. Anderson

THE SOUND OF LIBERATING TRUTH
Edited by Sallie B. King and Paul O. Ingram

BUDDHIST THEOLOGY
Edited by Roger R. Jackson and John J. Makransky

EMPTINESS APPRAISED
David F. Burton

THE GLORIOUS DEEDS OF PŪRṆA
Joel Tatelman

CONTEMPORARY BUDDHIST ETHICS
Edited by Damien Keown

INNOVATIVE BUDDHIST WOMEN
Edited by Karma Lekshe Tsomo

TEACHING BUDDHISM IN THE WEST
Edited by V.S. Hori, R.P. Hayes and J.M. Shields

EMPTY VISION
David L. McMahan

SELF, REALITY AND REASON IN TIBETAN PHILOSOPHY
Thupten Jinpa

EMPTY VISION

Metaphor and Visionary Imagery in Mahāyāna Buddhism

David L. McMahan

RoutledgeCurzon
Taylor & Francis Group

First Published in 2002
by RoutledgeCurzon
11 New Fetter Lane, London EC4P 4EE

Simultaneously published in the USA and Canada
by RoutledgeCurzon
29 West 35th Street, New York, NY 10001

RoutledgeCurzon is an imprint of the Taylor & Francis Group

Typeset in Sabon by LaserScript Ltd, Mitcham, Surrey
Printed and bound in Great Britain by
TJ International, Padstow, Cornwall

British Library Cataloguing in Publication Data
A catalogue record of this book is available from the British Library

Library of Congress Cataloguing in Publication Data
A catalogue record for this book has been requested

ISBN 0-7007-1489-8

Contents

Acknowledgements viii
Technical Note on Terms ix

Introduction 1

1 The Devaluation of Language and the Privileging of Perception 15

Language and Concepts in Early Buddhism 17
Abhidharma and Dharma Theory 23
Mahāyāna Views on Language and Concepts 25
Dialectical Patterns in the Perfection of Wisdom Literature 33
Dialectic, Paradox, and Discourse 39
The Paradoxical Dialectic and Buddhist History 41
Discursive Thinking and the Construction of the Lifeworld 43
Perception in Indian Buddhism and Indian Philosophy 47

2 Buddhist Visuality in History and Metaphor 55

Vision in Indo-European Language and History 56
Metaphors and Their Functions 62
Visual Metaphor in Buddhist Discourse 65
Related Metaphors for Knowledge and Awakening 71
The Meaning and Significance of Space in Buddhist Discourse 76
Conclusion 81

3 Orality, Writing, and Authority: Visionary Literature and the Struggle for Legitimacy in the Mahāyāna 83

Orality In Early Buddhism 87

Writing in the Early Mahāyāna 89

Writing and the Survival of the Mahāyāna 89

Sacred Text and Sacred Site 91

Writing and the Visual 95

The *Buddhavacana* and Strategies of Legitimation in the Mahāyāna 99

Visionary Literature and Grounds for Legitimacy 104

Conclusion 108

4 Realms of the Senses: Buddha Fields and Fields of Vision in the Gaṇḍavyūha Sūtra 111

Historical Context of the *Gaṇḍavyūha* 113

Visionary Literature and Thaumaturgy in India 114

Buddha-Fields and Images of Kingship 116

Elements of the Narrative 121

Vision and Doctrine 130

Dialectics of Words and Dialectics of Vision 133

Concretization of Metaphor 137

5 The Optics of Buddhist Meditation and Devotion 143

Vision and Visualization in Early and Non-Mahāyāna Meditation 144

Meditation and Mental Imagery 145

Vision and Devotion 147

Dharma, Buddha, Stūpa, and Saint 147

Recollection of the Buddha and Visualization Sūtras 149

Image Worship and Darśan 152

Asaṅga on the Buddha's Bodies 159

Tantric Visualization Practices 161

Stages of Tantric Sādhana 165

Maṇḍala and Sūtra Imagery 168

Embodiment and Resemblance 172

The Somaticization of Doctrine 174

Acknowledgements

I would like to express my gratitude to Gerald Larson, Ninian Smart, and William Powell for their valuable suggestions on this project, as well as Alan Wallace, William Paden, Kevin Trainor, Allan Grapard, Jeffrey Lidke, Marcy Braverman and Stephen Cooper for their helpful comments. I thank, as well, Gerald Larson, Ruth Katz, and Nandini Iyer for their guidance through the complexities of Sanskrit. Thanks are also in order to Mark Tatz for offering me his time in Tibetan language instruction and to Ninian Smart for studying Pāli with his tiny cadre of *upāsaka*s and *upāsikā*s. Finally, I thank Dwight and Mary McMahan, for their love and support, and Karen Sattler, who contributed little to this book, but so much to the rest of my life.

An earlier version of chapter 3 appeared as "Orality, Writing, and Authority in South Asian Buddhism: Visionary Literature and the Struggle for Legitimacy in the Mahāyāna" in *History of Religions*, Vol. 37, No. 3, 1998.

Technical Note on Terms

All parenthetical non-English words are in Sanskrit unless otherwise noted. Sanskrit, Pāli, and Tibetan terms have been italicized, except for those that occur frequently in the text (the first usage of these will be italicized) and those that have become commonly used in North America, such as karma and nirvāṇa. "Dharma," in the sense of Buddhist teachings, is capitalized and not italicized in order to distinguish it from other uses of the word, mainly to denote elements of existence or objects, which are rendered in lower case, i.e., "dharma." Names of cities or places still in existence are given in Romanized form without diacritical marks, for example, "Swayambunath."

Introduction

At the top of a hill overlooking modern-day Kathmandu, the horizon is punctuated by the tall spire of Swayambhunath, an ancient Buddhist *stūpa*. It and a similar stūpa, Bodhnath, are two of the most famous Buddhist monuments in the world. They draw many tourists and pilgrims, Hindu as well as Buddhist, who circumambulate them, spinning the prayer wheels which release to the winds the pent-up energy of mantras printed on their exteriors or rolled up within them. The specter of these large, white-domed stūpas is among the most famous images associated with the Himalayan regions of India, Nepal, and Tibet. Perhaps their most striking features are the sets of half-closed eyes painted on each of their four sides, representing the compassionate gaze of the Buddha looking out onto the world. Less obvious is what is not represented: beneath the eyes is ... nothing. No mouth, nose, chin, or ears; just disembodied eyes gazing out over the valley.

The eyes on the stūpas of Bodhnath and Swayambhunath are not the only oddly placed visual organs in the area. Just south of Kathmandu is the beautiful city of Patan, the artistic center of Nepal. In one neighborhood, the constant pinging of metal is heard all through the day – metal being fashioned into the wildly evocative sculptures of Tantric deities in copulation or with teeth bared and flames around their heads. Also at work are skillful thangka painters who precisely reproduce on large canvases another image seen frequently in this area: that of Avalokiteśvara, the bodhisattva of compassion who looks down beneficently upon the suffering of the world. In one common image, he has eleven heads, one thousand arms, and in the palm of each hand, an eye.

The meaning of the eye in Buddhism is multivalent. At the most basic level, the eye (*cakṣus*) is the organ of visual consciousness (*cakṣur-vijñāna*), which has form (*rūpa*) as its object. Vision, along with the other sense-capacities (*indriya*), are the conditions for the arising of various sensations, which in turn give rise to pleasurable, painful, or neutral feelings. The importance of the eye over against the other sense organs, however, begins with the rich web of symbolism surrounding it, for it is undoubtedly the most symbolically charged part of the body in Buddhist thought and practice. The various ways in which the eye and vision are embedded in philosophical, mythological, and praxiological discourse reveal much about the conceptual and cultural world of South Asian Buddhism. Throughout Buddhist literature knowledge and vision are paired, often in the standard phrase "the knowledge and vision (*jñāna-darśana*) of the Buddha." Being able to "see the Dharma" (in the sense of the Buddhist teachings) is synonymous with knowing truth, while "seeing the *dharma*s" (meaning here the constituent elements of existence) signifies the direct apprehension of the true nature of things. Various forms of higher knowledge are represented by different kinds of symbolic eyes: the divine eye (*divya-cakṣus*), the wisdom eye (*jñāna-cakṣus*), the Buddha eye (*Buddha-cakṣus*), and the Dharma eye (*Dharma-cakṣus*).[1] Two epithets of the Buddha also illustrate the association of vision with wisdom: Samantadarśin, "one having limitless vision," and Samantacakṣus, "one with the universal eye." The eyes of the Buddha are also an important symbol of his compassion for other beings: one episode in the legend of the Buddha's life relates that after his awakening, he looked down in compassion upon the world with his Buddha eye and was moved to teach the Dharma to others. Along with these various connotations of sight are often found light metaphors likening this apprehension to illumination and luminosity that dispels blindness or darkness.[2]

While much visual symbolism in Buddhism is associated with knowledge that penetrates through illusion and misconception, many texts also emphasize the constructive capacities of vision. The literary style of many Mahāyāna sūtras, contrary to that of the earlier Pāli corpus, uses a great deal of visionary material depicting fantastic apparitions and otherworldly scenes. Moreover, visualization practices have been a staple of Buddhist meditation from its inception. From early techniques of envisioning simple objects such as clay disks to the extraordinarily complex Tantric and Pure Land visualizations, the ability to maintain an image in the mind's eye has been highly valued, and many meditation manuals contain elaborate instructions for precisely constructing visualized images of various objects of concentration and devotion. A number of Buddhist texts also emphasize the benefits of seeing the body of a buddha, whether in ordinary, physical form or in the glorified, resplendent forms seen in visions or dreams. The selection of eyes, then, as the sole iconographic symbol on the stūpas of the Kathmandu valley is not arbitrary.

This study explores the roles of vision in certain phases of South Asian Mahāyāna Buddhism. I argue that seeing is the root metaphor for knowledge in certain Mahāyāna discourses, and further, that this visual metaphor is actualized in some of the most important features of the Mahāyāna, such as its visionary literature and visualization practices. Contemporary studies of metaphor – the most well-known of which is George Lakoff's and Mark Johnson's *Metaphors We Live By* – argue convincingly for the pervasiveness of metaphor and the degree to which the conceptual systems of a culture are fundamentally metaphorical. Further, the dominant metaphors of a culture are actualized in concrete social practice, literature, and material culture.[3] The Buddhist use of vision is an extraordinary example of this phenomenon. Visual metaphors inform not only Buddhist epistemology, but also its abundant visual practices, literature, and art by implicitly identifying the most important sensory locus of religiously significant meaning in the visual sense modality.

In addressing the roles of vision, however, it is also important to keep in mind the missing mouth and ears on the Nepalese stūpas. While it is unlikely that the omission of these parts of the body represents an explicit statement about their value, it does reflect a choice among the artists and architects to represent one particular sense faculty rather than others as the symbol of the Buddha's wisdom and compassion. In fact, the absence of mouth and ears on these structures is suggestive of the deep suspicion of words and language present in Buddhist literature from its earliest texts. Perhaps this suspicion is best summed up by the phrase often repeated in the Mahāyāna – a strikingly ironic one, considering the vast corpus of works purporting to contain the words of the Buddha:

> From the night when the Tathāgata [the Buddha] became fully awakened with unsurpassed, perfect illumination, until the night when he passed without remainder into final *nirvāṇa*, the Tathāgata did not utter or speak even a single syllable.[4]

The elevation of sight as a primary metaphor for knowledge and awakening in Buddhist discourses occurs against the background of the relative devaluation of language, voice, and sound. While the word of the Buddha has always been crucial to Buddhists of all kinds, and many texts praise the melodious sounds of buddhas' and bodhisattvas' voices or the supernal melodies of the pure lands, the general tendency of the philosophical literature has been toward suspicion of language and hearing. Hence the rather strange claim in a few Mahāyāna texts that the Buddha never actually condescended to use the medium of speech, but remained in a translinguistic state of concentration (*samādhi*) even while he appeared to be speaking.

The place where language and vision intersect in Indian Mahāyāna Buddhism is the arena of *world construction*, that is, the ways in which this tradition conceives of linguistic categories, sensory perception, and social convention as constituting a world of experience, or lifeworld. In Buddhist doctrine, language and conceptual thought construct this world, the categories within which thinking is limited, and the self-concepts within which awareness is imprisoned. The Mahāyāna philosophical schools looked askance at language – its limited capacities for expressing the truth of things, and its tendency to foster delusion – even while they admitted its necessity and practical utility. According to virtually all schools of South Asian Buddhism, language constructs a false sense of oneself and the things of the world and erects a labyrinth of artificial meanings within which consciousness becomes imprisoned, binding one to the repetitious cycle of birth and rebirth. The part language and conceptual thought plays in this process is spelled out fairly clearly in a number of texts, and the Mahāyāna understandings of the contribution of language and concepts to the constitution of this artificial lifeworld have been a staple of modern scholarship in Buddhist studies.

The role of vision in relation to language and world construction, however, is more nuanced and symbolic – it is also generally neglected by scholars.[5] Here we are not simply exploring a

Buddhist "philosophy of vision," although such theories will be relevant to a certain degree. What Buddhist texts *say* about vision in a technical sense is not as important to this inquiry as how they *use* visual metaphors and imagery, and what philosophical, praxiological, rhetorical, and social significance these uses had in Mahāyāna literature and practice. Visual and spatial symbolism provided a way for Buddhists to conceive of non-conceptual awareness that is free from the fabrications of the linguistically constituted world. While language obscured reality, vision, both in the sense of direct perception and in a metaphorical sense, was understood, under certain conditions, to provide an unmediated view of reality. How to evoke an awareness that is not mediated by language and concepts, as well as the philosophical problems this very notion suggests, are some of the key issues in Buddhist thought and practice among the elite monastic and literary traditions. Visual perception provided one of the most important metaphors for how this might be conceived. The modeling of awakened knowledge on the operations of the eye is an important factor in the construction of the epistemic paradigm of Mahāyāna Buddhism. The language of seeing provides a great deal of the metaphorical vocabulary of knowing in the Mahāyāna. Light, the Sun, fire, lamps, eye-diseases, sleeping and waking pervade Mahāyāna discourse on enlightenment or awakening (*bodhi*), the direct apprehension of reality.[6] Nor is this epistemic vocabulary confined to Buddhist traditions: visual models for knowledge abound in South Asian discourses on philosophy, meditation practice, and mythology.

Also at issue was what kind of mediation Mahāyānists regarded as best for evoking what was understood to be an unmediated vision of reality. This question involves a second use of vision characteristic of much Mahāyāna literature: the replacement of the ordinary linguistic-conceptual world with a perfected world envisioned in the imagination and described in great detail in a number of Mahāyāna sūtras. This literature and the visionary/ visualization practices that it recommended or influenced were crucial to the character of Buddhism, not only in India but also in Tibet, China, and Japan. The emphasis on, and celebration of, visionary experience formed a colorful complement to the often stark dialectics characteristic of texts that attempted to dissolve false conceptualizations. The role of visionary literature in Indian Buddhism, as well as its connection to the philosophical literature dealing with language, has been largely neglected by modern scholarship on Indian Buddhism. Yet these visionary aspects of Buddhism are as important as the philosophy, and attention to them is necessary in order to gain a fuller understanding of that philosophy and its ramifications for Buddhism more generally.

In addition to visionary literature, another important aspect of this visionary strain in Mahāyāna Buddhist traditions is the development of meditation and devotional practices in which the practitioner constructs in the imagination the object of devotion – a buddha, bodhisattva, or deity within a *maṇḍala*, or diagram representing a sacred realm. These practices must be understood in the context of the visually-based epistemological suppositions implicit in Buddhist philosophical discourses and of the visual and spatial metaphors present in both dialectical and visionary literature. The visualization practices common in the Mahāyāna, such as certain forms of "recollection of the Buddha," pure land visualizations, and Tantric visualization (*sādhana*s) translated into *praxis* the metaphorical underpinnings of earlier philosophical literature, rendering in concrete ritual actions the metaphor of knowing-as-seeing.

Another way in which vision is significant to the understanding of Buddhism in India is its relation to the problem of legitimation and authority in the Mahāyāna. Once the implicit tension between language and vision was in place, the Mahāyāna employed this opposition to argue for a more profound insight than that of the "Hīnayāna" and to establish the legitimacy of its scriptures on the basis of visionary experience.[7] The early Buddhist sūtras relied for their legitimacy on the claim that they were heard directly from the Buddha. The Mahāyāna sūtras also made this claim, but were met with considerable skepticism. In a variety of ways, visual symbolism and depictions of visionary episodes constituted part of the Mahāyāna's claims to authority and suppercession of the Hīnayāna. Visionary literature, then, not only presented the deepest spiritual inclinations of the Mahāyāna, it also formed an important aspect of its rhetoric of legitimacy.

Part of the broader significance of the exploration of language and vision, hearing and seeing, is that it allows us to examine the more general question of whether certain epistemologies, traditions, and cultural milieus are especially oriented toward particular sense modalities and what the ramifications of such orientations might be. Some scholars have insisted, for instance, that ancient

Greek thought and culture were *ocularcentric*; that is, that they tended to privilege vision in their orientation to knowledge and value. In contrast, Hebraic culture placed more emphasis on hearing, the word, and the voice.[8] Some have also argued that modern Western culture is the epitome of ocularcentrism, such that its socio-cultural milieu is constituted by a "hegemony of the visual." Certain languages also seem to privilege metaphors involving specific senses, suggesting underlying assumptions about the connections between knowledge and particular sense capacities. Putting the matter simplistically for the time being, it might make more sense either to see the truth, hear the truth, or feel the truth, depending on the cultural context. Links between sight and knowledge are pervasive in Indo-European languages, while other languages lack this linkage.[9] Close attention to metaphors, therefore, particularly those related to the senses, is important in attempting to clarify the epistemic presuppositions operative in any system of knowledge. The significance attributed to each sense modality and the ways in which it relates to knowledge and religious practice contribute to establishing the criteria for what counts as valid knowledge, what is valuable in experience, and what one should pay attention to in order to achieve the *telos* of a particular religious system.

The predominance of vision and the role of images in certain Western traditions has emerged of late as an important issue in cultural studies and philosophy, as well as religious studies. Martin Jay and David Levin, for example, have written extensively on the long history of ocularcentrism in Western philosophy, literature, and practice.[10] Visual models of knowledge, in their estimation, have in some cases had a dangerously limiting effect on the thought and practices of the West. They highlight the distancing and objectifying tendencies of vision, its preference for static representation over temporal process, its constituting of a representational model of knowledge, and its elevation of the object of vision over the spoken word. Late modern theorists have roundly criticized the representational model of knowledge, rooted in the idea of the correspondence of images in the mind to objective reality, which has dominated Western epistemology since Plato. The alleged hegemony of vision has been implicated in the failure of Western epistemology, the dominance of media images in modern life, disengaged spectatorship, sexism, racism, and a host of other crimes of the eye. Still other scholars suggest that the theories of vision emphasizing the viewer's distance and disengagement with regard to the visible world do not adequately account for all possible modes of vision, especially certain forms of religious vision that require engagement and intentional activity on the part of the viewer.[11]

Despite the variance in opinion on the functions and dangers of vision and visual models of knowledge, one constant is that the discussion so far has been exclusively Eurocentric. Since Mahāyāna Buddhism demonstrates modes of vision exemplifying the distancing and objectifying tendencies of sight as well as its engaged and interactive potencies, not to mention some unique uses not present in Western traditions, its introduction into this discussion should be thought-provoking and may open up possibilities for a more cross-cultural exploration of the roles of vision and the senses in philosophy and religious practice. Some of the aspects of Buddhism that we will examine are themselves not immune to critiques leveled at Western thinkers. Yet Buddhist visual concepts and practices also offer alternative models of ocular engagement that are quite provocative in light of recent critiques, suggesting different ways of conceptualizing the problem of ocularcentrism. We should not assume that Buddhism will fulfill fantasies of the East coming to the rescue of a spiritually deprived Western myopia, nor that Asian ways of vision can be homologized to European-based ways, and thus understood simply as further instances of ocularcentrism fraught with the same problems and contradictions. We can hope, however, to expand the discussion on the matter by introducing a fascinating array of material from the Buddhist world, material that may challenge scholars to rethink the parameters of this issue.

The emphasis on seeing in Buddhism is part of a wider set of Indian cultural tendencies in which the visual is elevated and privileged. In South Asian religious and intellectual traditions, the sense capacities that are most commonly associated with knowledge and religious experience are those of seeing and hearing. Certainly, tactile sensation is also found as a metaphor for knowledge and is significant in yogic practices, ethics, and monastic discipline, as well as sexual practices; texts also exist that mention the sweet smells associated with divinities. However, the significance attributed to vision and audition has been the most important in shaping the cultural and religious milieu of South Asian traditions. By the beginning of the common era, with the emergence of writing and the flourishing of visual arts, the image was beginning to displace the word – that which was held most sacred in Vedic culture – as the doorway to wisdom and religious knowledge. In this context, both Hindu and Buddhist traditions produced predominately ocularcentric epistemic systems that relied heavily on visual metaphors, practices, and literary genres. My selection of Mahāyāna Buddhist texts to investigate this phenomenon should not be construed as suggesting that this was an exclusively Buddhist phenomenon. Around the end of the pre-common era, India was captured by an explosion of the visual that included a flourishing of visionary literature, visual art, and vision-based epistemologies encompassing non-Buddhist traditions as well. The Buddhist metaphors, images, and practices discussed here constitute just a few examples of a much wider cultural phenomenon. Nevertheless, the way that these function in Buddhist literature are often unique to the specific concerns of Buddhists in India, and particularly to the arising of the Mahāyāna. And in that is their historical importance. The investigation of these ocular aspects of the Mahāyāna will lead us to considerations of the intersections between oral and written culture, the struggles between orthodox and unorthodox interpretations of the Buddha's teachings, conceptual and doctrinal changes accompanying shifts from oral to visual modalities, and more broadly, the predispositions that may be inherent in different sensory modalities and how they effect the production of knowledge and socio-religious practice.

The Mahāyāna in India was actually a plurality of traditions, many of which are likely lost to history, having no surviving written records and only ambiguous archeological data. It might, therefore, be overly ambitious to make sweeping claims about the general character of Mahāyāna Buddhism based on the evidence available. Moreover, this is primarily a textual study, and, as Gregory Schopen and others have pointed out, only an elite few ancient Indians read or wrote the often abstruse Buddhist texts that are our primary historical data. Any textual study, then, must be aware of its limitations and recognize that its conclusions may be valid only for a small segment of the Buddhist population. Nevertheless, the textual resources are rich and do tell us things about religion as it was lived beyond these narrow bounds. Since I am working toward some general conclusions regarding the character of these textual traditions in India, I must find a path between two untenable extremes with regard to choice of materials. One approach would be to draw randomly from all available Mahāyāna texts and archeological evidence, a project that could suffer from overgeneralization and decontextualization, as well as lack of coherence. Another would be to confine the inquiry to a single text or geographic region, an approach that runs the risk of being parochial and irrelevant to the larger context of Buddhism and Indian culture. Instead, I will look at a selection of particular texts, thematic issues, and practices as case studies illustrating how recurring visual motifs are played out in philosophy, religious practice, myth, and rhetoric. I begin with doctrinal materials, then move to visionary literature, and finally to materials concerning religious practice.

The source materials for this investigation are a selection of Mahāyāna texts, primarily the Perfection of Wisdom (*Prajñāpāramitā*) literature and the *Gaṇḍavyūha Sūtra*, with some attention as well to various meditation manuals and Tantric texts describing visualization practices. Since I am concerned with the construction of an epistemic system and its repercussions, I begin in chapter 1 with what are probably the earliest and most foundational doctrinal texts of the Mahāyāna, the *Aṣṭasāhasrikā Prajñāpāramitā* and the *Ratnaguṇasaṃcayagāthā Prajñāpāramitā*, dating from between the last century before the common era to the first few centuries of the common era.[12] Yet, what particularly interests me in these texts is not primarily the doctrines themselves, which have been studied extensively in a number of valuable works, but certain rhetorical features. First, these texts carry out a sustained critique of words and concepts alongside abundant use of visual metaphors for knowledge and wisdom. This carries certain epistemological implications that become clear in the Buddhist discussion of valid means of knowing (*pramāṇas*) and its emphasis on perception, especially visual perception. The second rhetorical feature important in these texts is a unique paradoxical discursive structure prevalent in the Perfection of Wisdom literature. This structure, which is essentially a linguistic pattern of assertion, denial, and reassertion, constitutes a specific way in which the texts play with language in order to circumvent the problems that their doctrines claim are inherent in language. In other words, this form of paradox is a way of using language to overcome the putative limitations of language itself. What is significant here is that this pattern not only structures a great deal of subsequent Buddhist writing, but also structures certain instances of visionary literature and visualization practice in the later Mahāyāna, its basic form being transposed from the verbal to visual. The pattern, then, serves as a kind of Mahāyāna leitmotif applied in a wide variety of contexts. This discursive pattern and a general history of the devaluation of language in general in Buddhist philosophical literature are the subjects of the first chapter.

Chapter 2 explores some historical and theoretical issues related to the role of vision as a metaphor for knowledge in Mahāyāna discourses. First, I locate this use of visual metaphor in the history of Indo-European languages and cultures, noting other cultures that have quite different conceptual-linguistic orientations to knowledge. Then, after a discussion of contemporary theories of metaphor, I address the ways that different sensory modalities, particularly vision and hearing, structure and process information, and how this might be significant to an understanding of Buddhist literature. Finally, I examine a number of uses of visual and spatial metaphor, showing how the Mahāyāna concept of knowledge and awakening was modeled primarily on the operations of the visual sense modality.

In the third chapter, I shift from a focus on knowledge-as-vision, as explicated primarily in the Perfection of Wisdom literature and related materials, to the roles of the "visionary" in Mahāyāna discourse and practice. Here I inquire into the emergence of lavish visual imagery in certain Mahāyāna sūtras, especially the *Gaṇḍavyūha Sūtra*, a circa. second-century South Asian Mahāyāna text later incorporated into the massive *Avataṃsaka Sūtra*. In contradistinction to much of the more philosophically-oriented literature of the Mahāyāna, this work makes explicit the extensive use of imaginative imagery, constructing elaborate visionary worlds rife with Buddhist symbolism. In this chapter I interpret one particular instance of this imagery as a use of the tension between language and vision for rhetorical purposes in the efforts of the Mahāyāna to legitimate its novel and heterodox sūtras. I discuss, as well, the importance of orality in the orthodox Buddhist traditions and the significance of writing to the survival, propagation, and character of the Mahāyāna in India. The rhetoric of the *Gaṇḍavyūha* suggests that it utilized this dialectical tension between seeing and hearing by asserting the superiority of the visionary bodhisattva over the "hearers" (*śrāvaka*s), orthodox monks who maintained a tradition of oral transmission of canonical Buddhist scriptures. This indicates two different ways of establishing scriptural authority and legitimacy. The orthodox monastic Buddhist *saṅgha*, or community, relied on orality for the legitimation of its authority; that is, on memorized and recited sūtras said to have originated with the Buddha's own voice. The Mahāyāna, by contrast, relied on writing and visionary discourse to establish its authority and legitimacy.

Chapter 4 continues the study of the *Gaṇḍavyūha Sūtra* as a repository of complex Buddhist imagery and symbolism. First I trace some of the imagery of this text to the reputed abilities of thaumaturges to conjure images and to Indian notions of divine kingship and buddhas or bodhisattvas as rulers in pure lands. Then I analyze how in this text many of the visual and spatial metaphors introduced in chapter 2 are concretized and actualized – in essence, transposed – into the visual realm, creating a fantastic mythical space in which the Buddhist principles and values elucidated in earlier literature are rendered in visual symbolism. The *Gaṇḍavyūha* becomes an imagistic reiteration of the metaphors, doctrinal themes, and paradoxical dialectic patterns set out discursively in the Perfection of Wisdom. This chapter addresses, additionally, concept change and formation and the generativity of metaphor and image. Specifically, the concretization of ideas in visual form creates images that then become the basis of further conceptual elaboration, yielding different doctrines when reconstituted back into the theoretical realm. The transposition of discursive doctrine into visual imagery, therefore, produced semantic shifts in key concepts; shifts that served as the basis for entirely new interpretations of traditional Buddhist ideas and practices.

Chapter 5 examines a further transposition of ideas and imagery into symbols and rituals by exploring the historical development of visualization in Buddhist meditation and devotional practices. These practices have roots in early meditation exercises designed to work with mental imagery, as well as in devotional cults dedicated to the Buddha Śākyamuni and a number of Buddhist saints and mythical figures. Beginning with relic cults and developing into icon veneration and complex visualization practices designed to evoke the presence of a buddha or bodhisattva, such deity visualizations arose in part out of attempts to address the fact of the Buddha Śākyamuni's absence. Visualization was thought to bring forth the actual living presence of a buddha, suggesting important links between seeing and being. The evocation of a deity not only enabled the practitioner to see the deity, but also to participate in his or her vision and see the world the way the deity sees it. This chapter also addresses perhaps the most elaborate visualization rituals in the Buddhist traditions, those of Tantric Buddhism. It suggests an interpretation of these practices as ritual re-creations of the settings of the visionary sūtras in which the Buddha Śākyamuni delivers his discourses – settings in which the devotee has direct access to a buddha's own visual/visionary space. Moreover, the attempt to encode doctrine in somatic images in the bodies of the deities, whether rendered in the visual imagination or stone and wood, further emphasizes the precedence of the visual and symbolic over the verbal.

In the concluding chapter I introduce the possibility that the exploration of these traditions, texts, and practices of Mahāyāna Buddhism might be significant to contemporary discussions of ocularcentrism. Here I address some contemporary critiques of ocularcentric thinking in the West, especially those claiming that such thinking involves a distancing, disengaged, and objectifying mode of knowing that is implicated in some of the shortcomings of Western Enlightenment philosophy. I then ask whether these critiques can be applied to the visually-oriented aspects of Buddhism that I have discussed, or if, on the other hand, Buddhist uses of vision might offer ways of redressing these alleged shortcomings. I suggest that Indian Mahāyāna Buddhist thought, as well as other trends in classical Indian reflection, developed a family of unique vision-oriented concepts of knowledge and truth, in some ways similar to Western ocularcentric models, but in many ways quite different. They are similar in the sense that they both emphasize dispassionate observation, synchronic appropriation, and passive contemplation. Much Buddhist thought, however, explicitly strove to avoid the hypostatization of phenomena, making rationalistic objectification less of a factor in Buddhist thought that in modern Western philosophical traditions. Furthermore, some Buddhist visualization practices utilized vision in ways quite different from that of Western ocularcentric practice, making the objects of vision less amenable to being appropriated as the static object of a reductive gaze – Tantric visualizations, for example, in which the practitioner merges with the visualized image. Thus, while these strains of Mahāyāna Buddhism do constitute forms of ocularcentric discourse and practice, they do not necessarily imply all of the cultural and philosophical ramifications of ocularcentrism in the West. Some Buddhist uses of vision do correspond to, and thus are subject to, the same critiques of ocularcentrism in the Europe and America; however, some forms of Buddhist visuality provide interesting alternatives to Western uses of vision.

CHAPTER ONE

The Devaluation of Language and the Privileging of Perception

> Subhūti said: It is wonderful, Blessed One, that the Tathāgata, the arhat possessed of perfect enlightenment, has shown the nature of all dharmas, yet this nature of all dharmas cannot be spoken of. If I understand the meaning of the Blessed One's teaching, then all dharmas are inexpressible.
>
> The Blessed One said: So it is, Subhūti, so it is. And why is this? Because the emptiness of all dharmas cannot be expressed in words.[1]

Among the many stories and theories that arose in Buddhist literature on the nature of the Buddha – his immanence or transcendence, the meaning and significance of his words, his experience of life in the world as an enlightened being – there exist a number suggesting that he existed in a strange, almost unimaginable state while here in the Sahajiya realm. Donald Lopez nicely illustrates this view in his summation of a passage in the *Tathāgatācintyaguhyanirdeśasūtra* (*Sūtra Explaining the Inconceivable Secrets of the Tathāgata*) whose dramatic speaker is the bodhisattva Vajrapāṇi:

> The ... sūtra compares the word of the Buddha to the sound of a wind chime, which without being played by anyone, produces music when stirred by the wind. So does the word of the Buddha arise when stirred by the minds of sentient beings, although he has not thought: it is due to his fulfillment of the bodhisattva deeds in the past that his speech conforms to the diverse needs of all sentient beings. ... Vajrapāṇi explains that the Buddha was actually silent throughout his life, remaining constantly absorbed in samādhi, without

> speech, without thought, without breath. The Tathāgata is thus like a prism; perfect, impassive, with no color of its own, it is touched by the faith, the development, the questions, the intentions of sentient beings and refracts the teaching that is appropriate to each.[2]

The Buddha's teachings are presented in this Mahāyāna text as arising spontaneously in response to the needs of individuals, rather than as a result of the ordinary activities of judgment, reflection, and evaluation. The words of the Buddha (*buddhavacana*), to which Buddhist scholastics gave considerable attention in their efforts to determine which teachings were authentic, actually were mirages. The Buddha, the text asserts, was silent throughout his tenure in this world, in a state of refined concentration even while he appeared to be conversing and teaching. The assertion that the Buddha never uttered a word is echoed in a number of Mahāyāna texts, and it is indeed an odd claim for a man to whom perhaps more words are attributed than any other historical figure. Here we glimpse a theme present in a number of Mahāyāna texts: the idea that it would in some way compromise the Buddha's pure awakened state to engage in the common cognitive-linguistic activities of ordinary beings. Though virtually all the sūtras present him as speaking, this one and others say that this speech was just an illusion, an expedient means by which the Buddha teaches people.

This passage brings to the fore the Buddhist suspicion of language through the image of an awakened being absorbed in silent meditative concentration. This is a figure that draws on a common theme in yogic traditions in India – that of the silent sage or *pure witness* who has transcended the ordinary, confused cognitive functioning of the mind and perceives, without mediation, the world as it is. The image of a witness, in turn, evokes some of the images already mentioned in the Buddhist metaphors for awakening – the Buddha or bodhisattva seated on a terrace looking out at the world as it is, the stūpas with disembodied eyes and no mouth, the Buddha having limitless vision. Throughout Buddhist literature, there exists an implicit tension between this supernal "seeing" and the entanglement of the mind in words and concepts. The *Samyutta Nikāya* declares: "Name soils everything; beyond name nothing is known. Everything is subject to this one thing: name,"[3] while repeatedly praising the "knowledge and vision of the Buddha." A Perfection of Wisdom texts declares: "Insofar as all names proclaimed in the world are left behind, [all] arisen things are transcended," while such a transcendence is often referred to as a "vision of the dharma."[4] From the sūtras to later Tantric texts, this tension displays itself: "What is the use of so much talk? The knower of Truth by means of true yoga will see everything there is to perceive."[5] To further clarify the abundant use of visual metaphor in the Buddhist vocabulary of awakening, it is helpful to explore just what this metaphor is contrasted with; i.e., what does this "seeing" that is supreme knowing see beyond? The answer in many Mahāyāna Buddhist texts, especially the Perfection of Wisdom literature, is: awakening sees beyond language, concepts and conventions.

This tension between language, concepts, conventions, and cognition, on the one hand, and perception and visual symbolism, on the other, has a long history in Buddhist thought. Reviewing some examples of the devaluation of language and concepts, as well as the implicit and explicit roles of perception and vision, will help contextualize the predominance of visual metaphor in Buddhist discourse. We begin with a brief overview of early Buddhist views on the roles and limitations of language, then explore some of the specific ways in which the Mahāyāna approached the problem of language and concepts, and finally examine how the primacy of perception and the symbolic privileging of vision is present in Mahāyāna philosophical reflection.[6]

Language and Concepts in Early Buddhism

The early Buddhist understanding of the role of language stood in sharp contrast to the prevalent view of Brahmanical India. The dominant conception of language during the time of the Buddha, that put forth by the Vedas, was that words had an intrinsic relation to the things they signified.[7] The *Pūrva Mīmāṃsā* school claims that there is an inherent relationship between words and their objects. In the *Bṛhadāraṇyaka Upaniṣad*, each thing has a specific name (*nāma*), form (*rūpa*), and function (*karma*) intrinsically its own that was given it by Brahmā when he created the world. Even if named things pass away, this eternally established name remains.[8] Furthermore, the words of Vedas themselves were understood to be revealed and absolutely authoritative.

Early Buddhist reflection on language, however, allowed a much smaller scope to the power of words, and this represented a significant break with what we know of the dominant ideas on language in ancient South Asia. Even though early Buddhist culture relied to a great extent on the spoken word of the sūtra, its philosophical reflection sought to limit the functions of words and language. Although early Buddhists certainly considered their sūtras true in that they were records of the wisdom of the Awakened One, they did not consider these scriptures to be divine and eternal revelations as the Brahmanical tradition considered the Vedas. Early Buddhist literature categorically rejects authoritative words (*śabda*, usually construed in this context to mean the authority of the Vedas, but also of any religious teacher or tradition) as a valid means of knowledge (*pramāṇa*), and recommended that even the words of the Buddha must be verified by the hearer him- or herself.

Further, the early Buddhist valuation of the function of language in human life was largely negative, insofar as words and concepts were considered to be among the primary factors in creating fundamental ignorance (*avidyā*; Pāli, *avijjā*) of the nature of things. This ignorance was understood to be the cause of baseless craving (*taṇhā*), which in turn leads to suffering and frustration (*duḥkha*). Moreover, Buddhist doctrine at this stage had no explicit notions of the inherent power of language to effect things in the world aside from its conventional efficacy in human life. It was critical of the idea, for instance, that the actual spoken words of the Vedas had inherent power and ritual efficacy whether they were cognitively understood or not. According to the Brahmanical tradition, the Vedic sacrifice depended not on conceptual understanding of ritual utterances but on the intrinsic power of the vocalized sounds themselves. For early Buddhists, language had no such function but was only efficacious insofar as it was understood cognitively. Thus the limitations placed on language in Buddhist reflection are homologous with the limitations of conceptual thinking. Indeed, the terminology translatable as "language" and "concepts" often seems to blur the distinction between the two.[9]

Buddhist ideas of language and conceptual thought are in part based on the fundamental Buddhist doctrines of impermanence (*anitya*) and of the interdependent and composite or conditioned nature of things. In this view, nothing permanent and stable is found in the world; everything is subject to decay and passing away. Yet name and form (*nāma-rūpa*) make things appear fixed and stable, thus serving as the basis for clinging and frustration. Giving names to things also creates the illusion of independent entities, even though all entities in the world are composite and dependent on other entities. According to early Buddhist texts, the things that words name are not self-existent entities, but rather, collections of fundamental elements or events called *dharma*s. All things, including the apparent self, are nothing in and of themselves, but rather are collocations of smaller components, which are reducible to their constituent dharmas.[10] Thus, the identities of what people take to be independent beings are actually constructs constituted by language, concepts and conventions, which impose an artificial unity and stability on what is really plural and evanescent.

Orthodox Buddhist doctrine asserts, further, that words are attached to things only through tacit agreement rather than through some intrinsic basis for the connection between words and their referents. The Sautrāntikas and Sarvāstivādins called this conventional designation (*prajñapti*), as opposed to the truth in the highest sense (*paramārthasatya*). The Pāli literature makes frequent reference to conceptual proliferation (*prapañca*; Pāli, *papañca*) as one of the fundamental aspects of bondage and delusion. Naming things and forming fixed concepts about them can reify them in such a way that they seem permanent and stable. In the Buddhist view this is a problem because, being composite and conditioned, these things are nothing in and of themselves and are bound to perish and change, creating frustration for those attached to them.

In addition to pointing out the delusory effects of discursive thinking in general, early Buddhist discourses attempted to curtail some forms of purely speculative inquiry and the development of definite views (*dṛṣṭi*; Pāli, *diṭṭhi*) on certain metaphysical matters, further limiting the scope of language and conceptual activity. This dissuasion from certain forms of metaphysical speculation had a number of purposes involving psychological, social, pragmatic, and epistemological concerns. In the *Paramaṭṭhaka-sutta* of the *Sutta Nipāta*, for example, the Buddha discourages his disciples from holding unnecessary opinions on every issue because it disturbs peace of mind and narrows one's thinking such that one is trapped in dogmatism, which leads to disharmony and strife with others.[11] One reason, then, for refraining from making judgments and holding views about every debatable issue is to promote and preserve personal peace and social and harmony.

Another reason for limiting the scope of speculative questioning was the pragmatic emphasis of the Buddha's teachings. In the *Cuḷamālunkya Sutta* the Buddha declares that having views on certain doctrinal questions that were commonly used to define one school of thought over against others does not aid one in achieving liberation. Here the Buddha enumerates the often-discussed "unanswered (*avyākṛta*) questions," points upon which the Buddha refused to express an opinion: whether the world is eternal or not; whether it is finite or infinite; whether the soul is identical or different from the body; and whether the Tathāgata exists after death, does not exist after death, both exists and does not exist after death, or neither exists nor does not exist after death.[12] The Buddha likens engaging in this kind of speculation to a man shot by an arrow who feels compelled to know everything about the composition of the arrow – what kind of wood the shaft is made from, what kind of material the arrowhead is, etc. – and about the man who shot the arrow – whether he was short or tall, which clan he is from, etc. – before having the arrow taken out. The fundamental issues that one should be concerned with, the Buddha indicates, are not metaphysical but existential, that is, the suffering and dissatisfaction inherent in human existence and the overcoming of these through certain prescribed ways of living that the Buddha had elucidated.

Also in the Buddha's treatment of the unanswered questions are epistemological issues and problems relating to the limitations placed on language and speculative reasoning. In the *Brahmajāla Sutta*, the Buddha mentions some of the same questions he refuses to answer in the *Cūḷamālunkya Sutta*, and says that to hold to fixed opinions on these matters is like being caught in a fine mesh net.[13] This seems to indicate the position that holding definite views on certain metaphysical matters is a conceptual trap that holds thinking in a certain pattern, thus preventing a broader, more encompassing view. Additionally, the Buddha's refusal to answer these questions reflects a general suspicion in Buddhist thought of "either/or" questions regarding the ultimate nature of things. This will become more significant in certain Mahāyāna texts which attempt to avoid all positions based on such binary oppositions.

Some modern scholars have interpreted the Buddha's refusal to answer these kinds of questions as a specific indication of his understanding of the limitations of language.[14] T. R. V. Murti likens these questions to the Kantian antinomies and the Buddha's silence on these questions as a critique of speculative metaphysics along the lines of the Kantian critique. In this view, the Buddha's response suggests the limits of reason and a caution against *a priori* reasoning.[15] K. N. Jayatilleke argues that the rejection of these questions often indicates that the question itself is "meaningless" in sense similar to that used by contemporary analytic philosophers. In this reading, not only are any of the possible answers to these questions inadequate but the questions themselves assume a misunderstanding from the outset.[16] The *Aggivacchagotta Sutta* indicates that these kinds of questions involve a misapprehension of language usage such as that involved in nonsensical questions like "Where does a flame go when it goes out?"[17] Indeed, one of the common ways in which the Buddha refuses to answer certain questions was to say that the question itself did not apply to the case. Such passages lend support Jayatilleke's interpretation that these questions are rejected because they are in some sense logically meaningless or they entail a misunderstanding due to the misleading structures of language.

Some of the modern interpretations of the unanswered questions, while perhaps too quick to assimilate these questions to both later Mahāyāna and modern Western philosophy, rightly point out the general notion of the limitations placed on language and discursive thinking even in early strands of Buddhist discourse. While the passages on the unanswered questions do not put forth any explicit theory of ineffability or inexpressibility, they do indicate the Buddha's refusal to engage certain issues because they either lead to needless disputation, are not conducive to enlightenment, or involve a misconception from the outset. It would be mistaken, though, to assume that this refusal amounts to a categorical rejection of anything that we would today call "metaphysics." In fact, the suttas do not remain silent on all issues of a "metaphysical" nature: for example, the Buddha does give doctrines in the Nikāyas on the interdependence of phenomena and on the nature of karma and rebirth, issues that are not merely "empirical," unless the definition of the term is stretched considerably.[18] Thus, part of the reason for refusing to answer the unanswered questions is not necessarily that all speculative questions on the ultimate nature of things are nonsensical *per se*, or that all of the unanswered questions necessarily imply that the "answers" are ineffable, but rather that the questions do not make sense within the context of Buddhist doctrine. For example, to ask whether the self is identical to the body presumes the existence of an individual self – something that Buddhism rejects, not because this assumption goes beyond empirical observation but because Buddhist doctrine counters it with the assertion that there is no substantial, individual self. Despite these considerations, though, the unanswered questions, along with the reluctance found throughout the Pāli cannon to engage in many purely speculative issues, do indicate a general skepticism regarding metaphysical language and a recognition of the limits of language, although they do not necessarily promote any explicit notion of ineffability.

One area in which early Buddhist doctrine *does* suggest ineffability is with regard to the inexpressibility of the nature of nirvāṇa or the unconditioned (*asaṃskṛta*). Language and concepts name impermanent, composite entities that have no identity in and of themselves, but are appropriated by the various mental functions into wholes that appear as independent entities. When the impermanence and interdependence of all things in the world are fully grasped, the objects to which name and concept cling are analytically reduced down to their component elements, the dharmas, and are no longer uncritically appropriated in the manner of a naive realism. Achieving liberation is understood to consist, in part, of the cessation of clinging to the compounded and conditioned things (*saṃskṛta*) and attainment of the unconditioned (*asaṃskṛta*). Language only deals with intentionally grasped objects of experience in the lifeworld, and in this sense is inapplicable to the unconditioned, since it is defined by the relinquishment of such grasping. Nirvāṇa is "signless" (*animitta*), that is, it has nothing whereby it might be recognized; therefore, it is not an object of discriminative, intentional consciousness, but a release from all such objects. Thus it is not, strictly speaking, an object of reference and is usually described negatively in the Pāli texts as the opposite of that which is undesirable in Buddhism – suffering, rebirth, death, and so on.[19] In this sense, then, nirvāṇa is ineffable in that it is realized, in part, by the relinquishment of linguistic-conceptual activity and also in that it is radically disjunct from the lifeworld that is constituted by this activity and which in turn makes up the object of any possible reference.

Language and conceptual activity in the Pāli cannon, then, are restricted and critiqued in roughly three ways: first, they are constitutive of a falsely constructed lifeworld; second, they can lead to fruitless speculation and dispute; and third, they cannot reach, and they hinder the attainment of, the ultimate goal of nirvāṇa insofar as this goal involves the dissolution of linguistic-conceptual activity itself.

Abhidharma and Dharma Theory

In the early sūtra literature, the overt concern was not with epistemology as such, but with the means for overcoming human suffering. More explicit concern with the theoretical understanding of language and its relation to the world was taken up in the Abhidharma literature, and the critical response of the Mahāyāna to its treatment of these issues proved to be the starting point of Mahāyāna philosophy. The Abhidharma is a body of literature developed by some of the Nikāyas, notably the Sarvāstivāda and the Theravāda, who gave Abhidharma literature canonical status alongside the sūtras and the Vinaya, texts elaborating on rules for monks and nuns. The currently extant Abhidharmas were most likely composed between the first two centuries B.C.E. and the first or second century C.E., and commentary continued for centuries after that.

The purpose of the Abhidharmas is no less than the exhaustive analysis and classification of all factors of phenomenal existence. We have seen that the early Buddhists conceived of the entities in the world of human experience to have no independent existence, but to be composed of a continuous series of basic constitutive events, the dharmas. The causally conditioned and ever-changing combinations of these dharmas create and compose experience in the lifeworld, and the hypostatization of these evanescent experiences by means of the conceptual, linguistic, and social activities of human beings creates the false impression of relatively stable and permanent entities in the world. One common Buddhist method of escaping from the bondage to this conventional reality is the analysis of constructed intentional objects into their constituent dharmas, which in turn eliminates craving and attachment to them. One of the primary goals of the Abhidharma literature is to aid in this analysis of the lifeworld into the dharmas, its constituent elements. This analytic exercise is a component of insight (*vipaśyanā*; Pāli, *vipassanā*) meditation, in which the meditator observes the arising and falling of dharmas without attachment.

In its efforts to clarify the process of the lifeworld and its constituent events, the Abhidharma developed rather complex systems of classifying the dharmas. The overarching division among dharmas is between conditioned (*saṃskṛta*) and unconditioned (*asaṃskṛta*) dharmas, that is, those that are part of the composite, causal process of the artificially constructed lifeworld, and those that constitute freedom from this process. In the Theravāda Abhidharma, the only unconditioned dharma is nirvāṇa, while the Sarvāstivāda includes nirvāṇa, space (*ākāśa*), and cessation (*nirodha*). Conditioned dharmas include physical constituents such as earth, water, elasticity, and malleability; mental constituents such as mindfulness, freedom from delusion, freedom from greed (morally good dharmas), wrong views, (a morally bad dharma), contact, sensation, and volition (morally neutral dharmas). Numerous other ways of classifying the dharmas exist, including divisions into the sense capacities and their objects, those which are influenced by craving and those which are influenced by wisdom. All of these classifications serve the ambitious purpose of providing a taxonomic map of all possible configurations of the human lifeworld.[20]

A prominent feature of Sarvāstivāda Abhidharma was the notion of dharmas as inherently existing substances (*dravyasat*) that subsist in both the past and the future, as well as in present time. In this view, dharmas are eternally existent entities that manifest momentarily in the causal-temporal flow of events, then disappear into back into an unmanifest state. Dharmas, whether they are manifest in their momentary appearance in the lifeworld or unmanifest in the future or past, all maintain their inherent, essential nature (*svabhāva*). The ordinary entities in the world such as chariots were not considered self-existent, but merely collections of dharmas given a sense of artificial unity in virtue of their being the objects of linguistic reference and intentional consciousness. Thus, in this system, two levels of reality exist: conventional existence, which consists of these artificial unities that make up the ordinary human experience; and substantial reality (*dravyasat*), that is, the self-existent dharmas which are the final unities into which human experience can be analyzed. This notion of the inherent existence of dharmas, as well as the attempt to classify all possible phenomena in human experience engendered particular skepticism in the Mahāyāna philosophers and served as the impetus for their most penetrating critiques and insights regarding the nature of language and concepts.

Mahāyāna Views on Language and Concepts

We begin an examination of the critique of language and discursive thinking in the Mahāyāna with its earliest extant texts, the *Aṣṭasāhasrikā Prajñāpāramitā* and the *Ratnaguṇasaṃcayagāthā Prajñāpāramitā* (hereafter cited as *Aṣṭa* and *Rgs*, respectively),[21] which are likely prose and verse versions, respectively, of the same text. These texts comprise the earliest versions of the Perfection of Wisdom (*Prajñāpāramitā*) literature, which are the foundational documents of the philosophical strains of Mahāyāna Buddhism. Before examining these texts, let us specifically identify the problem that early Mahāyāna thinkers faced regarding language and concepts. The early Buddhist critiques of language and discursive thinking deal primarily with propositional language, for example, "the world is finite," "the world is infinite," and also with the function of names and concepts in hypostatizing things in the world in such a way that they are mistakenly conceived as permanent and independent entities, thereby causing the mind to become entrapped in rigid patterns of attachment and aversion to them. This kind of reification involves primarily the referential and descriptive functions of language and implies a critique of what philosophers today might call a "correspondence theory" of language – the notion that words simply correspond to things objectively existing in the world, external to language. The Buddhist analysis of the objects of linguistic reference claims that the identity of things in the lifeworld is constituted in part by human conceptualization, naming, convention, and perception. The traditional Buddhist notions of interdependence, impermanence, and the composite nature of phenomena lead to the problematization of even the simplest of propositional statements. For example, the passages from *Milindapañha* already cited suggest that one falls prey to fundamental ignorance if one speaks uncritically about even seemingly self-evident things such as a chariot, no less than of complex matters such as the self (*ātman*). All referential statements, in this view, involve the potential for fostering further delusion by implicitly reifying conditioned and impermanent phenomena. Buddhist ontological analysis, therefore, problematized all cognitive language and conceptual thinking, and the Mahāyāna stepped up the claims of the ineffability of higher truth and the delusory tendencies of language. This, however, leads to the paradox inherent in all claims to the inadequacy of language or of ineffability: one can only make such claims by means of words, and there was certainly no lack of words that had come from the sūtra writers and commentators. In early Mahāyāna literature we see attempts to acknowledge this problem and find ways of dealing with it. Indeed, some of the most creative and influential theoretical work in the Mahāyāna revolves around this question of how the reality of things is ineffable, yet can and must be spoken of in order for one to realize that reality.

The Mahāyāna forced this problem upon itself by radicalizing the "constructivist" claims implied in the theory of dharmas. That is to say, it pushed the analytical tendencies, begun in the early sūtras and developed in the Abhidharma, to the extreme by way of the Mahāyāna's fundamental ontological claim that not only are the ordinary phenomena of the lifeworld constructed by concepts and formed from multiple dharmas, but that dharmas themselves are conceptual constructs and have no more inherent reality than any other named and conceived thing. With this move they attempted to reaffirm the impermanence and interdependence of all things that they perceived some of the Abhidharma commentators to have abandoned with their notions of the inherent and substantial existence (*svabhāva*) of dharmas.[22]

In the *Aṣṭa* and the *Rgs*, the notion of dharmas as verbal and conceptual constructs is clear and in obvious reaction to the Sarvāstivāda notions of dharmas as permanent entities. While the Abhidharma analysis of phenomena stops at the dharmas, considering them to be the endpoints in the analysis of the lifeworld, these Perfection of Wisdom texts claim that even dharmas are not self-substantiating entities, but are themselves products of human conceptual discrimination and designation. The Sarvāstivādin Abhidharma attempted to ground both human experience and discourse in a substratum of being consisting of permanent dharmas that could be apprehended and labeled. In this theory, the dharmas are the final, ultimately real entities (*dravyasat*) of which all things are composed. Perfection of Wisdom thought took the opposite view: "The lack of a basis of apprehension in all dharmas, that is called perfect wisdom."[23] For the Sarvāstivāda the conventional unities of the ordinary world exist only insofar as they are conceptual-linguistic constructs and function as linguistic referents, while the dharmas were inherently existing linguistic referents. For the Perfection of Wisdom texts, the dharmas are no more inherently existing than the ordinary entities.

The identification of different dharmas in the flow of experience is the same as the discrimination and appropriation of any other entity that is constituted by language, perception, and convention, and is not the discovery of a final, ontological substratum. The Perfection of Wisdom, and the subsequent associated wisdom traditions, attempted to undermine any idea of an ultimate ontological basis on which to anchor words, concepts, and taxonomies. Many passages in the *Aṣṭa* show that it afforded dharmas no more intrinsic existence reality than any other conventional realities such as the self:

> A bodhisattva should produce the thought: "As in each and every way a permanent self (*ātman*) is not found or apprehended, so in these same ways all dharmas are not found or apprehended." He should then apply this idea to all dharmas, inside and outside.[24]

> Foolish, undeveloped, common people have settled down in all of the dharmas. Having constructed them, attached to the two extremes, they do not know or see those dharmas. So they construct dharmas which are not actually found.... After they have constructed them, they settle down in name and form. ... But while they construct all dharmas which are not found, they neither know nor see the path that truly is.[25]

Thus, the *Aṣṭa* claims that those who had tried to establish a self-existent foundation for linguistic reference had failed and instead had made the very search for foundations into another activity enmeshed in the conceptual-linguistic trap. For Perfection of Wisdom literature it is precisely the lack of foundations, and the apprehension of this lack, that is celebrated as perfect wisdom, freedom, and enlightenment.

Another prominent element in the critique of inherently existing dharmas in the *Aṣṭa* and *Rgs* is the idea that all dharmas are limitless and boundless (*ananta* and *aparyanta*).[26] The boundaries of any dharma are not delineated by linguistic reference nor by the concept of that dharma; therefore, in theory they are without any intrinsic limitation. Thus, a person meditating and trying to identify specific dharmas in the flow of experience may isolate a particular dharma, but there is nothing inherent in that bit of experience that delineates its boundaries specifically; rather, it is simply another conventionally constituted event in the continuum of interdependently arising events. The delimitation of any particular bit of experience is a function of human appropriation and intentionality rather than any intrinsic characteristic (*svalakṣana*) of the bit itself. Taking any dharma as inherently delimited in the way that language and concepts divide it from everything else by means of applying a unitary name to it is called false discrimination or construction (*vikalpa*). This implies an attempt to undermine the Abhidharma's taxonomic project by claiming that dharmas have no essential nature whereby they could be distinguished from each other in an absolute sense. In this respect, they are all "like space" (*ākāśa*) in that they cannot be "placed side by side and ... compared" as the Abhidharma taxonomies attempted to do.[27] In their true nature, dharmas are boundless, meaning that the only thing that gives them a sense of having a unique characteristic is that they are discriminated from other things by designation and convention.

This fundamental boundlessness of all dharmas also implies a reformulation of the distinction between conditioned (*saṃskṛta*) and unconditioned (*asaṃskṛta*) dharmas. In the Abhidharma, as we have mentioned, the overarching division in the taxonomy of the dharmas is that between conditioned dharmas that make up the various entities and events in the lifeworld and unconditioned dharmas which constitute freedom from entrapment in the falsely constructed lifeworld. The claim of the Perfection of Wisdom texts that all dharmas are boundless is in essence a reconfiguration of this distinction: all dharmas lack inherent existence or essential nature (*svabhāva*); therefore, what is important is apprehending this true nature of all dharmas (that is, their having no essential nature!), whether conditioned or unconditioned. All dharmas in their true nature, even those classified as conditioned, are unconditioned and boundless, and the apprehension of this is what is important. According to the Perfection of Wisdom texts, then, dharmas have a twofold character: first, as nominal entities constituted by intentional consciousness; and second, in their actuality as indeterminate and empty of essential nature. Each dharma, then, is a "no-thing" that bleeds into the limitlessness of everything when unconstrained by conceptual reification. Awakening, therefore, is understood more in the sense of *seeing the true nature of all dharmas* rather than negating certain dharmas and actualizing certain others. The realm of causes and conditions is not ontologically distinct from the unconditioned, as the Abhidharma claimed; rather, the unconditioned is the true character of the conditioned world itself when apprehended with insight and wisdom (*prajñā*). Thus the Perfection of Wisdom attempts to disrupt the very foundation of Abhidharma theorizing on the relationship of the conditioned world to enlightenment, and of the taxonomy that made distinctions between unconditioned and conditioned dharmas its most fundamental classification.

This analysis begins to call into question the traditional distinction between *saṃsāra* and nirvāṇa, or the conditioned and unconditioned. Insofar as all dharmas in their actuality (*tattva*) are infinite, boundless, originally pure, and unconditioned, the ontological distinction between conditioned and unconditioned dharmas breaks down and becomes, rather, an epistemological issue; that is, whether one apprehends the world as *saṃsāra* or nirvāṇa depends not upon any absolute distinction among dharmas, but only upon how consciousness apprehends the world. The rejection of any absolute distinction between the conditioned and unconditioned in these texts makes the boundaries between the two more porous, both in theory and in practice, and directly links awakening to the world of phenomena in a way in which earlier Buddhism had not. The very reason perfect wisdom is infinite, says the *Aṣṭa*, is because of this limitlessness of *all* objects in the world, their limitations being only a product of human conceptual consciousness:

> Perfect wisdom is an infinite perfection by reason of the infinitude of objects. And further, a being is endless and boundless because one cannot get at its beginning, middle, or end. Therefore, perfect wisdom is an infinite perfection because of the infinitude of beings.[28]

And further, not only perfect wisdom and buddhahood are "unthinkable, incomparable, immeasurable, and incalculable," but so are all dharmas, including the factors of personal existence (*skandhas*) and visible form (*rūpa*), in view of their boundlessness and infinitude. Moreover, all dharmas are said to be "situated in emptiness,"[29] and "no dharma is excluded from enlightenment."[30]

The depictions of the bodhisattva in the early Perfection of Wisdom texts illustrate this new understanding of enlightenment that does not transcend or reject the world. The figure of the bodhisattva as someone who participates in the lifeworld yet who is free from the bonds of linguistic and conceptual fabrication was part of the Mahāyāna attempt to negotiate a way between life bound to *saṃsāra* and the complete absence of phenomenal expression implicit in nirvāṇa.

This rejection of the disjunction between the conditioned world and awakening represented by the bodhisattva ideal was to have profound effects on the subsequent development of Mahāyāna thought and practice. Rather than transcending *saṃsāra* altogether, the bodhisattva stands in between *saṃsāra* and nirvāṇa, able to comprehend them both. The *Rgs* says:

> Just as the leader [the Buddha] was not established in the unconditioned realm, nor was he situated in conditions, but wandered homeless, in the same way the bodhisattva stands without establishing a fixed position. This stand, the victor has said, is the position that is no-position.[31]

Here, the Buddha and bodhisattva are presented as "homeless," emphasizing that they neither live clinging to the world nor do they retire from it in the quiescence of nirvāṇa. The bodhisattva, then, is presented as living in an intermediate state in between the conditioned and the unconditioned, able to experience and cognize both. The *Rgs* and the *Aṣṭa* conceive of the alternative to "settling down" in either *saṃsāra* or nirvāṇa as comprehending the true nature of dharmas through wisdom: "Though he does not experience blessed rest [nirvāṇa], he nevertheless sees the dharmas."[32] For the bodhisattva, then, rejection of conceptual fabrication does not entail a cessation of being in the world. The contention is that although the bodhisattva still exists in the world and is involved in the transactions of everyday life, his wisdom surpasses that of the arhat who achieves transcendence of phenomenality in the quiescence of nirvāṇa. His "seeing" of the dharmas denotes comprehension of their true nature as empty of inherent existence. "The bodhisattva, the great being, in non-attachment awakens to unsurpassed enlightenment in the sense that he comprehends all dharmas."[33] This idea signals, again, the shift in the notion of awakening from the idea of transcendence of all conditioned dharmas to that of insight into the nature of all dharmas, conditioned and unconditioned. The idea of insight into the nature of dharmas, of course, is not a novel idea in Buddhist thought. However, the contention that this insight, occurring while still in the world, constitutes a higher kind of awakening than the attainment of nirvāṇa and cessation of phenomenality, was indeed new.

Another result of the extension of the constructive capacities of concepts and language to include the dharmas is that it rendered the issue of language more crucial, for it involved more radical claims of ineffability. Because all things appropriated by human conceptualization and discursive thinking are only nominal entities with conventional but not absolute reality, the unconditioned nature of things, independent of conceptual appropriation, is not amenable to linguistic expression. Not even the unconditioned dharmas are finally real referents. The *Aṣṭa* claims that the true unconditioned nature of things is beyond thought and language:

> The nature of form, Subhūti, is not thinkable, not amenable to thought, not conceivable, not subject to comparison. It is the same with feeling, perception, intentions, and consciousness ... and with all dharmas. [34]

Even the most sacred concepts in the Buddhist tradition are still concepts, and thus lack any inherent ontological grounding.

> "Buddha," "bodhisattva," "perfect wisdom," all these are mere words. And what they denote is something unproduced [i.e., that has no ultimate, substantial existence]. It is as with the self. Although we speak of a self, yet ultimately the self is something unproduced. Since, therefore, all dharmas are without inherent existence, what is that form, etc., which cannot be grasped and which is something unproduced?[35]

Here language is allowed a conventional function, but since, strictly speaking, no independent beings exist to which words refer, the truth of things cannot be a linguistic referent.

Not only were the doctrines of the Sarvāstivādins the subject of critique by early Mahāyāna thinkers, but their practices as well. In particular, the *Aṣṭa* frequently indicates the ineffectuality of "reviewing dharmas," a reference to mindfulness practices in which the meditator analytically observes the rise and fall of dharmas in his or her experience and tries to identify and classify them. The Abhidharma instructed meditators to attend to and analyze the conditions under which certain dharmas are produced in order that these dharmas might be pacified. The *Rgs* and *Aṣṭa* critique this form of meditational analysis, at least as recommended by the Abhidharma philosophers, because they understand these practices to entail discursive activities that, in the Mahāyāna view, still lead to subtle forms of attachment. For these Mahāyāna thinkers, the process of identifying elements of experience and verbalizing them simply creates another order of conceptual fabrication by means of discursive thought. The *Aṣṭa* repeatedly cautions against verbalizing and labeling of dharmas and making them an object of conceptual reflection: "If he does not perceive a thought, [identifying it] as 'this is that thought', he has no distorted perception, thought, or view."[36] To have no distorted thought, then, is to avoid constructing objects of reflection. The following passage in the *Aṣṭa* is typical among those that discourage attachment to any concept stated in propositions, including ones that give expression to Buddhist, and even explicitly Mahāyāna, doctrines:

> [The bodhisattva] should not abide in the skandhas, nor in their sign, nor in the idea that "the skandhas are signs," nor in the production of the skandhas, in their stopping or destruction, nor in the idea that "the skandhas are empty," or "I abide," or "I am a bodhisattva." And it should not occur to him, "he who abides thus, abides in perfect wisdom and develops it." He abides but he does not entertain such ideas as "I abide," "I do not abide," "I abide and I do not abide," "I neither abide not do I not abide," and the same [four] with "I will abide." He does not go near any dharma at all, because all dharmas are unapproachable and ungraspable. The bodhisattva then has the concentrated insight "not grasping at any dharma" by name, vast, noble, unlimited, and steady, not shared by any of the disciples or solitary buddhas.[37]

There is, then, an implicit suspicion of practices that use naming, labeling, or identification in propositional statements. Attachment to any thought is discouraged, and indeed the more refined states of being are indicated to be without thought and therefore without language.[38] The passage insinuates that thought and the verbalization of thought, especially in an attempt at the theoretical systemization of experience, creates a kind of second-order system of meaning that is one step removed from the primary experience of life as it is. One may indeed "abide" in perfect wisdom, but if one thinks "I am abiding in perfect wisdom," one is no longer abiding in perfect wisdom, for this activity has been made into an object of reflection. The caution against this kind of conceptual-linguistic activity focuses especially on self-referential statements that denote one's state of mind or that make specific predications about oneself. The activity of reflection is understood to create a kind of division or gap whereby a separate subject stands apart from the world or from itself as an object of reflection. Attaining wisdom in the Perfection of Wisdom sūtras implies the closing of the gap of self-conscious reflection.

Dialectical Patterns in the Perfection of Wisdom Literature

While the overall thrust of Mahāyāna wisdom literature tends to devalue cognitive language, this is admittedly only one side of the story. Ample scholarly attention has been given to Nāgārjuna's distinction between the two truths – truth in the highest sense (*paramārthasatya*) and conventional truth (*saṃvṛttisatya*), the latter of which has value for both practical functioning in the world and teaching of the Dharma. This allows a legitimate function for everyday language, avoiding the reduction of all truth to silence. Indeed these early Perfection of Wisdom texts upon which Nāgārjuna apparently based his dialectic introduce a linguistic pattern that allows for the re-affirmation of language in a provisional sense that discourages essentializing its referents. This pattern is a seminal discursive structure found in the Perfection of Wisdom texts, one that served as a foundational linguistic figure for many important developments in Buddhist thought in India and beyond. This structure is a unique pattern of paradoxical dialectic that arises from trying to solve the problems inherent in denying the ultimate validity of language while trying to preserve language in a practical sense, not only for teaching the Dharma but for ordinary comportment with the world. This form of paradox is important because it is a part of the Mahāyāna attempt to grapple with the problem of language. Moreover, it illustrates a basic pattern that we will see recurring in many different contexts more explicitly involved with the visionary literature and visualization practices taken up in later chapters.

All philosophical reflection that holds language in such suspicion, whether it consists of ancient notions of ineffability or contemporary deconstructive modes of thinking, is of course faced with a stark paradox: the elucidation of the functions and limitations of language must be given in language itself. The dilemma is presented quite clearly at the beginning of a later (5th–6th century) Perfection of Wisdom text, the *Questions of Suvikrāntavikrāmin*. When Suvikrāntavikrāmin asks the Buddha to explain the perfection of wisdom, the Buddha agrees to teach him, but then replies:

> The perfection of wisdom cannot be expressed by any teaching, since it has transcended all speech, and one cannot say about the perfection of wisdom: "this is the perfection of wisdom; he has the perfection of wisdom; through that is the perfection of wisdom; from that is the perfection of wisdom." A non-perfection of all dharmas is this; in this sense it is called "perfection of wisdom."[39]

These, the first words of the Buddha's teaching on the perfection of wisdom in this text assert that it is, in fact, impossible to teach it. Thus the problem is set up at the outset – how to speak about something that is not to be grasped by speech. The tension between what can be said and what is unsayable is a fundamental creative tension in the Mahāyāna.

In order to articulate the Mahāyāna understanding of emptiness, the Perfection of Wisdom texts find themselves flirting with the boundaries of intelligible language. Their authors appear to have realized that the assertion of ineffability combined with the doctrine of emptiness threatens to shut down language altogether if pushed to its conclusions. Not only does language not adequately describe or refer to the actuality (*tattva, tathatā*) of things, this actuality is itself precluded from being anything inherently existent. In order to articulate this vision, the authors of the Perfection of Wisdom literature developed a dialectical discourse in which the rhetorical style itself is designed to disrupt the referential function of language, not to circumvent reason altogether, but to attempt to develop a linguistic "game" that is transformative rather than strictly referential and that ultimately attempts to transcend words by means of words.

The most immediately noticeable feature of a number of Perfection of Wisdom texts is their concern with, and unusual rhetorical use of, binary opposition. The *Aṣṭa*, for instance, repeatedly warns against clinging to opposites and "clinging to 'is' or 'is not'."[40] In describing the Perfection of Wisdom teachings, it says: "This perfection does not follow in the duality of opposites because it does not settle down in all dharmas."[41] There is a caution, then, against seeing opposites like being and non-being or purity and impurity as given an any absolute sense. This, of course, is based on the doctrine of emptiness, which asserts that no referent has a fixed essence and, therefore, that the differentiations established by linguistic terms are not built in to the nature of things. The *Aṣṭa* presents binary oppositions in language as particularly prone to giving rise to the illusion of inherent existence.

The notion that in order to realize perfect wisdom, one should avoid "following in the duality of opposites" and "grasping to 'is' and 'is not'," that is, to avoid any kind of linguistic opposition, would seem to preclude the use of language itself. The Perfection of Wisdom literature does not, of course, manage to avoid opposition and distinction in its discourse (indeed, this would be impossible for any discourse), but in many passages it does use them in a very specific way that attempts to deter the tendency to reify the referents of linguistic opposition. This makes for some strange and fascinating dialogue that playfully utilizes paradox, irony, and perhaps even humor. One common pattern is the *assertion* of both terms of a particular opposition, making a rather concise paradox. For example: "The nature of all dharmas is no nature, and their no-nature is their nature."[42] Here the text asserts that dharmas have no nature, that is, that they are empty of inherent existence (*svabhāva*), and that this emptiness of essence is their only "essential" feature. Another way of dealing with binary opposition in the *Aṣṭa* is the *negation* of both terms, again on the basis of the doctrine of emptiness: "All dharmas are without either defilement or purification, for all dharmas are empty with regard to inherent existence."[43]

Other passages are more complex and often read like a mass of almost arbitrary contradictions, requiring more careful analysis to make comprehensible. Before analyzing such a passage from the *Suvikrānta*, it would be useful first to put it in context. This later Perfection of Wisdom text is interesting, in terms of both doctrine and rhetoric, in that parts of it read like a commentary on basic Buddhist terminology and concepts, systematically explicating some of the major ideas of both Orthodox and Mahāyāna Buddhism; for example, the truth of suffering, the cause of suffering, the cessation of suffering, the bodhisattva, the constituents of personal existence (*skandhas*), non-attachment, and perfection of wisdom itself. What on the surface promises to be a commentary, however, proves to be a radical critique and reinterpretation of each of these classical Buddhist ideas – one that puts a very Mahāyānistic spin on these doctrines and attempts to negate any possible "essentialist" readings of them. Thus it serves a polemical function in taking traditional concepts employed by all Buddhists and re-framing them in terms of the doctrine of emptiness. For example, the cessation (*nirodha*) of birth and becoming discussed frequently in the Pāli cannon is reinterpreted as "penetration" (*prativedha*) or understanding of the fact that no intrinsically existing beings are born and become in the first place; cessation, therefore, becomes a matter of one's cognition rather than whether one will be reborn or not.

Again, the most striking feature of these unorthodox readings of Buddhist doctrines is the rhetorical technique of holding together binary oppositions in such a way that the given idea is both asserted and denied at the same time. To see how this technique is executed, let us look closely at a passage dealing with the notion of "world-transcending wisdom" (*lokottarā prajñā*).

> That which is clear understanding is direct realization, and this is what is called "world-transcending wisdom." But world-transcending wisdom is not as is thus spoken. And why? Because the world is not ascertained; how much less, then, world-transcending wisdom. And how much less will speech transcend the world by means of world-transcending wisdom. And why? [Wisdom] does not ascertain a world and so transcends nothing at all – this is what is called "world-transcending wisdom." "World" is said to be a verbal conception, and a verbal conception does not go beyond the world. Going beyond all verbal conception – that is what is called "world-transcending"; so world transcending is not transcendence and non-transcendence is world-transcending. And why? Because no dharma whatsoever is found that one might transcend or by which one might transcend – this is what is called "world-transcending." But "world-transcending wisdom" is not as is thus spoken. And why? Because that which is world-transcending cannot be spoken of; it has crossed over, and nothing, again, is to be transcended – this is what is meant by "world-transcending wisdom."[44]

As confusing as such a passage may be to those unfamiliar with these texts, it would be inadequate simply to interpret it, on the one hand, as convoluted and self-contradictory or, on the other, as an attempt to confuse the rational functioning of the mind in the service of mystical realization; for there exists a logic in this dialectic that is intelligible and at the same time attempts to show the authors' understanding of the relationship between words and their referents.

The first few statements of the passage show a form found in most Perfection of Wisdom texts. First something is posited – in this case a description of "world-transcending wisdom" as clear understanding and direct realization. Then the statement is immediately retracted by a critical analysis of the term or terms – in this case "world" – that attempts to show that the use of the term is misleading in light of the doctrine of emptiness. After this some of the common philosophical themes of emptiness philosophy are condensed and applied to the term. First, the highest form of wisdom does not ascertain or conceive (*upalabhate*, Tib. *dmig pa*) the world as an inherently existing thing or referent; therefore, "world-transcending wisdom" cannot make sense if understood in this way. Second, since linguistic referents are not intrinsic existents, and "world" is itself linguistically constituted, there is nothing essential to transcend through wisdom. When the "world" is shown to lack intrinsic nature, the notion of transcending it falls away.

After carefully dismantling these interpretations of world-transcending wisdom, however, the text does not abandon the notion but, surprisingly, revives it at each stage, claiming that the negation of the notion in terms of emptiness is, itself, the true sense of the idea and the one presumably intended by the Buddha all along. The author of this text was obviously concerned with maintaining continuity with the earlier tradition and with the authority of the Buddha; therefore, he has the Buddha regularly claim that he actually taught this quite "non-Hīnayāna" doctrine right in the midst of the Pāli sūtras, but couched it in early Buddhist terminology, only teaching the Mahāyāna doctrine "in a hidden sense."[45] What is extraordinary is that the "hidden sense" of a particular term or doctrine often turns out to be expressed as a simple negation of the traditional use of the term or doctrine (as in the previously-mentioned example of the cessation of birth and becoming).

After this critique of the concept, the point is driven home further as the dialectic jumps to another stage: "But 'world transcending wisdom' is not as is thus spoken. And why? Because that which is world-transcending cannot be spoken of. ... That is what is called 'world-transcending wisdom'." This move appears to be a negation of the very critique that the text itself just proposed; yet it is a logical and necessary consequence of that critique. If wisdom is truly ineffable in the sense that there are no intrinsically existing things to which to refer, then wisdom entails the negation of all discourse, *including the exposition that the text itself has just given*. And yet, again, there is no resting in the silence of that negation, for immediately after ineffability is claimed, thereby negating all of the previous assertions and negations and threatening to shut down the discourse completely, there is another re-assertion of the concept of "world-transcending wisdom" as the very insight into this ineffability and the emptiness of any inherent existence with regard to the term being considered.

Complex dialectical formulations such as this one are found throughout the Perfection of Wisdom literature and are nicely condensed in the *Vajracchedika* by means of a formulaic structure that is similarly applied to various concepts drawn from Buddhist literature. For example:

> The Blessed One said: "Subhūti, when you consider the number of particles of dust in this world system of three million world systems, would they be many?" Subhūti answered: "Yes, Blessed One, many. And why? Because what was said by the Tathāgata to be particles of dust, the Tathāgata has said are no-particles. In this sense, the Tathāgata has said 'particles of dust'. Moreover, that which is a world-system is said by the Tathāgata to be no system. In this sense, he says 'world-system'."[46]

The formula repeated throughout this passage makes the general form of the dialectic more easily discernible. Expressed in logical symbols, it is the three-term formula: A, ~A, "A". The first move of the dialectic introduces and sometimes describes the subject matter at hand. The subject matter to which the dialectic is applied is virtually negligible – it can be any topic with which Buddhists are conversant, but is usually confined to specifically Buddhist doctrines and themes. The initial presentation of the term (A) indicates the naive appropriation of things in the lived world as well as its philosophical counterpart, the positing of inherent existence and the reification of conceptual structures. The second move in the dialectic is a negation of the previous assertion and whatever has been said about it. In the passage from the *Suvikrānta*, this stage is sometimes introduced by the phrase 'but it is not as is spoken' (*na punar yathocyate*), indicating that what has just been asserted is actually not the case. The negation that constitutes the second stage (~A) is the assertion of the doctrine of emptiness with regard to the given subject matter. In the *Suvikrānta* passage, this stage goes through a number of negations. In most of the *Vajracchedika* passages it is one simple negation, for example: "That which is a world-system is said by the Tathāgata to be no system."

The third stage in the dialectic ("A") reaffirms the first term, indicating a way of understanding the expression in light of emptiness. The re-affirmation takes the form of a commentarial gloss on a term that can be read: "In this sense, 'world-system' is spoken [i.e., by the Buddha in various sūtras]" (*tenocyate loka. . . . iti*). The passage, therefore, is in the odd position of saying that the sense in which the Buddha intended a particular idea is the negation of that very idea. But this is not an unqualified negation indicating that the subject at hand (and by inference, anything else) does not exist in any sense whatsoever – it exists in a qualified, conventional sense insofar as it is conditioned by and interdependent with other things. In this sense, therefore, what was negated is re-affirmed and can be spoken about and used in everyday discourse. This re-affirmation is important to the Mahāyāna, for it allows the emptiness philosophers to avoid the charge of nihilism and to assert the pragmatic use of language and activity in the world.

Dialectic, Paradox, and Discourse

The dialectical formulations of the Perfection of Wisdom sūtras served as a means of linguistically demonstrating this tradition's understanding of the limits of language as well as its re-affirmation for practical purposes.[47] This form of dialectic is one that attempts to avoid the unqualified positing of statements about the ultimate truth of things. Instead, it tries to point indirectly to its understanding of nonlinguistic truth by disrupting the inclination of the reader to "settle down" (*avābhinivisati*) in any statement, or in "the two extremes" of any binary opposition.[48] By developing a discourse that in certain specific ways undermines its own statements, the authors attempt to disclose the labyrinthine trap of language and show a way beyond it. This trap specifically entails attachment to the terms of any set of binary oppositions; thus, one goal of the dialectic is to show the interdependence of binary conceptions so that the reader is less inclined toward their reification. Since binary oppositions go to the very heart of language, the reader is rendered "unsupported" or "ungrounded" (*apratiṣṭhitā*)[49] when these oppositions are undermined; that is, unsupported by any concept or assertion implying an underlying substantial ground supporting the life-world.

Recall the Buddha's warning at the beginning of the *Suvikrānta* that, despite his agreeing to discuss perfect wisdom, it cannot really be an object of discussion. It is in light of this statement, and of the critique of language and concepts that we have examined in Buddhist thought, that the dialectic must be understood. The authors of the Perfection of Wisdom literature saw the philosophical problems inherent in attempting to make the unconditioned (*asaṃskṛta*) into an object of discourse and attempted to resolve these problems by a move away form referential language about the unconditioned, toward a specific mode of discourse that attempted to trace the horizon of referential language, thereby suggesting what is beyond it. The purpose of the dialectic is not to *say what* the unconditioned is, but to *show how* it is.[50] The "thesis" of the Perfection of Wisdom literature is that all elements of existence have no intrinsic nature; they are groundless in and of themselves and exist only in relation to other elements. Since all objects of reference are interdependent and linguistically constituted, to discuss something called "the unconditioned" as an unqualified referent would implicitly contradict this thesis. The thesis, then, cannot be set forth as a theoretical "view" (*dṛṣṭi*) in an unqualified sense. The discursive form itself, therefore, demonstrates the notion of emptiness by continuously shifting perspectives so that no position within the context of the dialectic has any ultimately final, solid ground upon which to establish itself. In this way the text relativizes its own statements by not allowing them to stand as self-sufficient propositions, and this constant relativizing of statements by means of continuously shifting from one frame of reference to another has the vertiginous effect on the reader of constantly having the rug pulled out from under one's feet. This, in effect, is part of the "preformative" aspect of the text, in that what it is supposed to *do* is more than just convey propositional meaning; it is designed to have a specific effect on the reader.

The unique dialectical form put forth in the Perfection of Wisdom leaves the contradicting elements in tension, rather than resolving them in a final synthesis. Assertions give rise to negations, which in turn give rise to negations of the negations, not for the purpose of coming to a final conclusion – an endpoint in the dialectic at which the final truth can finally be stated – nor for the purpose of establishing an infinite regress. Instead, the movement of the dialectic itself shows the continual ungrounding of all affirmation and negation as the empty interplay of all binary opposition – indeed of all language. It is a demonstration of the endless shifting of perspectives that constitutes the emptiness of language and the lifeworld. This ungrounding dialectic, then, attempts to show what it cannot say by serving as a model that presents the ungrounded movement of things in general. It is, thereby, an attempt to use language to reveal the emptiness philosophers' understanding of the truth of things, not by means of unqualified propositional statements, but by a qualification and relativization of all such statements. Insofar as the dialectic resists any final closure or coming to rest in an unqualified statement of truth, it *evokes* the truth of what it cannot say by outlining the limits of propositional language, its paradoxes standing in sharp relief against the background of what is left unsaid and unsayable.

The Paradoxical Dialectic and Buddhist History

The Perfection of Wisdom literature has been perhaps the most influential sūtra literature of the Mahāyāna. We will have occasion to refer back to this literature in the foregoing chapters, because in many ways it sets the agenda for a great deal of Mahāyāna literature and practice. Its paradoxical dialectic established an underlying conceptual and literary form that is recapitulated in various writings, philosophical discussions, and meditation practices throughout the history of Buddhism. For example, Malcolm David Eckel shows how Bhāvaviveka, the Mādhyamika philosopher, constructed his arguments in the same three-part structure as that presented in the *Vajracchedika*.[51] Gadjin Nagao demonstrates the influence of this structure on Madhyamaka, Yogācāra, and Tathāgatagarbha thought.[52] As we will discuss later, this form was also recapitulated in a number of meditation practices, including the transposition of the dialectic of words into a dialectic of images and of the seer and seen.

The dialectic was formative as well in that the tension it attempted to maintain between its positive and negative poles was a highly creative tension, and entire schools of Buddhist philosophy assumed their particular character influenced by whether they leaned toward one side or the other in their interpretations of emptiness. Not only each school but each textual tradition, each form of discourse, including the Perfection of Wisdom tradition and the Madhyamaka themselves, had to deal with this problem, for it is impossible to maintain an "ungrounding" discourse except in highly specialized rhetorical forms such as Nāgārjuna's *catuṣkoṭi*, the famous "four cornered negation," or the paradoxical dialectic. Unqualified statements must be made for language to maintain itself as viable communication, and the balancing act between being and non-being cannot be maintained except in this highly specialized linguistic game. Even the Perfection of Wisdom literature, of course, makes many unqualified statements without putting them through the paces of the dialectic. Therefore, while virtually all the schools of Indian Mahāyāna thought embraced the impulse of the Perfection of Wisdom literature, their appropriations of emptiness revealed the cleavages between and within the groups, each leaning toward one side of the dialectic or the other – toward being or non-being, toward presence or absence, toward speech or silence.

The Madhyamaka tended toward a negative formulation of emptiness, relying on ruthlessly exposing what it considered to be the delusions entailed in any assumption of inherent existence. The founder of Madhyamaka, Nāgārjuna, developed his notion of the two truths as an attempt to account for and harmonize the two sides of the dialectic – the first assertion in the dialectic (A) is the equivalent of Nāgārjuna's conventional truth, naively conceived, that is, of all "views" and of the positing of inherent nature. The subsequent negation (~A) corresponds to the application of emptiness – to Nāgārjuna's series of negations applied to various concepts and to truth in the highest sense. Yet he claims that this truth cannot be apprehended without resort to conventional truth, thus he re-affirms it in light of emptiness in a move corresponding to the third term ("A") of the dialectic.[53]

But even the Madhyamaka was split between the Svātantrikas, who maintained that it was possible to make certain self-authenticating claims, and the Prānsaṅgikas, who denied such a possibility. Other Buddhist schools, accusing the Madhyamaka of nihilism, tended toward a more positive expression of emptiness. The Yogācāra, for example, attempted to compensate for this perceived negativism by developing the notion of the storehouse consciousness (*ālayavijñāna*). Theories of Buddha nature and *Tathāgatagarbha* were also efforts to develop a more positive conception of reality while maintaining the doctrine of emptiness. The basic conflict between positive presentations of reality and negative ones can be seen working its way through Buddhist history outside of India as well, in the anti-cognitive tendencies of Ch'an and Zen, and in their conflicts with Pure Land Buddhist in China and Tantric Buddhists in Japan; also in the disagreements between dGeluk pas and rNyingma pas on the nature of emptiness, the dGeluk pas taking a more negationary stance and rNyingma pas, who posited a kind of metaphysical absolute behind appearances. Further, the abundant use of paradox in the Ch'an/Zen traditions is rooted in the Perfection of Wisdom literature, and the famous saying attributed to Ch'ing-yuan Wei-hsin recapitulates the dialectic with the characteristic concretness of this tradition: "Before a man studies Zen, to him mountains are mountains and waters are waters; after he gets an insight into the truth of Zen through the instruction of a good master, mountains to him are not mountains and waters are not waters; but after this when he really attains to the abode of rest, mountains are once more mountains and waters are waters."[54]

Discursive Thinking and the Construction of the Lifeworld

While the Perfection of Wisdom texts fervently critiqued notions of inherent existence and highlighted the role of language and concepts in the construction of a falsely apprehended lifeworld, it was the philosophical schools of the Mahāyāna that worked out the theoretical intricacies and implications of these doctrines. The Mādhyamikas, Yogācārins, and logicians developed systematic accounts of the dynamics of language and conceptualization and their relation to soteriological concerns. Although the various schools developed different interpretations of this process, they all used similar technical terminology indicating the various stages of conceptual construction. At the risk of obscuring the nuances of the various schools of Buddhist thought, it would be worthwhile now to cull from various texts the general features of this "world-construction" as conceived by most South Asian Mahāyāna philosophers in order to provide a more thorough understanding of what we have been calling "language," "concepts," and "discursive thinking" – terms not unproblematic in contemporary philosophy and theory, and no less so in Buddhist thought. Buddhist philosophers developed a rich and subtle array of terminology dealing with conceptual-linguistic activity, which should now be elucidated in order to clarify the multiple functions and subtle shades of meaning implied by these terms. I will draw primarily from the Madhyamaka school for this terminology, but will also mention other school's interpretations.

In his useful article "Some Aspects of Language and Construction in the Madhyamaka," Paul Williams discusses a number of these terms, pointing out especially the significance of *saṃjñā*, often translated as "perception," "idea," or "impression." Williams points out that the function of *saṃjñā* is not simply bare perception, but the classification of what is perceived in terms of subject-predicate sentences. A sentence, for example "*x* is blue," does not designate the transient, conditioned instance of blue, but rather articulates the specific instance as belonging to a particular *class*, in this case that of blue things. *Saṃjñā* establishes the "sign" (*nimitta*) of an object – that by which it is differentiated from other things – by indicating the class of things to which the object belongs. Thus, the sign functions as the predicate of the statement "*x* is blue."[55] Williams cites a number of sources indicating this interpretation of the role of *saṃjñā*: For instance, the *Ch'eng-wei-shih-lun*, a Chinese translation of a Sanskrit Madhyamaka text, defines *saṃjñā* as "the apprehension of the *nimittas* of an object (*ching*). Its function is the production of different sorts of words and discourse."[56] The *Abhidharmasamuccaya* states that the function of *saṃjñā* is to "recognize and know diverse things, and to set them forth as empirical and linguistic referents."[57] *Saṃjñā*, therefore, is already involved in a kind of reflective consciousness that articulates the objects of perception and re-presents them linguistically, differentiating them on the basis of class inclusion. This involves a degree of abstraction from what Buddhists considered the immediate presentation of phenomena – which is a unique and momentary occurrence – and thus a degree of falsification of the actual occurrence of dharmas. Hence the frequent admonitions throughout Buddhist literature not to cling to these signs, as well as descriptions of wisdom as "signless" (*animitta*)[58]. *Saṃjñā*, although often translated as "perception," should be differentiated from *pratyakṣa*, which indicates a more immediate, non-verbal level of perception literally meaning "seeing before the eyes, witness, perceptible, immediate."[59]

Other terminology important to the Mahāyāna understanding of conceptual-linguistic construction is the group of frequently used words having $\sqrt{}$*kḷp* as the root. Candrakīrti's *Prasannapadā* indicates that *kalpanā* is the act of construing as permanent that which is impermanent. Thus, the function of *kalpanā* is the hypostatization of that which has been discerned and distinguished from the continuum of becoming and passing away.[60] The term *vikalpa*, with its divisive prefix *vi-*, generally denotes the discriminitive function of intentional consciousness. *Vikalpa* abstracts a particular referent by negating what it is not; thus, rather than the apprehension of a positive entity, this process constructs a denotative referent by negating everything but the particular intentional object. By determining particular configurations of background and foreground, this aspect of conceptualization creates binary divisions, attachment to which is a fundamental characteristic of bondage in Buddhist thought. Madhyamaka texts tend to emphasize the delusiveness of *vikalpa* insofar as it creates binary oppositions that manifest as either/or questions resting on false premises, while Yogācāra texts often present the basic illusion engendered by *vikalpa* as the absolute distinction between subject and object.[61]

We have already noted the term *prapañca* in the context of pre-Mahāyāna Buddhism, denoting conceptual proliferation. What is distinctive about this aspect of conceptual-linguistic construction is that it emphasizes not just a single instance of hypostatization, objectification, or verbal construction, but rather the tendency of conceptual-linguistic activity to proliferate, thereby creating a network of meanings based on these false conceptualizations. In general, the term has the implication of enlargement and multiplication, false statements, and vain imaginings.[62] In a more technical sense it may be understood as denoting the expansion of a mistaken apprehension from an initial and particular instance of the reification to the increasing implications and conclusions based on this initial fabrication. Williams argues that *prapañca* indicates a "widening" of the opposition between *x* and *not-x* that is initially produced by *vikalpa*[63] and thus "designates the tendency and activity of the mind, weakly anchored to a (falsely constructed) perceptual situation, to proliferate conceptualization beyond its experiential basis and therefore further and further removed from the foundation which could lead to a correct perception via impermanence."[64] He also suggests that *prapañca*s indicate verbalizations that articulate inferential structures which in turn lead to the extension of verbalization, thereby creating more and more artificial referents.[65] Whether the focus is on conceptual activity or overt articulation, *prapañca* implies the prolific web of false concepts and verbalizations within which consciousness becomes entangled.

Two things are noteworthy here: first, the assumption that perception (*pratyakṣa*) in and of itself, free from any conceptual appropriation, is closer to the unmediated truth of things than verbalized sentences, particularly propositional subject/predicate statements; and second, language, concept, classification, and reflection are presumed to distort the true apprehension of things and can conceal more than they reveal. The state which reveals that actuality of things is a pre-reflective state prior to conceptualization and articulation; the state in which *prapañca*, *saṃjñā*, and *vikalpa* are relinquished is frequently described as tantamount to enlightenment. Indeed, the *Bodhicaryāvatara* says that a monk who has destroyed *saṃjñā* and *vikalpa* has nothing more to attain.[66]

Recall in the previous discussion of language in the *Aṣṭa* that the bodhisattva is frequently discouraged from articulating his experience in sentences such as "I am a bodhisattva," "I abide in perfect wisdom," and so on. Now we can make more sense of this, as well as the vigorous criticism of Abhidharma methods of "reviewing" the dharmas by labeling them as they arise in consciousness with the intent of classifying them in an all-embracing taxonomy. While for the Madhyamaka and other Mahāyāna schools it is useful and even necessary to organize and classify the world in certain ways, all dharmas are only distinguishable by conventional organization and designation, not by absolute ontological distinctions. Dharmas do not fall into natural taxonomic categories, for any categorization is already a second-order activity removed from the pre-reflective apprehension of things. Insofar as the division of things into subjects and predicates is present even at the level of *saṃjñā*, the most rudimentary stage of conceptualization, language and discursive thought are at the heart of the construction of a lifeworld that is fundamentally misconstrued. In this respect, discursive thinking is considered distortive and impure, so much so that some Mahāyāna texts claim, as we saw earlier, that the Buddha did not really engage in speech at all. Thus Bhāvaviveka says, in the *Chang-chen-lun*, that when all dharmas are understood free of conceptualization (*niṣprapañca*), only then does there arise correct speech – which is ceasing to speak at all.[67]

Perception in Indian Buddhism and Indian Philosophy

Behind the critique of language and concepts, therefore, is an inclination to think of the apprehension of truth in the highest sense as modeled on perception (*pratyakṣa*) rather than conceptual-linguistic activity. To a great extent, this is due to the fact that perception is understood in most of Indian philosophy, and especially Buddhist thought, to be the most reliable way of knowing something in an ordinary sense. Perception and its relationship to knowledge is one of the pervasive issues in Indian thought, and in order to discern the roles of vision in Buddhist discourse we must first address briefly the primacy of perception as a whole in not only Buddhism, but all of Indian philosophy. The initial impetus for most schools of Indian philosophy was scripture – the Vedas, Upaniṣads, epics, sūtras. Systematic philosophy attempted to organize, analyze, interpret, and defend the positions and particular interpretations of these positions against rival schools. All of the schools of Indian philosophy (*darśana*s) asserted that there were definite means for coming to valid knowledge (*pramāṇa*s). The most commonly accepted and debated means of valid knowledge included perception (*pratyakṣa*), logical inference (*anumāna*), and testimony of a reliable witness, (*śabda*, usually meaning a scripture). Some schools accepted others such as analogy (*upamāna*), implication (*arthāpatti*), memory (*smṛti*), and the perception of absence (*anupalabhadhi*).

Without exception, all schools of Indian philosophy not only accepted perception as a means of valid knowledge, but accorded it a primary position. All other forms of knowing and cognition were understood to be based on this *pramāṇa*. The agreement ends there, though, and the range of divergence on the nature of perception and its relationship to cognition can be illustrated by the conflict between the Vedic philosopher Bhartṛhari and Buddhist theorists. For Bhartṛhari, all perception and cognition is linguistic, and without language there is no apprehension of objects. Drawing from the Vedic understanding of the word, he asserts that words themselves call things into being from Brahman and that names of things are essentially identical with the things themselves. Perception, therefore, while primary to other forms of knowledge, is fundamentally linguistic, and language is rooted in being itself. J. Mohanty summarizes Bhartṛhari's principle: "There is no awareness in this world without its being intertwined with the word."[68]

I have already pointed out the sharply differing orientation of Buddhist thinking on this issue, be it that of the orthodox Buddhist suttas or the early Mahāyāna sūtras, both of which consider language to be derivative and deceptive if understood to refer to inherently existing realities. Later systematizers of Buddhist thought attempted to develop and refine this position in a number of ways, some of which utilized the primacy of perception as a basic element in their theories of knowledge. Many agreed that perception was primary in the sense that it reveals the world prior to the imposition of conceptual elaboration. The Yogācāra philosopher Asaṅga defined perception (*pratyakṣa*) as being direct (*aviparokṣa*), not judged (or reasoned) or not-to-be-judged (*anabhyūhitānabhyūha*), and having no error.[69] Vasubhandu agreed, calling perception a kind of consciousness (*vijñāna*) that occurs on account of an object (*artha*) only, as opposed to consciousness depending on mistaking one thing for another or consciousness based on linguistic conventions.[70]

Perhaps the most detailed theory of perception and knowledge was that of the sixth century philosopher Dignāga. We can in no way do justice to this complex thinker in this short space, but will be content to mention his basic views on the issue at hand, for he draws out the some of the important themes regarding perception implicit in Buddhist thought for centuries before him. For Dignāga, correct knowledge and epistemology were paramount, and most important to his epistemology was perception (*pratyakṣa*). In his text on the theory of knowledge, the *Pramāṇasamuccaya*, Dignāga asserts that perception is an unmediated apprehension of a particular, a given that is untouched by conceptual construction.[71] Names, classifications, assignations of specific qualities and actions, and association with a particular substance are impositions upon this apprehension and do not refer to real objects.[72] In other words, all qualifiers add a constructed dimension of generality to the unconstructed and specific nature of a perception. The real particulars apprehended by perception are always unique, and perception alone apprehends the unique characteristic (*svalakṣana*) of each. Words, in contrast, refer to classifications (*jāti*) constructed by the intellect, rather than to these real entities. Language serves to make distinctions and dichotomies, and to divide up the totality of the world of perception.[73] Dharmottara and Dharmakīrti expand on this notion, saying that these second-order activities of naming and conceptualization involve memory (*smṛti*), since a name or classification can only be given to something when it is associated through memory with something encountered in the past. Recognition is not produced by the object of perception itself, but by its entering into a network of associations, memories, and categories derived from past experience. Only perception yields direct, unconstructed knowledge (*nirvikalpa-jñāna*).[74]

In Dignāga's and his successors' accounts, then, perception is prelinguistic, prereflective, and revelatory of what is most fundamentally real. It does not, however, incorporate what is given in perception into a class of things, as does *saṃjñā*. This is the function of inference and language. On this point, Dignāga clarifies the boundary between the linguistic and the non-linguistic by citing the *Abhidharma*, which, again using the example of *perceiving blue*, explains that consciousness of perceiving blue is different than the conception of "something blue," which makes the perception into a predicate. Warder summarizes this point: "[I]n sensation (*pratyakṣa*) and in consciousness of sensation one is conscious of for example blue, but not of: 'It is blue'. In the object (*artha*) one has perception (*saṃjñā*) of the object, but in the object one does not have perception of a 'predicate'."[75] Here we see a continuation of the theme we noticed in the Perfection of Wisdom texts: the suspicion of propositional language and of the assigning of predicates in any absolute sense.

Because of their views on perception and conceptions, Buddhists tended to be minimalist in their acceptance of *pramāṇa*s. Generally, they accepted perception and inference, noting that inferential knowledge is derivative, secondary, and more prone to delusion. Some accepted reliable testimony, particularly that of the Buddha, but Dignāga and others argued that this testimony was based on the Buddha's perception and inference and therefore did not constitute a separate means of knowing.

Also noteworthy in this regard is the difference between Dignāga and the emptiness philosophers on the matter of *pramāṇa*s. For Dignāga and the logicians, along with Abhidharma theorists, perception "reaches" the object – a real particular –

while for Nāgārjuna nothing, including the barest data of sensation, has any inherent existence or unique characteristic. The constituted, conventional nature of things, for the Madhyamaka, extends to all things and itself becomes the "object" of the highest knowledge. Dignāga understands perception to reveal the unique character of an object, while Nāgārjuna claims that no self-evident, irreducible character is found. Any notion of a "given" is problematic in the Madhyamaka. In fact, Nāgārjuna appears to reject the entire discussion of *pramāṇa*s, claiming that any set standard of validity has no way of validating itself. This leads either to an infinite regress or an arbitrary choice of such a standard.[76]

Proponents of the Svātantrika Madhyamaka school gave a more important place to inference than their rival school, the Prasaṅgika, as well as the Yogacārins and Logicians, who unambiguously favored perception as the most reliable *pramāṇa*. Bhāvaviveka, arguing from the Svātantrika side, asserts that inference is necessary for the discernment of ultimate truth in order to sort out this truth from falsehood, something that perception alone is incapable of. On this basis, Eckel claims that Bhāvaviveka gives priority to inference while at the same time liberally using visual metaphor to designate the attainment of awakening.[77] Reality itself cannot be an object of inference, according to Bhāvaviveka, but inference and its necessary concomitants, language and conceptuality, are needed to clear the way to the apprehension of reality. Yet whether or not inference ever completely drops away, he expresses the final apprehension of reality as a *vision*, and never itself an object of inference.

While Dignāga and his disciples, then, did not agree in some important respects with either the Nikāyas or the emptiness philosophers, they all maintained a polemic against reliance on language, understanding perception to be superior. The significance to our study of Dignāga and the other Buddhist theorists who dealt thematically with perception and *pramāṇa* theory is that they make explicit the privileging of perception that runs throughout the Buddhist tradition. Even among those who rejected systematic accounts of perception, the perceptual metaphor still remained the most pervasive metaphor for knowledge. The preference for vision as the sense modality most representative of the capacities of the senses, and in many ways most important, is obvious in Buddhist literature. Seeing is often used as a metonym standing in for perception in general, making it the paramount sense capacity both in literal and symbolic terms. In Buddhist thinking, vision is paradigmatic of what the senses are and what they do in contrast to other faculties; the vast majority of examples of perceptual acts in Indian philosophy, Buddhist or otherwise, are acts of seeing. The word *pratyakṣa* itself, recall, literally means "before the eyes."

This paradigmatic place of vision among the other senses has to do in part with the Indian understanding of visual perception as *immediate*. Visual perception is often considered by different intellectual traditions to have an immediacy that is absent in audition, particularly the hearing of words. Greek, European, and Indian thought have often claimed, on the basis of widely divergent theories of perception, that vision has a direct access to its objects, while hearing is mediated. An object of vision is directly disclosed to the eye, but hearing discerns *activities* of things. The hearing of words involves further mediation, conceptualization, and processing. While contemporary cognitive science has revealed the high degree to which visual perception is also mediated, what is important here is how vision is understood phenomenologically – in this case, by Mahāyāna Buddhists, but perhaps cross-culturally – as a more immediate disclosure of the world than that given in auditory experience.[78] This apparent immediacy of visual perception – the implicit facticity of the seen – contributes to the structuring of Buddhist discourse, and it is from this structuring that we can begin to discern the place of vision in this discourse. Hearing is often associated with the word and language in Buddhism, which was intrinsically linked to conceptual thought, whereas the paradigmatic sense capacity in Buddhist thought, vision, represented unmediated knowing. Even though hearing was, of course, perception as well, the primary thing to be heard was language, which requires inference, conceptual thinking, and processing and is, therefore, inevitably prone to delusion. Perception, represented by vision, is used to express the simple and direct access to what is there. Thus the act of seeing becomes prototypical of the act of knowing – not just knowing facts, but apprehending truth in the sense of awakening.

The notion of seeing as prototypical of the act of knowing, especially knowing as "higher knowledge," is common in other Indic traditions as well. Again, the Buddhist emphasis on vision is part of a wider pan-Indic tendency to understand knowledge on the model of vision. For example, in Vedic and Upaniṣadic literature we find vision being self-consciously used to indicate non-sensory apprehension of the supermundane truth. I have mentioned that in the Vedic tradition, hearing was of supreme importance in certain respects. Seers (*ṛṣi*s) "saw" the ultimate truth, but this truth was not a vision *per se*, but the *words* of the Veda, memorized, repeated, handed down from teachers to generation after generation of disciples, and never written down until relatively late. Yet "seeing" was what provided direct access to the Veda. The notion of seeing words might not be surprising to those of us who quite literally see them every day on the printed page, but it is quite surprising that the apprehension of the Veda was conceived as an act of seeing long before the development of writing. While the spoken word of the Veda was *śruti* – that which is heard – this refers to the words as repeated and passed on generation to generation, heard by the disciple from the guru: the primary apprehension, however, is represented by sight. This suggests that, even in the much more oral/aural world of early Vedic culture, with the supreme value given to the word, seeing may have been understood as the most direct mode of apprehension.

The Upaniṣadic literature seems to elevate further the value of seeing. Hearing is still quite highly valued as it relates to the Veda, the Bṛhadāraṇyaka Upaniṣad, for example, identifying the eye with worldly wealth and the ear with divine wealth, or the Veda itself.[79] Here the ear is the vehicle for the authority of the Veda while the eye, although the most reliable means of determining ordinary facts, sees only worldly forms.[80] But Jayatilleke points out that in the middle and later Upaniṣads, verbal forms from $\sqrt{}$*dṛś* and $\sqrt{}$*paś*, both meaning "to see," began to acquire new significance. The *Kaṭha Upaniṣad*, for instance, claims that the *ātman* cannot be seen with the physical eye,[81] nor attained from scriptures;[82] yet it is seen (*dṛśyate*) by "those who can see subtle things."[83] The *Muṇḍaka Upaniṣad* likewise asserts:

> It (the *ātman*) is not grasped by sight, nor even by speech,
> Nor by the other senses, austerity, or works.
> Purified by the light of knowledge (*jñāna-prasādha*),
> In that way, by meditating, one sees (*paśyate*) that which is without parts.[84]

Jayatilleke identifies this as a new way of knowing, a way presumably distinct from both the seeing of the Veda and ordinary physical seeing and that was not recognized by the earlier tradition.[85] This more figurative notion of seeing became prevalent in Indian thought, especially during and after the late Upaniṣads and is particularly evident in Buddhism. Terms for seeing, in fact, came to be used in Indian philosophical discourse as virtually synonymous with knowing.[86]

We can discern, therefore, an implicit tension between language and perception that runs through Indian discourses on knowledge and awakening – especially in Buddhism, but also in the Vedānta and other Indian schools – in which perception won out as the mode of access to the world considered to yield knowledge in a more direct and unmediated way. Vision being the most representative of the senses in Indian philosophical discourse, it became a prominent symbol of unmediated access to truth. Two of the recurring images in Mahāyāna texts, therefore, should be clearer: that of the silent Buddha and that of the awakened being on top of a hill or terrace looking out upon the world from an elevated distance. The image of the silent Buddha and the claims that he never actually spoke a word are not nonsensical or arbitrary. Behind them is the accumulated weight of a long tradition of suspicion regarding language and concepts. Despite the fact that a number of Buddhist traditions would eventually come to a different relationship with words – for example, embracing mantras understood to have inherent power in much the same way the Veda did – the dominant attitude, especially in the contemplative traditions, was that words and concepts were instrumental in constructing a delusory understanding of oneself and the world, despite their necessity on a practical level. The image of the Buddha or bodhisattva perched on a high terrace surveying the world is no arbitrary image, for it represents the spacious "seeing" of reality as a whole from the vantage point of one who has opened his or her eyes from the sleep of language and "seen" beyond its obstructions. This understanding of seeing carries with it rich symbolism in Buddhist traditions, as well as a specific history – subjects to which we turn in the next chapter.

CHAPTER TWO

Buddhist Visuality in History and Metaphor

> We never cease living in the world of perception, but we bypass it in critical thought – almost forgetting the contribution of perception to our idea of truth.
>
> *Maurice Merleau-Ponty*[1]

Vision is a natural phenomenon, and it can be studied as such – a matter of rods and cones, light waves and neurons. Vision also has a history, a natural history as well as various cultural histories. One pivotal chapter in the natural history of human vision, for example, was when hominids began to stand on their hind legs, reducing the importance of smell, the principal sense for quadruped mammals. Upon homonids' rising on two legs, vision gained a new and important place in the sensorium; Freud even speculated that this transformation was the basis of human civilization.[2]

While there are undoubtedly universal features of vision based on physiology that constitute its natural history, it is important that we attend also to the cultural histories of vision and the other senses as well – ways they are appropriated, understood, and given specific places in systems of meaning and value within particular cultures. These culturally and historically particular ways of seeing and understanding seeing have been called "visuality."[3] The many different kinds of visuality have varied considerably: theories of "extramission" in which the eyes emanate light rays in order to see; the Medusa's gaze, capable of turning a person to stone; notions of the evil eye; mystical visions and delusionary apparitions. Vision has been presented variously as a way to break free from egoistic limitations to the unconditioned light of truth, or as a self-reflective trap capable of drowning Narcissus in the waters of self-absorption. These are just a few of many ways in which the eye and vision have functioned in particular philosophies, myths, and practices.

We have noted that "seeing the dharmas" or "seeing the truth" is a frequent metaphor for knowledge and awakening in the Perfection of Wisdom and other Buddhist literature, and that this seeing contrasts with language and conceptual thought, which are considered to foster delusion. Now I will examine in greater detail the role of visual metaphors for knowledge and awakening, as well as some of the historical influences that may have contributed to the forms visuality assumed in the context of South Asian Buddhism. The two main points I wish to make in this chapter about visual metaphor in Mahāyāna Buddhist discourse are, first, that these metaphors are *generative*. That is, by focusing attention on visual experience as a model for knowing enlightenment, they produce a particular way of understanding what constitutes knowledge, especially enlightened knowledge. They help to constitute, in other words, a specific epistemic paradigm. Second, the metaphor of vision is not left to perform this task in isolation, but invites the use of several other metaphors related to vision, such as light, the sun, fire, lamps, sleeping and awakening, eye-diseases, and space, the medium of vision. This family of metaphors, clustered around the central trope of "knowing-as-seeing," forms a major part of the symbolic vocabulary of the epistemic system implicit in South Asian Mahāyāna Buddhism.

Vision in Indo-European Language and History

It may seem quite natural to the speaker of modern English that vision is strongly associated with knowledge and the intellect, for such an association pervades this language. Often *seeing* is understood as synonymous with knowing or understanding, for example: "I see what you mean," or "I see your point of view." We have a general *outlook* on life and try to gain *insight* into another person's *perspective*. We *speculate*, *inspect*, *introspect* (from the Latin *spectare*) and *survey* subjects of broad *scope* (cf. the Greek *scopos*, "watchman," from skeptomai, "to look out"). The special relationship between knowledge and vision is attested to by the fact that "seeing is believing," and an eye-witness is more convincing than hearsay or a gut feeling, both of which are associated with other sense faculties. What is not immediately apparent, however, is that this linkage of knowledge and vision that is common sense to the speaker of modern English is deeply rooted in the Indo-European language family and so is present in Indian culture as well. Moreover, it may *not* be common sense to those in other cultures or language families.

Indo-European, the ancient ancestor of both European and Sanskritic languages, contains a number of roots whose historical development in many of its descendants suggests an ancient pattern of connection between eye and mind. Few people who rent videos today are aware that the word for what they watch is from the Latin *videre*, which means "to see" and is cognate with the Sanskrit √*vid*, "to know," the root of *Veda*, the ancient Indian scriptures considered the ultimate source of knowledge. The common Indo-European root is **weid-* "to see, to know truly." From this word we get the English "vision," as well as "wisdom," and "wit." The Indo-European **sekw-* is also the root of the English "see" and the Hittite "to know."[4]

Although other senses sometimes take on intellectual connotations, there is a systematic correlation between vision and the intellect in this linguistic lineage that does not obtain for other sense modalities. Eve Sweetser suggests that vision and intellection are linked, in part, because of the ability of the visual sense to focus on particular objects and select one item in the visual field at will – a function closely resembling the workings of intentional awareness. Moreover, she asserts that the two are connected because vision is "our primary source of data about the world."[5] Vision simply provides more information than do the other senses – we see many more things than we can hear, taste, touch, and feel. The ability of vision to access data from a distance is also important.

> The ability to reach out is a significant parallel between vision and intellection, since the objective and intellectual domain is understood as being an area of personal *distance*, in contrast to the intimacy or closeness of the subjective and emotional domain (we may keep someone *at a distance* by keeping the conversation intellectual; and if we feel too *close* to someone, then maybe we can no longer be objective about that person).[6]

Although the example is highly specific to modern Western culture, the distancing tendency of vision and the linkage of this tendency to the intellect and objective knowledge also has a history deeply embedded in Western intellectual traditions from the time of the Greeks. The ocularcentrism of Greek culture in philosophy, religion, and the arts is well-attested. Hans Jonas claims that the Greek philosophical emphasis on vision and the ability of sight to observe a thing at a distance, disengaged from the object, was directly connected to the development of the notion of objective truth in the West – the thing as it is, independent of how it affects the person. The distinction between the thing in itself and the thing "as it affects me" gives rise to the notion of *theoria* and theoretical truth.[7] Theory, or *theoria*, which has the same root as theater, denotes in its root meaning "the outward look, the aspect in which something shows itself" and meant in the ancient Greek context "to look at attentively, to look over."[8] In Jonas's and others' readings, this meant a distancing between subject and object. Because vision tends toward static representation rather than the more dynamic structuring of hearing and touch, it emphasizes static being over dynamic becoming and fixed essence over transitory appearances.[9]

The Greeks also celebrated vision in their anthropomorphic gods and goddesses, who were depicted in sculpture and worshipped in visible form. They loved spectacle and theatrical performance, idealized the nude body, developed mathematics with a geometrical emphasis and a science of optics that was crucial to their philosophy.[10] While they celebrated vision, they also feared its immense power, as is suggested by the myths of Narcissus and Medusa, and by the widespread use of amulets designed to protect from the evil eye.[11]

Stephen Tyler claims that Greek thought can be analyzed in terms of two tendencies: the Platonic, which understands things in terms of substances or objects, and the Heraclitian, which understands things in terms of attributes, actions, events, and relations. The former, he argues, won out over the latter in the ancient Greek world and continued to form the underlying structure of Western metaphysics until the twentieth century. According to Tyler, the privileging of vision in the history of Western thought is inextricably connected to the emphasis on *things*, which take precedence over processes, events, and possibilities, inevitably entailing a metaphysics of substance and the notion of thinking as *representation* rather than as communication, a notion more tied to a verbal model. The "hegemony of the visual," he claims,

> (a) necessitates a reductive ontological correlation between the visual and the verbal; (b) creates a predisposition to think of thinking/knowing as seeing; (c) promotes the notions that structure and process are fundamentally different and that the latter, which is only sequentiality, can always be reduced to the former, which is simultaneity, so that being dominates becoming, actuality dominates possibility.[12]

Like Jonas and Sweetser, Tyler also sees this linking of vision and thinking/knowing as an ancient pattern embedded in the Indo-European language family. The rendering of speech in visible form through the technology of writing was also a constitutive factor, in that it assimilated the word to the visual realm and contributed to the reduction of the verbal model of thinking to the visual. The verbal/auditory aspects of thinking and communication in this way become another object of sight.[13]

But now we face the issue with which we began this part of the discussion: it seems quite natural that vision should be a privileged sense, especially with respect to knowledge; as Sweetser says, we simply get more information from the visual sense than from any other and the link between the visual and the intellectual may be universal and indeed "natural." Seeing, in fact, would seem to be a subset of knowing – to see something is to have some knowledge of it. The link is not symmetrical, of course, since to know or know about something does not necessarily entail seeing it, despite the figures of speech suggesting such. Nevertheless, part of the prevalence of visual metaphors for knowing must be connected to general body-mind correlations in language by which mental events are expressed in somatic terms. Sweetser claims that this is a systematic, and probably universal, cognitive process whereby meanings on a physical level become regularly linked to categories at an abstract mental level. This is part of the "Mind-as-Body Metaphor" whereby words for thinking and emotions are regularly taken from the somatic realm – from sensations or physical actions – and generally proceed from the concrete to the abstract.[14]

Nevertheless, despite the regularities and physical bases of such metaphorical understanding of thinking and knowing, the predominance of a particular sense modality in the language of knowledge is also highly mediated by culture and patterns of the language itself. This point takes us closer to our primary subject matter in India. Tyler, comparing the vocabularies of knowledge in the Indo-European and Dravidian language families, shows that far fewer Dravidian words expressing thinking or knowing concepts make reference to sensory representation, and even fewer are visual tropes. Instead, the common metaphors for thinking and knowing in Dravidian languages are drawn from the realm of intentionality, translatable as "desire," "intention," "hope," "wish."[15] The sensory metaphors that are present are about equally divided between visual, verbal, and kinesthetic terms and reveal no pattern of preference for one sense faculty over the other in expressing notions of knowing. Often the use of indirect discourse is the primary model for reporting thoughts; in the Koya language, for example, it is most common to report a thought using a speech metaphor, for example: "'I will go to Nallabali', he thought." In this case "he thought" is a metaphorical use of a word that literally means "he said" (*ittōṇḍu*), indicating a verbal rather than visual modeling of thinking.[16]

Insofar as the linguistic and cognitive habits of Dravidian languages do not contribute to vision being the dominant metaphor for thinking and to the *thing* as the dominant metaphysical category, they suggest more of an action, event, or process orientation. They do not have the sensory and metaphysical patterns that contributed in Indo-European philosophy to framing thinking in terms of *ideas representing things*, the formative notion in Western metaphysics.[17]

This leaves us with two points regarding the metaphorical linkage of vision with knowledge. First, there is a cognitive/linguistic habit or pattern in Indo-European languages that predisposes both common sense and intellectual discourse to understand thinking and knowing in terms of seeing. This is to some extent grounded in the natural structure of human physiology and bodily activity, since the eyes provide us with a substantial amount of information, and seeing itself could be conceived as a kind of knowing in a limited sense. Second, however, is the fact that, while the visual metaphor is a likely choice for expressing concepts of knowing, it is *not* a cultural universal. The fact that so much information comes by way of vision perhaps predisposes human beings to make strong associations between vision and knowledge in general, but not all cultures place the same emphasis on the visual or use vision as a root metaphor for knowledge. Our case of Dravidian, as well as Hebraic language and culture, offer counter-examples to the notion that structuring knowledge in terms of vision is inevitable. Judaism and Islam have often distanced themselves from certain aspects of vision, especially in their aversion to pagan "idolatry." The visual orientation of Greek culture is often contrasted, albeit perhaps too simplistically, to the more verbally oriented Hebraic traditions,[18] and the anti-visual tendencies have been strong in Judaism even up to recent Jewish theology.[19] José Faur, for instance, says:

> The Greek truth is visual. Therefore it is related to the spatial World-Out-There. For the Hebrews the highest form of truth is perceived at the auditory level. . . . Verbal representation of God, even in anthropomorphic terms, is common both to Scripture and to the rabbis. What was offensive to the Hebrew was "to see" God; that is, to express His reality at the visual level.[20]

Some cultures, then, have historically tended to think of knowledge, truth, and religious value more in terms of hearing than of vision. Even if understanding knowledge in terms of vision is common, the ways in which visual experience, visual knowledge, and other kinds of knowledge are all related in a conceptual system are based to a high degree in cultural experience.[21]

But what of the situation in ancient India, where the Indo-European and Dravidian traditions mingled? Here Tyler underestimates the degree to which static being and thought about "things" in an abstract sense achieved prominence in Indian thought. He assumes that Indian philosophy, with intentionality and desire occupying a central place, the cosmos being an illusion (*māyā*) (a standard overgeneralization of Indian thought), and a process of endless flux, eschewed notions of unchanging essence or static being.[22] But most of the philosophical systems of ancient India in no way rejected concepts of essence. In fact, the tension between static being and dynamic becoming is pervasive in Indian philosophy, both as an internal dynamic within individual schools of thought and as points of rivalry between schools (the *ātman/anātman* debate between Vedāntins and Buddhists being the most obvious example). While Indian thought was heavily influenced by the indigenous Dravidian-speaking population, it was dominated by Indo-European cognitive/linguistic habits derived from the same root language as Greek. It would be premature and perhaps simplistic to trace this tension to influences of Indo-Aryan culture versus Dravidian culture, but these respective influences were important factors in the overall shape of Indian philosophy. The Aryan language and religion emphasized permanence (the eternal Vedas, eternal Brahman) and vision (with its *ṛṣis*), while the elements that we know of in the indigenous Indian religions (goddess worship, fertility cults, cyclical understanding of time) were arguably dominated more by temporal process and interaction. The combinations of both of these influences permeate Indian religion and philosophy. There were, then, two streams of thinking about *things* in India, whether or not they can be tied to Aryan and Dravidian influences respectively, as there were two streams in Greece. One, rooted primarily in Upaniṣadic literature, held to a static, absolute reality behind illusory phenomena, while the other, represented mainly by Buddhism, held to a dynamic, essenceless view of reality. The first was a substantialist metaphysics – a "metaphysic of presence" often given to discussion of "existents" or "being" (*sat*, *bhāva*), while the other, sometimes ruthlessly critiquing the very notion of being and essence, and at other times coming rather close to it, maintained a constant polemic against Indian substantialism.

We shall see later in this chapter that Indian uses of visual metaphor, like that of the Greek, sometimes implicitly de-emphasized temporal flux in favor of representation of the world as a state of static simultaneity. Yet these metaphors were well-ensconced in Indian language and were used by Buddhist anti-substantialists as well as Vedāntin substantialists. Ocular vocabulary in India, then, was not as inevitably tied to substantialism. In the case of Buddhist discourse, which is traditionally anti-substantialist, visual metaphor was often used not so much to evoke the sense of static representation of an object, but rather an unimpeded vision diffused throughout empty space – a vision of the insubstantiality of things that constitutes awakening.

Metaphors and Their Functions

It has been said that metaphor is not a "transfer of meaning but a restructuring of the world."[23] If this is so, the understanding of a world – meaning for our purposes a cultural world in which are found particular meanings, values, and practices – should benefit from the study of the prevalent metaphors of that cultural world. Before discussing specific instances of how metaphor and other tropes in South Asian Buddhist literature both reveal and structure

Buddhist meanings, it is necessary to discuss metaphor in a more general sense. Since the meaning and functions of metaphors are not immediately obvious, I will first outline some basic concepts derived from contemporary linguistic theory which will be guiding ideas in my analysis of Buddhist metaphoricity.

Contemporary studies in linguistics and cognitive science in the past few decades have revolutionized the understanding of metaphor. Until recently, metaphors were often taken to be non-literal expressions having little or no place in scientific or philosophical discourse, those being attempts to accurately and neutrally describe reality and account for the causation of phenomena. Everyday language and, even more so, scientific language were understood to be, at least ideally, unambiguous, literal, and largely devoid of the imprecisions of metaphor. Andrew Ortony summarizes this position:

> Science is supposed to be characterized by precision and the absence of ambiguity, and the language of science is assumed to be correspondingly precise and unambiguous – in short, literal. For this reason, literal language has often been thought the most appropriate tool for the objective characterization of reality.[24]

Metaphor and other tropes, in this view, are considered exceptions to the usual rule of literal language – deviations belonging mainly to the domain of the poet.

Recent studies, however, demonstrate that metaphors permeate both ordinary and scientific language and, far from being an exception, are the norm. Metaphors do not dwell exclusively in the realm of poetic and purely figurative language but, rather, are pervasive in virtually all linguistic domains and, moreover, are major determinates of how human beings understand their world. George Lakoff and Mark Johnson, in their groundbreaking *Metaphors We Live By*, claim that "metaphor is pervasive in everyday life, not just in language but in thought and action. Our ordinary conceptual system, in terms of which we both think and act, is fundamentally metaphorical."[25] Lakoff, in a later article, claims that metaphor is one of the main ways in which we not only comprehend many ordinary activities, but also perform abstract reasoning.[26] In this sense, metaphorical language that is embedded in scientific or philosophical discourse serves to highlight – as well as hide – different aspects of reality.[27] Moreover, metaphors are rooted in human conceptual systems and are not simply linguistic phenomena.[28] In fact, a metaphor is not just a word or concept used outside its usual meaning to express a similar idea, but is, rather, a way of conceiving one entire realm of concepts in terms of another realm. Metaphoricity is a way of "cross-mapping in the conceptual system" of one domain of experience and terminology with another.

To illustrate this notion of how metaphors work, let us look at one of the now well-known illustrations of this view given by Lakoff and Johnson: ARGUMENT IS WAR. This is a conceptual metaphor illustrated by a number of expressions in everyday language.

> Your claims are *indefensible*.
> He *attacked every weak point* in my argument.
> His criticisms were *right on target*.
> I *demolished* his argument.
> I've never *won* an argument with him.
> You disagree? Okay, *shoot!*
> If you use that *strategy*, he'll *wipe you out*.
> He *shot down* all of my arguments.[29]

The metaphor ARGUMENT IS WAR is a cross-mapping of the vocabulary of one conceptual domain (war) upon another (argument).[30] More than just figurative expressions, these examples illustrate that the vocabulary of war is deeply embedded in our concept of an argument and that this vocabulary actually structures the very practice of argument. Lakoff and Johnson further suggest that this is deeply cultural and invite the reader to imagine a culture in which the primary metaphoric vocabulary of argument is that of, for example, dance rather than war. In such a culture, people would view and carry out argument rather differently, perhaps emphasizing aesthetic balance and performance rather than winning or losing.[31]

The view of metaphor as primarily a poetic device and a deviation from scientific, philosophic, or other discourses that attempt to describe reality and account for phenomena, is challenged by a few simple illustrations to the contrary. For example, Richard Boyd shows that there are cases in which scientific metaphors are "an irreplaceable part of the linguistic machinery of a scientific theory" and that such metaphors contribute to the constituting of scientific theories rather than just expressing aspects of them figuratively.[32] He illustrates this claim with the example of some metaphors of cognitive science that draw from the terminology of computer science:

> 1. the claim that thought is a kind of "information processing," and that the brain is a sort of "computer;"
> 2. the suggestion that certain motoric or cognitive processes are "pre-programmed;"
> 3. disputes over the issue of the existence of an internal "brain-language" in which "computations" are carried out;
> 4. the suggestion that certain information is "encoded" or "indexed" in "memory store" by "labeling," whereas other information is "stored" in "images."[33]

The point is that these metaphors are not simply exegetical but are *theory constitutive*, shaping the way we understand cognitive functioning, contributing to how questions about the mind are framed, fostering certain types of experimentation, highlighting certain aspects of cognitive functioning, and obscuring aspects that do not fit the MIND IS A COMPUTER metaphor.

A final point that is significant to our subject is that metaphors are "realized" in objects, situations, myths, symbols, and other cultural products. They often impose structure on material culture, for example, thermometers and stock market graphs, which are realizations of the metaphor MORE-IS-UP, a metaphor that holds even in cases where there is no physical connection between more and up. They are also realized in other cultural products such as literary works (*Pilgrim's Progress* and the *Gaṇḍavyūha* are examples of the metaphor PURPOSEFUL LIFE IS A JOURNEY), dream interpretation, social institutions and practices, laws, and forms of discourse.[34] Thus, metaphors not only offer different ways of viewing the world, they help constitute those views and give rise to activities and cultural products that are realizations of metaphors basic to particular cultures.

Visual Metaphor in Buddhist Discourse

Of the numerous ocular metaphors found in Buddhist literature, perhaps the most pervasive, and that which grounds some of the others, is the correlation of awakening, or the most profound kind of knowing, with vision. From the earliest stages of Buddhism, seeing has connoted the direct cognition of truth. Even verbal truths, when understood fully and directly, are "seen"; for example, in the *Suttanipāta*, "one comprehends the Noble Truths and sees (*passati*) them," and the Buddha is said to know and see all things.[35] The frequent pairing of knowing and seeing indicates intimate, direct, and full knowledge.

I will use the phrase KNOWING IS SEEING to stand for this basic metaphor, of which there are numerous expressions. A sampling of just a few found in some Mahāyāna texts are:

> Thus has the vision of the Dharma been taught by the Tathāgata ... whoever sees thus, sees all elements of existence (dharmas).[36]

> Without wisdom, these five perfections are without eyes.[37]

> When they are taken hold of by wisdom, they obtain an eye.[38]

> Deep is the dharma of the leaders, and hard to see. ... those who are grasping and unintelligent are blinded.[39]

> Without the perfection of wisdom, they are as if born blind.[40]

> The bodhisattva looks down upon (*vyavalokana*) dependent arising ... [while] seated on the terrace of enlightenment ... and thus attains all-knowledge.[41]

> This king of concentrations (*samādhi-rāja*) entails withdrawing from all sense fields ... [and] the seeing of dharmas (*darśana-dharma*).[42]

> [The king of concentrations entails] not rejecting knowledge and vision ... it is the eye of those desiring to see.[43]

> Even as those not suffering from eye disease do not see the hairs and mosquitoes and such things which are perceived by those with eye disease, so the Buddhas in no way whatsoever see self and non-self as self-existing realities in the way ordinary people imagine them.[44]

> Someone who has opened the wisdom-eye, stopped the sleep of ignorance, and woken up does not see things as they are seen conventionally.[45]

These metaphorical expressions all draw in different ways from various aspects of visual experience, suggesting a coherent system of metaphors for understanding knowledge in terms of seeing.

This, of course, does not mean that all forms or instances of knowledge in Buddhist discourse are understood in terms of sight, nor that sight is in every case associated with higher knowledge and enlightenment. It does mean that there exists in Buddhist discourse a coherent and systematic way of understanding the concept of knowledge and access to ultimate truth in terms of visual experience. Among the elements of visual experience that these examples draw from and incorporate into ways of thinking about knowledge and enlightenment are the following:

1. Seeing is relatively passive in comparison to speaking, moving, and acting. Buddhist scriptures do not discuss actions of the body, speech, mind, and *eyes*; the eyes are understood as receptive, not imposing anything on what is simply there, and not entailing karmic consequences. Activities of the mind, body, and speech in Buddhism create karmic reactions and have potential to produce delusion. When warnings are given in Buddhist literature about the dangers of the senses, it is with the understanding that it is the *attachment* to sense objects that is the problem, not the senses in and of themselves. The eye may draw a monk into temptations of the flesh, but it is really not the eye that does the damage but the mind's attachment to what the eye sees.

This implies certain assumptions about knowledge, namely, that what is ultimately "there" is apprehended in a state of passivity and receptivity. This applies whether "what is there" is conceived of as raw sense data (as in Dignāga) or empty phenomena (Nāgārjuna). *Tattva*, reality as it is, presents itself to the mind that has pacified conceptual-linguistic constructions. In Buddhist thought, the "vision" of things as they are is usually presented as prior to language, non-conceptual, and pre-theoretical (or perhaps "post-theoretical," insofar as it is often presented as occurring after working through dialectical reasoning).

I suggested earlier that the apparent immediacy of vision was an important factor in its being chosen to represent awakening. Why not then choose sense capacities that could be conceived as being even more immediate, such as tactile sensation? Part of the answer concerns the issue of passivity. In Buddhist philosophy, the most commonly used tactile metaphors, grasping (*gṛha*) and clinging (*upādāna*), are associated with conceptual appropriation and the desiring of objects thus appropriated. These metaphors indicate the fundamental activities of the deluded mind. Thus, while *gṛha* is sometimes a knowledge metaphor – for example, sometimes Buddhist texts refer to *grasping* the truth – it became most often associated with delusive mental activity. Letting go of such activity and allowing things to be as they are leads to true apprehension of the world. This is a more passive mode of knowing, one of simply perceiving the state of things as they present themselves directly to the eyes rather than grasping for them.

2. Knowledge as vision is entailed in the central metaphor of Buddhist discourse, that of sleeping and awakening. Ordinary experience under the influence of delusion is often compared to dreaming, and the Buddha, whose title means, of course, the Awakened One, is a person who is not under the influence of these delusions. Opening the eyes indicates waking from sleep and is a standard image found throughout Buddhist literature. Bhāvaviveka, the Mādhyamika philosopher, illustrates this trope nicely:

> Someone who feels drowsy and falls asleep sees such things as young men, women, and a palace, but does not see them when he wakes up.
>
> Likewise, someone who has opened the wisdom eye, stopped the sleep of ignorance, and woken up does not see things as they are seen conventionally.[46]

3. Seeing in the metaphorical sense often highlights an ambivalence in Buddhism regarding vision and the senses in general. One of the above passages from the *Samādhirāja Sūtra* states that the King of Concentrations involves "withdrawing from all sense fields . . . and seeing of dharmas." This suggests the inadequacy of the physical eye and the notion common in Buddhist meditation techniques that the apprehension of the highest truth is often obtained in a deep state of concentration in which there is not only no conceptual activity, but also no sensory awareness. Despite the prevalence of visual metaphor for awakened knowledge, Buddhist traditions maintained a suspicion of vision and the senses because of their role in providing the "data" for attachment and delusion. The notion of the various non-physical eyes – the Dharma-eye, the Buddha-eye, etc. – represented a devaluation of 'ordinary' vision and its potential defects, and a corresponding substitution with the more profound vision offered by these non-physical eyes.

4. The ability of the visual system to apprehend vast areas, long distances, and many things simultaneously is often highlighted in Buddhist literature and associated with a sense of spaciousness. When the "wisdom eye" is opened, it sees "all dharmas" or "dependent origination," the network of interrelated events that makes up the entire cosmos. This sense of sight as capable of encompassing wide spaces and penetrating to the furthest depths of the cosmos is important to the development of the imagery of Mahāyāna sūtras, as I will show in later chapters.

5. On the other hand, the complementary capacity of sight is the ability to search the visual field and focus on small details. Visual metaphors for acute mental perception and analysis draw on this capability; for example, the term *vipaśyanā* (insight), having the verbal root √*paś*, "to see," with the divisive prefix *vi-*, indicates seeing in a sharply focused and discerning manner and is also a name for a collection of meditation exercises involving examination of the mind and its contents or meditation on certain doctrines. Thus the abilities of the mind either to focus intently on a subject or to broaden even to embrace all things are both rendered in terms of visual experience.

6. Vision serves as a particularly apt metaphor for knowledge in relation to the notion held by many Buddhist schools that the mind is inherently pure or luminous, whereas mental afflictions (*kleśa*s) are adventitious accumulations. This entails the image of an eye having an obstruction or defect rendering it incapable of seeing the distances beyond the obscuration. Having a disease of the eye is a standard trope in Buddhist discourse, representing the mind deluded by mental afflictions such as craving, hatred, and jealousy. A standard list of states not conducive to correct knowledge are called obstructions (*nivaraṇa*) – lust, ill-will, sloth, listlessness, restlessness, worry, and skeptical doubting.[47] Conversely, having overcome these afflictions is often represented by having "unobstructed" or "unimpeded (*anāvaraṇa*, *aniruddha*) knowledge," again evoking the image of something in the line of vision being removed.

7. Visual terminology in Sanskrit (especially derivations of √*paś* and √*dṛś*) has a multivalency denoting a number of things related to knowledge and awakening. The English word "vision" can refer to physical sight, mental clarity, foresight, or mystical vision; these

Sanskrit visual terms have a similar semantic range. For example, in addition to its more primary meaning – seeing physical objects – *darśana* can denote intellectual discernment or a "philosophical vision" of things, as in the six *darśana*s, or philosophical systems, of Indian philosophy. It can also mean an inspired vision or vision in the religious or mystical sense. It is used in Buddhist literature to indicate sharp intellectual discernment as well as broad, non-conceptual apprehension.

The pervasiveness of visual metaphors in Buddhist discourse becomes particularly interesting when it encounters the doctrine of emptiness. This is a case in which metaphorical resources of a tradition have potential to work against explicit statements of doctrine, for the idea of emptiness implies that on the level of ultimate truth (*paramarthasatya*) – that level often represented by ocular tropes – nothing is really "seen." That is, the lack of inherent existence means no independent, self-subsisting thing is present; therefore, "seeing" reality in fact means seeing no objects at all. Here we might expect that the metaphor would fall by the wayside or at least no longer have any constitutive power in the discourse. This is not the case, however, perhaps because ocular metaphors are so deeply embedded in Buddhist thought. Instead of leaving the metaphor behind, many Madhyamaka texts retain and use it quite self-consciously in the form of the paradoxical dialectic discussed in the previous chapter. For example, from Bhāvaviveka:

> If [dependent] arising does not exist, does not *not* exist, and does not both [exist and not exist], what kind of thing can it be? How can anyone think that he sees the Teacher by seeing this [dependent arising]?
>
> . . . By removing the stains of errors [others] have made and being illuminated by the rays of the true Dharma, one sees the Buddha in a relative and beneficial way.
>
> [But] ultimately [this seeing] is no seeing because whatever is illusory is non-existent. [Dependent arising] cannot be analyzed, discerned, compared, or specified.[48]

And from Kamalaśīla:

> [The yogin] is established in the understanding that all dharmas have no inherent existence and, thus established,

> enters into the highest truth (*paramatattva*), having entered into a state of concentration free from conceptual construction. ... Established in this highest truth, he sees the Mahāyāna, which is said to be that highest truth. And that vision of highest truth (*paramatattva-darśana*), which is the vision of all dharmas seen by the eye of wisdom, is according to the sūtra, a non-vision (*adarśana*). ... This non-seeing (*adṛśa*) is what is meant by non-vision. But this non-vision is not like having one's eyes closed or being blind, nor is it from a defective condition.[49]

Here, in Bhāvaviveka's passage, we again encounter the paradoxical dialectic in which the particular image, in this case the Buddha himself, is discerned and asserted in a relative, conventional sense and negated in an absolute sense. In Kamalaśīla's passage, the vision of the highest truth is akin to "non-vision" or seeing nothing. Seeing the particular, the Buddha, is a function of the focusing, discerning aspect of sight, while the vision of highest truth, which is beyond any particular that could be "analyzed, discerned, compared, or specified" is a vision that includes no such particulars. The analytical vision is subordinated to the vision that sees nothing and yet is still vision – a vision that is non-vision.

Related Metaphors for Knowledge and Awakening

The use of words relating knowing to seeing in Buddhism implies specific patterns of inference relating the two concepts. To map out more carefully the topology of these relations, we must examine some of the metaphorical uses of concepts related to knowledge in Buddhism. When I refer to words denoting knowledge and awakening, I am referring primarily to words derived from the Sanskrit roots √*jñā*, √*vid*, and √*budh*. Words most commonly linked to vision tend to be those derived from √*jñā*. *Jñāna*, a generic term for knowledge that can mean ordinary knowing or knowing of the highest truth, is the word often paired with vision in the stock phrase, "the knowledge and vision of the Buddha." *Prajñā* tends to be used in more specific ways, often indicating the highest form wisdom. Technical uses of these terms, however, vary from school to school. We have examined some visual metaphors for awakening or knowing higher truth. Some other metaphors and similes that occur with significant frequency in Buddhist texts are:

KNOWING IS PENETRATION (*nirvedha*, *nirvadhana*, etc., "penetrating" wisdom; also *tīkṣṇa-prajñatā*, "sharp" wisdom[50])
KNOWLEDGE IS LIGHT (*prakāśa*, *prabhā*, *āloka*, etc.)
KNOWING IS CUTTING (*cheda*, *uccheda*, etc.)
KNOWING IS ENTERING INTO A REALM (as in "entering into truth" (*satyānupraveśa*))[51]
KNOWLEDGE IS SPACE (*ākāśa*)

Some of these metaphors may seem to have nothing to do with our central metaphor likening knowing to seeing, but the place of each in Buddhist discourse is implicitly related to vision, and together they form a network of concepts, each of which is coherent with this central metaphor.

1. LIGHT METAPHORS

We begin with the most obvious, KNOWLEDGE IS LIGHT, or as it may be understood in some contexts, TRUTH IS LIGHT. That this is part of a system of metaphors coherent with KNOWING IS SEEING should not need extensive demonstration. Light is obviously the prerequisite for vision; it spreads itself out in space so quickly that it may seem to have little to do with time; it is a symbol in many traditions for religious truth, knowledge, and revelation. Light in the Mahāyāna Buddhist traditions serves as a particularly interesting metaphor and symbol, because it bridges the scholastic aspects of Buddhism with its visionary elements. This is because it serves as a metaphor for knowledge in a more philosophical sense, as in knowing emptiness, as well as a symbol for sacrality in the rich imagery of Buddhist visionary literature.

Just a few of many possible examples will suffice to give a basic idea of how the light metaphor is used in Buddhist literature: perfect wisdom is said to be both a light and a source of light;[52] bodhisattvas are "lights and leaders of the world";[53] the six perfections are a bodhisattva's light, torch, and illumination;[54] the bodhisattva's compassionate work is an abundant light that purifies the eyes of all beings, freeing them from *saṃsāra*[55] and a light to the blind.[56] The essential nature of mind or wisdom in many texts, both Mahāyāna and non-Mahāyāna, is said to be transparently luminous (*prabhāsvara*, Pāli: *pabhassara*) by nature and only adventitiously obscured by mental afflictions.[57] All dharmas are often declared to be by nature transparently luminous as well.[58]

2. INSIGHT METAPHORS

I have mentioned that many instances of the metaphorical use of vision as knowledge imply knowledge in a high degree of generality – understanding the principle underlying things, the sameness of all dharmas, the emptiness of all phenomena, seeing the entire process of dependent origination or numerous universes in one sweeping vision. As we have seen, though, visual terminology is also used to indicate the more focused knowing sometimes implied in the metaphor KNOWING IS PENETRATION.[59] This metaphor involves the concept of a sharp, discerning intellect able to cut away (*cheda*, *uccheda*) illusion from truth, evoking as well the metaphor KNOWING IS CUTTING.[60] It is closely related to insight (*vipaśyanā*, again meaning, literally, "discerning vision") and insight meditation, in which the practitioner closely observes the contents of consciousness or contemplates a specific subject matter. KNOWING IS PENETRATION also likens the object of knowledge to a realm or container that a piercing mind probes to discover truth, thus evoking the metaphor KNOWING IS ENTERING INTO A REALM. Also present are sexual implications which were elaborated upon and concretized during the development of Tantric practice. Such metaphors of entering and penetration cohere, as well, with the various metaphors for knowing and understanding that are associated with movement in space, such as *pratipatti*, whose more literal meaning is "movement or going."[61]

Penetration, as used in some Mahāyāna texts, can also have the implication of broad, general knowing when it is indicated that the meditator, in penetrating the nature of one thing, penetrates the nature of everything or penetrates nothing.[62] Kamalaśīla ties penetration in this sense directly to light, likening it to the light of knowledge possessed by the yogin, which "penetrates everywhere, unimpeded" when mental obscurations have been removed. He likens it also to the light of the sun on a cloudless day when no impediments exist to keep it from pervading the sky.[63]

3. SPACE

The association of knowledge with space is one of the more interesting and quite neglected features of Buddhist discourse, and while on the surface space may seem to have little to do with vision, it is in fact connected in a number of ways with our primary metaphor, KNOWING IS SEEING. Simply from a linguistic standpoint, connections between vision and space are apparent. For example, the primary meaning of the verb *locate* (√*lok*) is "to see," and it also means, in some texts, "to know" or "to perceive." The noun derived from this root is *loka*, the primary meaning of which Monier-William's *Sanskrit-English Dictionary* lists as "free or open space."[64] In many contexts, it then comes to mean "world" or "realm." Moreover the term *ākāśa* (space) itself is derived form the root √*kaś*, whose verb forms are associated with light and luminosity, for example: *kāśate*, "to be visible or appear, to shine."

While it is impossible to reconstruct precisely the process by which seeing and space became associated in the same family of words, it is not unexpected, for they are *phenomenologically* associated. To clarify this, we must briefly digress into some further discussion of how vision and hearing structure models of knowing. David Chidester notes a number of ways in which vision and space are associated on a phenomenological level. Visual coherence, he notes, is structured by the simultaneous presence of objects in the visual field. This simultaneity contrasts with the temporality that structures hearing.

> The major structuring principle of visual experience is space; that of auditory experience is time. Vision is diffused in space, words move in time. As a corollary to this, it is important to note the capacity of sight to present simultaneity and the capacity of hearing to present sequence.[65]

Although temporality is, of course, a part of visual experience insofar as the visual field is scanned in time, this temporal dimension of vision is different than that of audition. Hans Jonas elaborates on this point:

> The present, instead of being a pointlike experience, becomes a *dimension* within which things can be beheld at once and can be related to each other by the wandering glance of attention. This scanning, though proceeding *in* time, articulates only what was present to the first glance and what stays unchanged while being scanned. The time thus taken in taking-in the view is not experienced as the passing away of contents before new ones in the flux of event, but as a lasting of the same, an identity which is an extension of the

instantaneous *now* and therefore unmoved, continued present – so long as no change occurs in the objects themselves.[66]

These characteristics contrast with the temporality of sound, which is always in flux and structured by sequence and discontinuity. The simultaneous presence of things in the space of the visual field also incorporates the objects within the field into a coherent unity and continuity, as opposed to the sequentiality and discontinuity presented by audition. Vision, then, presents a manifold that suggests the continuing presence of things that can remain virtually unchanged while the eye rests on or scans them, rather than an emergence and passing away of successive phenomena. A painting remains the same during the time one is looking at it, but music cannot remain fixed in what Cézanne called "the world's instant" – it cannot be music without movement in the temporal dimension that is its home. While vision can, of course, apprehend change – the moving of a bird or the passing of a train – it does not depend on change, as does hearing, for its operation.[67] Chidester captures the point succinctly: "Hearing is dependent on action, events, and occurrences in the outer world, a world in the process of becoming, while seeing has a constant and continuous access to the world's state of being."[68]

Such tendencies, along with the capacity of the eye to see things at a great distance, may predispose the visual mode to detached contemplation and a distancing of its object. We have mentioned the distancing capacity of vision and how it may have impacted ideas of knowing in ancient Greece. This capacity of vision and the Greek modeling of knowing as *theoria* upon vision, had reverberations throughout the history of Western intellectual life. Jonas notes that sight is the only sense that can gain an advantage by spatial distance, being capable of taking in ever greater vistas the more the intervening space, while other senses lose effectiveness with distance. This capacity of sight to apprehend great distances and the inclusion in this apprehension of the terminus of such distances, forming a background for other possible presences even beyond this terminus, is according to Jonas the "birthplace of the idea of infinity."[69]

In the visual field it is this continuous blending of the focused area into more and more distant background-planes, and its shading off toward the fringes, which make

> the "and so on" more than an empty potentiality; there is the co-represented readiness of the field to be penetrated, a positive pull which draws the glance on as the given content passes as it were of itself over into further contents. ... The unfolding of space before the eye, under the magic of light, bears in itself the germ of infinity – as a perceptual aspect. ... The fact that we can look into the unbounded depth of the universe has surely been of immense importance in the formation of our ideas.[70]

These observations suggest some of the phenomenological connections between vision and space, and how these connections may contribute to the formation of ideas and systems of knowledge. With this as a background, let us investigate the role of space in Buddhist discourse and its place, along with vision, in a nexus of concepts that constitutes certain ways of knowing and understanding knowledge in the Mahāyāna.

The Meaning and Significance of Space in Buddhist Discourse

Space has always occupied an important place in Buddhist thought and symbolism. It receives notable attention in Abhidharma and meditation literature, and some early Buddhist schools considered it an unconditioned dharma, alongside nirvāṇa. Sometimes it is a synonym for the sky and is listed among groups of other primary elements. Different texts, and even different passages within the same text, reflect an ambiguity as to whether Abhidharma philosophers understood space as simply the nothingness that surrounds all physical things or as a fine material or ether that is omnipresent and eternal.[71] The *Abhidharmakośa* describes it as that which does not impede and is unsupported by anything.[72] The *Visuddhamagga* says that it is free from impact and multiplicity and, in a surprising comparison to sentient beings, declares it free of the problems involved in having a physical body and having constant sensory impact.[73] In the sequenced stages of meditation, the *jhāna*s, presented in a number of Pāli texts, having endless space as a base of concentration is one of the refined states of meditational development. Space is often compared to nirvāṇa, and Conze gives an evocative impression of these comparisons based on sūtras and commentaries:

> Both exist, though their form, location, age and measure are unascertainable. Both are unobstructed, supportless and infinite, without origin, life or death, rise or fall. In meditation space can be considered as a sort of likeness of the emptiness which is the ultimate reality. A vast capacity, it is not nothing. Not subject to conditions or restrictions it is free from obstructions and obstacles, and cannot resist, fetter, entrance, estrange or lead astray. It is everywhere, and everywhere it is the same. In it nothing is wanting, nothing owned. In perfect calm it remains by itself outside time, change and action. Nothing can be predicated of it, and nothing adheres to it as its attribute.[74]

While *ākāśa* can mean space in a local and ordinary sense, such as a finite space in between two objects, the primary symbolic force of space comes from considering it as infinite and connoting vastness, undifferentiatedness, formlessness, sameness, extension in all directions, non-resistance – that part of the lived world that is most akin to perfect, transcendent freedom as conceived in Buddhist thought. In addition to all these characteristics, its etymological connection to light and vision is not overlooked by Buddhists, and it is sometimes said to shine brilliantly.[75]

Mahāyāna texts are often less concerned than Abhidharma scholastics with systematic analysis of space and instead exploit the symbolic richness of the concept, making it one of the primary tropes for awakening and wisdom. In the *Rgs*, the boundless knowledge of the Buddhas is compared to the boundlessness of space.[76] The sameness of space is also emphasized, as is its being unbroken, undivided,[77] and without multiplicity or differentiation.[78] In the *Aṣṭa*, the Mahāyāna itself is identified with space in that it is infinite, immeasurable, and self-identical everywhere; as in space, there is room in the Mahāyāna for innumerable beings.[79] Perfect wisdom is said to be like space in that it is pure, unconditioned,[80] deep, not able to be measured, calculated, or compared.[81] Dharmas, as elements of existence, are often compared to space or to objects in space:

> Bodhisattvas, upon becoming fully awakened buddhas, teach that form is situated in the space of the world; likewise with feeling, perception, volition, and consciousness. All dharmas are situated in space, and like space they do not come or go.

> Space has not come or gone, it is not made or unmade, not constituted, not fixed, not in a particular form, indeterminate, it neither arises nor ceases. Likewise, all dharmas are unconstituted, indeterminate, unarising and unceasing. And why is this? Because the emptiness of form neither comes nor goes. Likewise for [all the skandhas] and all dharmas. And why is this? Because all dharmas are situated in emptiness, and from that situation they do not depart. They are situated in signlessness, wishlessness, not constituted, not arising, having no birth and no substantial being ... they are situated in immobility.[82]

> All dharmas are inactive and cannot be grasped, because they are inactive like space.[83]

Note how different the image of dharmas presented here is from their representations in non-Mahāyāna traditions as impermanent, always in flux, and flashing in and out of existence. While it would be misleading to say that the Mahāyāna abandoned the doctrine of impermanence, some texts implicitly de-emphasize it with such imagery as this. While the very doctrine of emptiness derives from impermanence – things lack self-identity in part because they are in constant flux and interaction – emptiness takes on its own semantic life in the Mahāyāna, sometimes forgetting its basis in impermanence. Indeed, this foundational notion in Buddhism often recedes somewhat in Mahāyāna texts and becomes subservient to the now more privileged concept of emptiness, which assumes connotations beyond just lack of identity because of impermanence. Images and metaphors likening emptiness and dharmas to static space are among the vehicles whereby emptiness takes on such new semantic overtones. This, therefore, is an example of the role imagery and metaphor can play in subtly enhancing and shifting meanings.

The concept of "all-knowledge" (*sarvajñatā*) is often likened to space, and space is said to be a subject the contemplation of which can lead to all-knowledge. In this passage of the *Aṣṭa*, the Buddha responds to Subhūti, who asks by what means a bodhisattva should understand the perfection of wisdom:

> The Blessed One said: "The perfection of wisdom is understood by the bodhisattva with a disposition inclined towards all-knowledge.

> Subhūti said: "How, Blessed One, does one develop a disposition inclined toward all-knowledge?
>
> The Blessed One replied: "By developing a disposition inclined toward space, being intent on space, and oriented toward space, Subhūti, the disposition toward all-knowledge becomes understood. And why is this? Because all-knowledge is neither an object of proof nor is it measurable. ... The immeasurability of all-knowledge is the immeasurability of space.[84]

Perfect wisdom is said to be deep, limitless, inexhaustible and boundless like space. Space is even used as a model for certain kinds of behavior and is favorably compared to deluded humans in that space does not self-consciously reflect on its own state:

> It does not occur to space in any way that it is placed near or far, for space makes no such conceptually constituted distinctions. Similarly, it does not occur to the bodhisattva practicing the perfection of wisdom, "I am near to complete awakening and far from the [lower] stages of the hearer and solitary buddha." Why? Because perfect wisdom makes no such conceptually constituted distinctions.[85]

The themes articulated in some of these examples drawn from the *Rgs* and the *Aṣṭa* illustrate how the Mahāyāna drew upon spatial experience to formulate an understanding of wisdom and awakening. The dominant image of dharmas in early Buddhist thought was of the elements of existence flashing into the world and then disappearing, enjoying only a transient moment of becoming. This is a picture of the world as fundamentally impermanent and in dynamic flux. In the examples cited above, however, we see the image of dharmas fixed in space, immobile, neither coming nor going. Rather than a plurality or hierarchy of dharmas, all dharmas in this Mahāyāna image are the same, sharing a fundamentally empty nature, and in this way leveled so that none is intrinsically higher or lower than others. Instead of the series of plural moments of existence arising and falling in time, we see the elements of existence as a continuity, without any essential differences, inactive, and unified in a homogeneous and infinite space.

This de-temporalizing of time by representing it as subordinate to space is significant in Buddhist thought and imagery. For example, the image of time as contained within space provides the basis for maṇḍalas like the Mahākāla maṇḍala in which time is represented as a circle in space. Nor is it arbitrary that space is a metaphor and symbol for awakening, while time tends to be devalued. The passage and ravages of time is a – perhaps *the* – fundamental problem of human existence in Buddhist and other forms of Indian thought. Siddhārtha's "four sights" – of an old man, a sick man, a corpse, and an ascetic – graphically depict his realization of the passing of time and its horrifying effects. Birth, old age, sickness, and death are the stock examples in Buddhism of what is wrong with temporal existence. Temporal life, represented in the Mahākāla maṇḍala as a monster gripping the circle of birth and re-birth, is to be overcome in one way or another. While the Nikāyas emphasize flux and discontinuity with regard to the world of dependent origination and present a pluralistic event ontology emphasizing impermanence, this world of flux is devalued; impermanence is not to be celebrated but transcended. This changes somewhat in the Mahāyāna, with its assertion of the non-duality of *saṃsāra* and nirvāṇa; the Mahāyāna found ways to conceive of the transcendence of time within time itself. Part of this is the spatialization of time – assimilating temporality to the always present dimension of space, which presents a symbolic abrogation of temporality by representing the world not as a series of things coming and going, but as a space within which the events of the world are contained, events which are all present together as if unified in one ever-present field of vision.

The representation of dharmas as static or contained in a spatial field is also conducive to the injunction not to cling to worldly phenomena. Descriptions of dharmas as equal, with none being more inherently attractive or repulsive than others, are meant to induce a sense of neutrality and equanimity toward all phenomena in a way that presenting them as dynamic phenomena flashing in and out of existence could not. The image of dharmas as contained within infinite space or as spreading out and pervading endless space invites a calm sense of detached contemplation and non-attachment. Seeing the *state* of things in the present dimension of space is more conducive to non-attachment than perceiving the unidirectional flow of *events* impinging upon the subject, calling for response. Spatial representation of dharmas, then, allows for the *distance* needed in order to release the inclination of the mind to cling to phenomena.

Finally, space occupies an elusive place in the lived world as something that both is and is not, something all-pervasive yet elusive and insubstantial. This makes it a ready symbol for emptiness, which is often associated with boundlessness, infinity, non-hindrance, and great distance, as is space. Throughout Mahāyāna literature, emptiness itself is often symbolized by empty space. In one episode of the *Vimalakīrti-nirdeśa Sūtra*, the great teacher Vimalakīrti, using a feigned illness as a means to draw people to receive teaching from him, empties his house of all attendants and furniture except for his sickbed. When asked why his house is empty, he evokes the classic doctrine of emptiness replying that all Buddha lands are similarly empty, as is emptiness itself.[86] Thus he makes the abstract notion of emptiness concrete, symbolizing it with the empty space of his room. The *Gaṇḍavyūha* frequently refers to unimpeded space of the Dharma-realm (*dharmadhātu*), which is conceived of in this text as the state in which dharmas in their emptiness mutually penetrate each other, their boundaries dissolved in light of their lack of inherent existence. Awareness of emptiness is often described as "spacious," a notion that Tibetan Buddhist literature, both modern and ancient, takes up in doctrine and practice. This resonance of emptiness and space, even though they are distinct concepts in Buddhist thought, reinforces the coherence of the symbolic system within which vision, space, and emptiness co-exist and mutually reinforce each other.

Conclusion

From these examples, the implications regarding these notions and images of space and their relationship to vision should be clear. I have suggested that vision structures experience in certain definite ways: it presents the world more as a static state than a dynamic flux; it presents a manifold of co-present things rather than an impermanent process of arising and passing away; it evokes the notion of infinity through its ability to see things at great distance and take in large areas, the limits of which always draw the imagination on to penetrate further possible spaces; it can view objects at a removed distance, inviting detached contemplation. The symbolic discourse of space in Buddhism recapitulates all of these ways in which the world is presented to the sense of sight: dharmas as immobile objects in space, overcoming temporal flux through remaining within the eternal present of a unified field of vision or spreading infinitely throughout all of space like light. Moreover, space is the medium of vision; therefore, a system of metaphors that models awakening on visual experience is more likely to find coherency with spatial concepts and metaphors than those of hearing or other sense modalities.

Our discussion of metaphor suggested that the mapping of one conceptual realm onto another is not just exegetical but theory-constitutive; that is, metaphor is not simply a figurative way of expressing something that is already understood, but is itself a way of conceiving and structuring the understanding of a thing or activity. This should not be construed as a kind of linguistic determinism in which language exhaustively determines cognition; rather, the linguistic and metaphorical concepts in a given conceptual scheme (whether that of an entire language or a set of technical vocabulary and concepts in a tradition) constitute the primary possibilities and most likely choices for construing various phenomena. In the case of the development of Mahāyāna thought, knowing itself is conceived in terms of seeing, and conceiving it as such constitutes a particular way of knowing. Visual experience, then, is a significant constituent of some of the fundamental concepts of knowing and enlightenment in Buddhist thought insofar as these concepts are modeled on ocular capacities. Whether they draw on the focusing and discerning abilities of the eye, as in concepts of *insight*, *penetration* and *cutting* or its ability to take in expansive vistas, as in *space*, *light*, and in some cases *penetration*, the vocabulary of knowledge is taken in large measure from phenomena having to do with various aspects of sight. The structure of the very concept of awakening (*bodhi*) and many of its associated ideas are understood on the model of the operations and capabilities of the eye. These concepts shape and constitute a coherent discourse on knowledge and awakening, marking the parameters of the Mahāyāna paradigm of knowing. There exists an intentional aspect to this as well – if the attention is trained to attend to the visual system (including the visual imagination) as a reservoir of religious meaning and a locus for religious truth, then visual thinking and its associated concepts, such as space, continuity, as so on, will occur "naturally." Thus, a natural family of concepts arises that significantly contributes to constituting a coherent epistemological paradigm.

CHAPTER THREE

Orality, Writing, and Authority: Visionary Literature and the Struggle for Legitimacy in the Mahāyāna

The tension in the Mahāyāna between seeing and hearing, sight and language is not confined to doctrine and symbolism, nor is it exclusively a metaphorical or epistemological question. It is evident in a quite different issue that the fledgling Mahāyāna movement faced: its attempts to justify and legitimate its often heterodox ideas and apocryphal sūtras. The case study I will use to illustrate this issue is a particular interface between doctrine and literary style in the *Gaṇḍavyūha Sūtra*. Scholars have commented widely upon the doctrinal differences between the sūtras of the Pāli cannon and the Mahāyāna sūtras composed in South Asia, but seldom have they given attention to what the strikingly contrasting literary styles of the Pāli and Mahāyāna sūtras themselves might reveal about Buddhism in South Asia. Scholars have had many productive debates on whether the doctrine of emptiness is a radical departure from early Buddhism, whether the Mahāyāna introduces a subtle self (*ātman*) that contradicts the doctrine of *anātman*, and whether the Yogācāra was really "idealist" or not. But the literary styles in which these doctrines emerge in some Mahāyāna sūtras is so dramatically divergent from that of the Pāli sūtras that an exploration of what contributes to this divergence may be as fruitful for the study of the Indian Buddhist world as that of their doctrinal differences. Indeed, even attention to only the introductory passages of certain sūtras opens up a number of important issues in the study of Buddhism.

Notice, for example, the introductory passages to two sūtras. The first is an early Pāli text, the *Saḷāyatanavibhaṅga Suttam*, which discusses the sense fields (*āyatanas*). It begins:

> Thus have I heard. At one time the Blessed One was staying at Sāvatthi, in Jeta Grove at Anāthapiṇḍika. The disciples greeted the Blessed One, and the he said: "Disciples, I will now discuss the distinctions between the six sense fields. . . ."[1]

This, of course, is the standard introduction common to virtually all of the Pāli sūtras. The Buddha then goes on to give a straightforward presentation of the doctrine of the six sense fields (*āyatanas*) in the typical repetitive style of the Nikāyas, with many formulary expressions repeated often throughout the text for purposes of memorization. Compare this with the introduction to the *Gaṇḍavyūha Sūtra*, a Mahāyāna text from about the second or third century C.E., set in the same location:

> Thus have I heard. At one time the Blessed One was staying in Śrāvasti, in a magnificent building in the garden of Anāthapiṇḍika in Jeta Grove, together with five thousand bodhisattvas, led by Samantabhadra and Mañjuśrī.[2]

So far, except for the mention of the building (*kūṭāgāra*) and the bodhisattvas, the two passages are almost identical – but the similarities dissolve quite abruptly. After the names and admirable qualities of a number of the bodhisattvas present are listed, the bodhisattvas observe that most beings are incapable of comprehending the great merits and abilities of the Tathāgata, and they ask the Buddha, not to *tell* them about these qualities, but to *show* them (*saṃdarśayet*). In response, the Buddha enters a state of profound concentration, and suddenly:

> . . . the building became boundlessly vast; the surface of the earth appeared to be made of an indestructible diamond, and the ground covered with a net of all the finest jewels, strewn with flowers of many jewels, with enormous gems strewn all over; it was adorned with sapphire pillars, with well-proportioned decorations of world-illumining pearls from the finest water, with all kinds of gems, combined in pairs, adorned with heaps of gold and jewels, with a dazzling array of turrets, arches, chambers, windows, and balconies made of all kinds of precious stones, arrayed in the forms of all world-rulers, and embellished with oceans of worlds of jewels, covered with flags, banners, and pennants flying in front of all the portals, the adornments pervading the cosmos with a

> network of lights. ... The Jeta grove and buddha-fields as numerous as atoms within untold buddha-fields all became co-extensive. ...[3]

The text goes on in this vein for quite a few pages, describing in the most lavish terms the luxuriant scene that suddenly arises before the group right there in Jeta Grove, the sight of so many of the Buddha's talks. There are endlessly winding rivers of fragrant water which murmur the teachings of the Buddhas; palaces that float by in the air; countless mountains arrayed all around; clouds laced with webs of jewels and raining down diamond ornaments, garlands, flowers, and even multi-colored robes; celestial maidens fly through the air trailing banners behind them while countless lotus blossoms rustle in the incense-filled air. After the initial description of the scene, bodhisattvas from distant world-systems begin to arrive, and with each of their appearances, more wonders are revealed, penetrating to the farthest reaches of the most remote worlds, then zooming back to the body of the Buddha, to the tips of his hairs or the pores of his skin, within which are revealed countless more world-systems.

What can account for the striking stylistic differences between these two texts, and why would many Mahāyāna sūtras make such a radical departure from the accepted genre of sūtra composition established by the earlier sūtras of the Pāli canon? The standard answer might be that the Mahāyāna, being originally a lay movement, was more disposed toward literary extravagance, mythical imagery, and themes appealing to the popular religious imagination. While the Mahāyāna literature, no doubt, contained elements appealing to lay Buddhists and the popular culture of its time, pandering to popular tastes is an unsatisfactory explanation; furthermore, the lay origins of the Mahāyāna are now in serious doubt.[4] For a fuller understanding of the stylistic differences between "Hīnayāna" and Mahāyāna sūtras, at least two more factors must be addressed. One is the fact that the Mahāyāna was a written tradition, while many pre-Mahāyāna Buddhist works of literature are written versions of a vast corpus of orally transmitted sayings. One of the important changes in Indian culture at the time of the arising of the Mahāyāna was the development of writing. The beginnings of the widespread use of writing in India contributed to some of the transformations Buddhism faced a few hundred years after the founder's death and was crucial to some of its most significant cultural and religious developments. Literacy disrupted the continuity of the oral tradition and reoriented access to knowledge from the oral/aural sense-world to the visual world. The transition from pre-Mahāyāna to Mahāyāna Buddhist literature, then, provides a valuable case-study of the changes that may occur during the transition from oral to written culture.

But the transition from orality to literacy was part of a wider concern for the Mahāyāna – the difficulty of establishing legitimacy and authority as a fledgling heterodox reform movement facing a well-established monastic orthodoxy. The orality of early Buddhism was not only an instance of historical happenstance but also an important means by which the early Saṅgha made its claim to authority. Pre-Mahāyāna Buddhism was, in fact, quite self-consciously an oral tradition, relying on the oral recitation and hearing of the Buddha's discourses – talks that were maintained in the memories and mouths of monks who were, according to tradition, repeating, generation after generation, the very words that the Buddha himself spoke. This tradition of recitation, then, was the way by which the Saṅgha established its claim to the *Buddhavacana* – the words of the Buddha – which conferred authority and legitimacy to the early Buddhist community.

Initially, the Mahāyāna sūtras, composed hundreds of years after the Buddha's death, enjoyed no such institutional maintenance and legitimacy and, thus, had to look elsewhere for legitimation. That "elsewhere" was the higher visionary worlds supposedly visible only to those more advanced followers of the Great Vehicle, whose visionary capacities revealed the bases for the unorthodox doctrinal claims of this new form of Buddhism. The Mahāyāna sūtras bear the marks of the movement's efforts to legitimate its novel doctrines and practices in the face of orthodox monastic communities that had implicit authority, and by and large rejected the Mahāyāna's innovations. The otherworldly imagery in the *Gaṇḍavyūha* and other Mahāyāna sūtras has roots not only in the vivid experiences and religious inspirations of early Mahāyānists, but also in the challenges that this heterodox minority movement faced in its struggle for legitimacy, patronage, membership.

Orality In Early Buddhism

Early Buddhist culture was an oral culture. The earliest archeological evidence of an Indian language being written in India, with the exception of the Harappān seals, are the inscriptions of Aśoka dated circa 258 B.C.E. The early Buddhist sūtras were not written documents but verses committed to memory and recited by monks who specialized in the memorization and recitation of what were understood to be the words of the Buddha. The orally preserved teachings were the substitute for the actual speaking presence of the Buddha; they were not merely the words of the teacher, but, after his death, the teacher itself. As the Buddha says in the *Mahāparinabbāna Sutta*:

> It may be, Ānanda, that some of you will think 'The word of the teacher is a thing of the past; we have now no teacher'. But that, Ānanda, is not the correct view. The doctrine and discipline, Ānanda, which I have taught and enjoined upon you is to be your teacher when I am gone.[5]

Hearing and the spoken word were also inextricably tied to authority in early Buddhism. The *śrāvaka*s (literally, "hearers") claimed to have directly heard and reported the words of the Buddha when he taught in India, and elaborate institutional efforts were employed by the Saṅgha to keep these words alive. The source of authority for the early teachings was the fact that they were heard from the self-authenticating presence of the Buddha. The repetition of these words was itself the Dharma and was the link to the living presence of Gautama who was now gone forever.

In an article on orality in Pāli literature, Steven Collins shows that the monastic Buddhist tradition was, even after the introduction of writing, largely an oral/aural one.[6] The traditional method of educating monks and nuns was for these students to hear and commit to memory the words of their teacher, and most of the words in the Pāli literature referring to the learning process are related to speaking and hearing.[7] The monumental task of committing the received words of the founder to memory and reciting them regularly was based on the need to maintain the Dharma and protect it from corruption and innovation, as well as on the mandate to train disciples and maintain mindfulness of the teachings. Collins maintains that the oral/aural aspects of Pāli literature are important "both as a means of preservation and as a facet of the lived experience, the 'sensual dimension', of Buddhist 'scriptures'."[8] From Collins's arguments, it is evident that this "sensual dimension" was, in the first few centuries after the Buddha's death, primarily oriented toward one particular sense – that of hearing.

While Buddhist vocabulary always had an abundance of visual metaphor, vision in a literal sense and visual imagery were not emphasized as a way of communicating the early teachings, as the aniconic nature of early Buddhism indicates. The earliest phases of Buddhism produced none of the elaborate monuments and sculptures so characteristic of its later developments. Making images of the Buddha was discouraged, and the only early representations of the awakened one were aniconic suggestions of his life and teachings such as the footprint symbolizing both the Buddha's absence and the path that he left behind. Hearing the words of the awakened one, either through being in his presence during his lifetime or by hearing his teachings recited, was the primary way of receiving the teachings. Even after texts were being written down, it was not for the purpose of their being read privately – the Vinaya gives detailed lists of all the items of property a monk may have, which does not include books or writing utensils.[9] Rather, they were committed to palm-leaf so that they would be preserved and read aloud in the context of instruction or public recitations.

It is only after Gautama had been gone for some four hundred years that the Saṅgha undertook to systematically write down what were believed to be his words. In and of itself, writing seems to have been held in some degree of suspicion: "Knowledge in books [is like] money in someone else's hands: when you need it, it's not there," says a *nīti* verse.[10] Writing was dangerous in that it relinquished control over the distribution of the Dharma and removed the words of the Buddha even further from their original source in his living speech and presence. Lance Cousins has argued that systematic oral transmission within institutions such as the Saṅgha is more likely to preserve texts intact than writing would, because in the former situation, it takes the agreement of a large number of people to make changes to the text. Manuscripts, on the other hand, can be changed by any individual scribe.[11] For an orthodoxy trying maintain the authenticity of its founder's teachings, writing was probably seen as a danger that eventually became a necessary evil. Pāli commentaries claim that the writing down of sūtras began only after there was merely one man left alive who had a particular text committed to memory, and that the text was written down for fear of its being lost forever.[12] Donald Lopez suggests that the reluctance of the Saṅgha to commit the sūtras to writing may have to do with an "ideology of the self-presence of speech," that is, the notion that only the Buddha's *speech* could truly present the Dharma, the uncreated truth, as he discovered it and that writing stands further removed from this truth – derivative, displaced and dead.[13] The repetition of words that were heard from the Buddha by a disciple, then transmitted to his disciple, and so on through a lineage of hearers, not only had the effect of rendering the Dharma in the manner that most closely approximated its original utterance, it also provided a source for genealogical legitimacy. The introduction of writing could not help but rupture this sense of authentic presence and continuity. In the early Buddhist tradition, then, the written word had little inherent value; it was seen, at best, as a merely instrumental vehicle for the spoken word.

Writing in the Early Mahāyāna

In the Mahāyāna, however, the written word took on quite a different significance, especially with regard to Mahāyāna sūtras. Writing was crucial to the development and character of the Mahāyāna in at least three respects: first, written texts were essential to the survival of this heterodox tradition; second, they provided a basis for one of the most important aspects of early Mahāyāna practice, the worship of written sūtras themselves; and third, writing contributed to a restructuring of knowledge in such a way that vision, rather than hearing, became a significant mode of access to knowledge.

Writing and the Survival of the Mahāyāna

The first point is offered by Richard Gombrich, who has suggested that the rise and sustenance of the Mahāyāna was due in large part to the use of writing.[14] He notes that the task of preserving the immense Pāli cannon orally was made feasible only through the considerable efforts of the Saṅgha, which was organized enough to train monks in the memorization and recitation of the oral teachings. The Saṅgha had standards for determining whether or not an utterance was authentic and should be considered the word of the Buddha; if it did not meet these standards, it was not preserved.[15] Because the preservation of extensive oral teachings required the institutional organization and systematic efforts of the Saṅgha, teachings that were not accepted and preserved by this collective effort most likely withered away. Gombrich speculates that many monks and nuns may have had unique visions or inspirations that led them to formulate new doctrines and teachings, but if those teachings were not preserved by the Saṅgha, they were lost forever. The Mahāyāna, however, arose at about the same time writing was becoming prevalent in India, and this provided a means by which heterodox teachings could be preserved without the institutional support of the Saṅgha. Gombrich argues that this was a major factor in the ability of the Mahāyāna to survive.

I would add to this that the sacred status that many Mahāyāna sūtras ascribed to themselves, both as bearers of doctrine and as material objects, encouraged their reproduction and dissemination and thus contributed to their survival. Many Mahāyāna sūtras present the copying of these texts as a highly meritorious act, and devote a considerable amount of space to extolling their own greatness and telling of the immense benefits to be gained from reading, copying, memorizing, promoting and distributing them. The *Saddharmapuṇḍarīka Sūtra* (the *Lotus Sūtra*), for example, promises to those who promulgate even one of its verses incalculable moral and spiritual benefits, including great wisdom, compassion, rebirth in luxurious heavenly realms, and intensification of the sense capacities for receiving broad ranges of stimuli; also included are more mundane benefits, such as an abundance of food, drink, clothing and bedding,[16] and freedom from disease, ugliness of countenance, bad teeth, crooked noses, and imperfect genitals.[17] Even illiterate devotees of sūtras copied their script in hopes of gaining such benefits.[18] Thus writing, combined with the promise of merit through reproduction of the texts, gave many sūtras a built-in promotional device and distribution system. Evidently, what made the orthodox tradition wary of writing – fear of losing control over teachings – was worth the risk for Mahāyānists, who were attempting to expand and spread their movement.

Sacred Text and Sacred Site

Some recent scholarship suggests that some of the earliest forms of the Mahāyāna may have been cults centered around worship of the movement's new sūtras. These cults played an important part in the growth of the Mahāyāna. Certain Mahāyāna sūtra manuscripts were considered sacred objects with the power to consecrate places, thereby establishing sacred sites and Mahāyāna centers of worship similar to, and modeled on, stūpa cults that were already prevalent. To understand the importance of this phenomenon, it is first necessary to consider briefly these stūpa cults and their socio-religious significance.

Many sacred sites in the early Buddhist tradition were designated by stūpas – reliquaries containing remains of the Buddha, and later, disciples or revered monks. Stūpa building and stūpa reverence was a widespread form of devotional practice among the laity as well as some monastics. The eight stūpas within which the Buddha's relics were supposedly housed after his death became places of pilgrimage and thriving centers of both religious and commercial activity, populated by religious specialists as well as merchants who would all gather for religious services and festivals. These centers may have been more popular among laypersons than the monastic community, who were not permitted to participate in commercial activities, pluck living flowers for offerings, listen to worldly stories and music, or watch dancing, all of which were part of the festivities at the stūpas.[19] According to Akira Hirakawa, the congregations that developed around these centers of worship gradually developed into lay orders that were stūpa cults not directly tied to monastic Buddhism.[20] As iconic art began to develop, the stūpas often contained illustrated scenes from the *Jātaka* stories, detailing the amazing and selfless deeds of Gautama in his past lives. Hirakawa speculates that the repeated telling and interpreting of these scenes to pilgrims by the religious specialists gave rise to forms of Buddhism that emphasized the salvific power of the Buddha and promoted worship and devotion toward him. The stūpas, therefore, were important factors in the development of the devotional elements that would constitute certain aspects of the Mahāyāna. Hirakawa also suggests that this was the origin of groups which considered themselves to be bodhisattvas, distinct from the śrāvakas and arhats, and who would be presented as the most advanced disciples in most Mahāyāna texts.[21]

As much as stūpa culture may have directly contributed to the Mahāyāna, it also served as a complex arena of tension and conflict between these cults and the wisdom schools. While Hirakawa makes a good case for the contributions of stūpa cults to the development of the Mahāyāna, he admits that the origins of the some of the most important Mahāyāna literature, the Perfection of Wisdom sūtras, must be sought for elsewhere.[22] This body of literature, along with a number of Mahāyāna wisdom texts, downplays the value of stūpa/relic worship in comparison to devotion to the text itself, that is, the written manuscript of a Perfection of Wisdom Sūtra. The reason for the devaluing of stūpas in Mahāyāna literature is both doctrinal and pragmatic. One of the earliest Perfection of Wisdom texts, the *Aṣṭa*, contains an interesting discussion indicating the ambivalence and tension between stūpa cults and the emerging groups devoted to Mahāyāna wisdom texts. In one passage, the Buddha questions Śakra about the value of the relics contained in stūpas compared to the Perfection of Wisdom, asking which he would prefer if he had the choice between an enormous number of relics of all the Tathāgatas and one written copy of the text. He of course chooses the Perfection of Wisdom, arguing for its primacy over relics, since the Perfection of Wisdom[23] is the *cause* of the wisdom of the Tathāgatas, rather than its depository. The value of relics is derivative in that they, being identified with the enlightened buddhas, are the results of, and are pervaded by, the Perfection of Wisdom. Furthermore, he claims, the Perfection of Wisdom supersedes relics (*śarīra*) insofar as it is itself the "true body of the Buddha," which is the body of the Dharma (*dharmakāya*).[24] This illustrates the effort by the followers of the Perfection of Wisdom to replace, or at least augment, devotion to the physical remains of the Buddha enshrined in stūpas with both the message and physical presence of the written text of the *Prajñāpāramitā*, invoking the traditional notion of the functional equivalence of the Dharma-body, as the collected teachings of the Buddha, with the Buddha himself.[25]

In addition to the doctrinal disagreements between the emerging textual traditions of the Mahāyāna and the stūpa cults, more concrete concerns regarding the establishment of places of worship may have been operative. During the earliest developments of the Mahāyāna, sacred places associated with the life of the Buddha were controlled by the stūpa cults connected to the orthodox traditions. Evidence exists in the Perfection of Wisdom texts that the Mahāyāna polemics against the Hīnayāna stūpa cults were not only about doctrine but also about the struggle of the Mahāyāna to establish its own sacred places. Gregory Schopen deals with this issue in his well-known study of the early Mahāyāna as loose federation of different "cults of the book" in which sūtras themselves become objects of worship, and the cults who worshipped them were structured along the lines of stūpa cults.[26] Schopen argues that the tradition of the cult of the book drew from the idea that the presence of the Buddha in a particular place during a significant episode of his life rendered that place sacred. This was also the rationale behind early stūpa cults. The idea was combined with the notion expressed in the stock phrase, "Whoever sees the Dharma, sees the Buddha," indicating that wherever the teachings were set forth, the Buddha is effectively present. From this

> ... it followed naturally that if the presence of the *Bhagavat* at a particular place had the effect of sacralizing that spot, then by extension, the presence (in some form) of the *dharmaparyāya* [setting forth of the Dharma, i.e., a sūtra] must have the same effect.[27]

Reciting a text purporting to be the words of the Buddha over a particular place, then, would render it sacred in the same sense in which a stūpa is a sacred place, that is, in that the Dharma was taught there, and even in that it contained 'part' of the Buddha himself, in this case his Dharma-body rather than merely his physical remains. Schopen argues that this was one way in which early Mahāyānists dealt with the problem of "localization of the cult of the book" by way of "authoritatively legitimating that spot as a cultic center."[28] This was a way of establishing new sacred places which probably served as permanent teaching centers that were not tied to those sacred cites associated with the Buddha's life, which were under the control of more orthodox groups.

Furthermore, the recitation of a sūtra or formula at a particular place was not the only way to consecrate the site; the presence of a *written copy* of a sūtra was understood to have the same effect. Schopen argues that the shift from a primarily oral to a primarily written tradition was important to the establishment of these Mahāyāna cultic centers, because the presence of the written sūtra eliminated the need for oral consecrations by the monks who specialized in reciting sūtras (*bhāṇaka*s). The written sūtra could serve as a focal point of the cult and as a permanent source of the power and presence of the Dharma, independent of the need for recitation.[29] This, in turn, freed Mahāyānists from the need to have the institutional sanction and support of the Saṅgha.

The transposition of the Dharma into physical form to be worshipped, combined with the promises of great benefits gained from copying and promoting the sūtra, insured that devotees would reproduce and distribute the texts widely, expanding the influence and power of the Mahāyāna cults and contributing to its devotional flavor. The *Aṣṭa* presents a compelling picture of some of its cult's practices in passages suggesting what activities are most meritorious with regard to the sūtra:

> If a son or daughter of good family has genuine confidence and trust in this Perfection of Wisdom [i.e., the *Aṣṭa*], is intent on it, has a clear mind, has thoughts raised to awakening, has earnest resolution, and hears it, grasps [its meaning], speaks it, studies it, spreads it, demonstrates it, explains it, expounds it, repeats it, makes it manifest in full detail to others, makes its meaning clear, investigates it with the mind, and with superior wisdom, examines it thoroughly; then copies it in the form of a book, bears it in mind and preserves it so that the good Dharma will last long, so that the guide of the buddhas will not be disappear, and so that the bodhisattvas may incur benefits by means of this flawless guide; indeed, that son or daughter of good family who makes this Perfection of Wisdom his or her teacher, honors and respects with flowers, incense, perfume, garlands, ointments, powders, raiment, parasols, emblems, bells, banners, with lamps and garlands all around it; whoever pays obeisance to it in these various ways will generate great merit.[30]

In addition to its emphasis on promotion and distribution, this passage shows how a text like the *Aṣṭa*, usually known for its early enunciation of the most abstract philosophical concepts of the Mahāyāna, had more uses than just the development of the movement's theoretical foundations. In fact, it and other early sūtras were among the important objects of Buddhist devotion. This suggests how intertwined the traditions of high philosophy were with devotional practices. It also shows another facet of the importance of the physicalization of the Dharma in the form of the written book in the early Mahāyāna.

Closely connected to this issue is another implication of the uses of writing in the Mahāyāna, and particularly in its written sūtras: writing challenged the traditional notions of sacred space. As a heterodox minority movement, the early Mahāyāna was enabled through writing to expand and develop by granting to the book the sacrality of the Buddha himself, thus providing lay followers with forms of devotion and, through the consecrational power of these manuscripts, creating new sacred sites under its control. Cults of the book also attempted to establish a new relation to sacred space that was not tied inevitably to those traditional sacred sites associated with the life of the founder and which were controlled by orthodox monks or stūpa cults. The fact that anywhere the text was placed could now become a sacred place equivalent to those associated with the life of the Buddha had the effect of de-emphasizing the significance of the specific, localized, and temporal presence of Śākyamuni. Sacred space was now mobile. This is perhaps the beginning of a marked tendency in the Mahāyāna toward a more general dislocation of sacrality from the locus of the "historical" life of Śākyamuni in favor of more abstract and unlocalizable understandings of sacrality and of the Buddha.

Writing and the Visual

A further way in which writing was significant to the Mahāyāna in particular, and to all of Buddhist and South Asian thought, practice, and literature in general, was that it shifted access to and organization of knowledge from a primarily oral/auditory mode to a primarily visual mode. To call the introduction of writing a "shift" from an oral to a literate culture is, perhaps, an exaggeration, since elements of the oral culture – recitation of sūtras, memorization, oral teaching, and so forth – remained as a strong component in Buddhist life in both Mahāyāna and non-Mahāyāna schools. Moreover, "shifts" from orality to literacy happen gradually and among specific members of a society; for the majority of South Asians who remained non-literate, there simply was no such shift. Yet, despite tendencies of scholars to exaggerate the momentousness of the introduction of literacy to a culture, important changes do accompany the use of writing – changes that effect the entire culture and not just those who themselves read. In order to explore some of the implications of the introduction of writing in Indian Buddhist culture, it is necessary to make a digression into some general observations regarding the ways that seeing and hearing structure cognition and about the introduction of writing and the effect that they may have on culture and scripture. While these observations about hearing, vision, and writing may be useful to a greater or lesser extent depending on the specific cultures to which they are applied, I outline them here because of their relevance to the case of South Asian Buddhism.

Recall, first, the points in chapter 2 on the structuring of experience by different sense modalities: that hearing structures sound in a temporal sequence, while vision can apprehend and unify a manifold into synchronic configurations in space, making them more amenable to analysis. These observations apply to oral and written discourse as well. Merleau-Ponty calls spoken language "an indefinite series of discontinuous acts."[31] Because words are always disappearing as they are pronounced, Walter Ong says that orality is essentially dialogical and that in oral cultures, thought must be "shaped into mnemetic patterns ordered for oral recurrence," and consist of rhythmic and repetitious patterns and formulary expressions.[32] This, of course, is precisely the constitution of the early Buddhist sūtras, such as the *Saḷāyatana-vibāṅga*, cited at the beginning of this chapter. Regarding the written word, Ong asserts that the introduction of writing "restructures consciousness," and that the literate mind is forever changed in its thinking and orientation to the world, not only when engaged in reading or writing, but even when speaking, hearing, and composing thoughts orally: "More than any other invention, writing has transformed consciousness"[33] because, among other things, it "moves speech from the oral-aural to a new sensory world, that of vision [and therefore] transforms speech and thought as well."[34]

The implications of these suggestions on ways in which oral-aural and literate-visual modalities structure consciousness and culture cannot be fully drawn out in the limited space of this inquiry, but we can note some points about South Asian Buddhism in this regard. The difference between accessing the teachings of the Dharma through hearing and through reading undoubtedly had significant effects on the ways Buddhists appropriated the sūtras. Writing was a medium that was uniquely appropriate to the Mahāyāna and its creative reinterpretations of doctrine in that it freed access to texts from being dependent on the collective activities of chanting and recitation, and thus from the need for the institutional sanction of the monastic saṅgha. Further, because the written manuscript frees the reader from being locked into the temporal flow of the recitation and to the particular place where the recitation is performed, it lends itself to appropriation in ways very different from those that are possible in either the performing or hearing of oral recitation. Since the manuscript is present in its entirety, rather than constantly passing away in time, as is the case with oral utterance, a greater degree of analysis and reflection upon the material is possible. A reader can move back and forth through a text at will, drawing correlations between different passages, analyzing and comparing statements, cross-referencing with other texts, and so on. These activities allowed more individual reflection, interpretation, and analysis, which may have predisposed readers to novel interpretation, individual insight, and embellishment.

The analytic and interpretive activities to which writing lent itself were not confined to the Mahāyāna, but had an impact on all Buddhist schools. It is around the time of the emergence of writing that systematic philosophy and analysis of doctrine, such as that found in the Abhidharma, begins to take shape. Ong has suggested that analysis and philosophy are only possible in a literate culture.[35] If the early Pāli sūtras that we possess today are anything like their oral antecedents (which they most likely are), this is obviously not true in the case of Indian Buddhism. Considerable theoretical reflection and analysis is present in these texts. However, it seems clear that extensive analysis of the sūtras themselves arose in conjunction with the development of writing. The attempt to systematize the teachings of the sūtras into a consistent order came about with the relative freedom from temporal sequence that writing afforded. Fully developed Abhidharma thought, with its extensive lists, categories, correlations, headings and subheadings, bears the marks of literate composition in that it culls teachings from multiple sources and attempts to systematize, synthesize, and categorize them. Such activities would be extremely difficult if one were limited to the sequentiality that structures oral recitation of memorized utterances. The simultaneous presence of written texts in visual space is necessary for such work. The multiple categories and subcategories in the Abhidharma and other commentarial literature are, in part, the products of the ability to represent complex classificatory schemas spatially. One can scarcely come across a discussion of Abhidharma literature that does not contain at least one chart in which the various elements of existence (*dharmas*) are laid out, allowing all the complex classifications and their relationships to present themselves spatially.

The fixed, static nature of the book, and its passive unresponsiveness may also give it a sense of implicit authority and unchallengeability on an intuitive level, particularly to those for whom writing is a new or even mysterious phenomenon. Ong suggests that writing establishes a "context free" or "autonomous" discourse that is more detached from its authors than oral discourse, and therefore cannot be questioned directly.[36] These points are helpful when thinking about the Mahāyāna and heterodox movements in general. Writing helps in establishing an unorthodox movement because written words may have their own implicit authority; they do not call for justification, response, and argumentation as easily and immediately as spoken words. Their soundless presence is perhaps more likely to evoke a sense of implicit legitimacy than a human voice, whose authority depends on the social position of the speaker in a given context. The impassivity of the written word may evoke a sense of authority that gives the appearance of being free from or floating above social context, since the conditions of its production (at least in the case of Mahāyāna sūtras) are obscure. Its very unresponsiveness may seem to elevate it above the spoken word, which tends to call for an immediate response. In many cultures in the early stages of literacy, writings confer to themselves a self-authenticating and sacred quality,[37] perhaps because of the mute, unresponsive authority that they present or because sacred words are among the things most likely to be written down. Furthermore, by providing a technology by which any literate person could access and interpret the Dharma outside the context of the saṅgha, writing encouraged unorthodox insight, creativity, and dissent. The writer could compose his or her own ideas, which would be present before the eye, laid out with the same seeming permanence and unassailability as the *Buddhavacana*. The physical presence of the written manuscript, in turn, contributed to likelihood that these ideas would not die the moment the author's voice fell silent. Therefore, the inherently conservative tendencies of the oral tradition, which strove to maintain the integrity of the words of the founder through its various institutional practices and rules, were subverted in part by the introduction of writing.

Finally, in looking at the introductory passages of the sample sūtras, the most obvious difference is that they are unmistakably structured around different sense modalities, the sūtra on the sense fields being composed in mnemonic patterns for oral memorization and recitation and the *Gaṇḍavyūha* being written as a visual extravaganza, not only in its barrage vivid of imagery, but in its frequent use of visually-oriented language and metaphor. The emphasis throughout the text is on what is seen rather than what is heard. The emergence of visionary literature is not confined to Mahāyāna Buddhism, but is a pan-Indic phenomenon beginning around the first or second century before the common era – the same time as the emergence of writing. Parts of the *Bhagavad Gītā* and the Pure Land texts are the most ready examples of such visually oriented literature emerging around this period. It is also noteworthy that visualization practices became more elaborate and important in both Buddhism and Hinduism at this time. Certainly we cannot attribute all of this exclusively to the emergence of writing, but the co-incidence of a wave of visionary literature and practice sweeping India at about the same time as literacy was becoming widespread does suggest that writing and the attendant shift to the visual sense modality played a significant part in the development of visionary literature in India.

The *Buddhavacana* and Strategies of Legitimation in the Mahāyāna

Of course, the implicit advantages of writing and written sūtras were not the only factors in the relative success of the Mahāyāna movement(s) in South Asia. Aside from being composed in the propitious medium of written language, the content of Mahāyāna sūtras written in South Asia went to great lengths to attempt to establish the movement's authority and legitimacy, something that would have been quite difficult for what was probably a minority movement facing well-established and powerful monastic institutions with their own claims to authority and legitimacy. At least one factor in the evocative visionary imagery and rhetorical style of many Mahāyāna sūtras involved its use as such a strategy of legitimation. Before examining a specific instance of such a use, though, it would be helpful to place this claim in context by discussing some of the ways in which the early Mahāyāna struggled against the more orthodox schools' claims to exclusive authority based on possession of the *Buddhavacana*, the words of the Buddha. As we have seen, the early Buddhist community's identity entailed its role as the keepers of the *Buddhavacana* given by Gautama and, according to tradition, memorized by his disciples and passed orally from generation to generation. This community considered itself to be those who heard, either directly or through others, the words of the Buddha. Thus, the hearers of the *Buddhavacana* were not only those who were actually present at the talks of the Buddha, but also disciples who received the teachings through hearing oral recitation. Although not the only criterion for legitimacy, the most important and unambiguous way in which a teaching was understood to be authentic was that it was considered to be the very words that the Buddha spoke.[38] The *Buddhavacana*, therefore, was the primary seal of authenticity.

Concern for the word of the Buddha continued in the Mahāyāna, but became a more complex issue. A sūtra, in the Buddhist tradition, is a composition purportedly containing a talk given by the Buddha, and is therefore by definition *Buddhavacana*. Whether from the Pāli cannon or the Mahāyāna, all sūtras start out with the narrator uttering the same words: "Thus have I heard . . ." (*evaṃ mayā śrutam*). Following this is a note of the particular place the sermon was heard, as well as mention of individuals and groups that were present – all reports that would seem to provide verification that the original hearer was in fact in the specified place at the time of the talk. Yet it is clear to modern scholars, as it probably was to many Buddhists in ancient India, that the Mahāyāna sūtras were composed quite a long time after the death of Gautama and that it is highly unlikely that the "historical" Buddha ever spoke any of them. Thus, the need to explain the existence of these sūtras and the attendant novel doctrines was of great concern to the Mahāyāna and is an issue addressed, directly or indirectly, in many sūtras and commentaries.

It is impossible to precisely reconstruct the attitudes and motivations of these early Mahāyāna sūtra writers – to imagine what they conceived of themselves as doing when, hundreds of years after the Buddha's death, they wrote the words "*evaṃ mayā śrutam. . . .*" (Thus have I heard. . . .) Perhaps they had powerful insights that they were convinced were inspired by the Buddha, or perhaps stories and ideas generated in the environments of the stūpa cults eventually were considered to be part of the Buddha's dialogs. These late sūtra writers may have simply had a far more liberal interpretation of what counts as the word of the Buddha than that of their orthodox contemporaries. It is conceivable that many doctrines and practices that we now consider uniquely Mahāyāna were in existence from very early, but were simply marginalized by those who determined the legitimacy of teachings; thus we know nothing about them until the Mahāyāna became more organized and began writing its own texts.

Despite the inevitable obscurity to historical investigation of the intentions of these late sūtra writers, many indications do exist as to how Mahāyānists construed their creative reformulations of the Dharma and justified them to themselves and to outsiders once they were written. A number of explanations were offered for the emergence of these new sūtras. According to one ancient reconstruction of the Mahāyāna, the *śrāvakas* did not have the capacity to understand the advanced teachings of the great vehicle, so they were taught to otherworldly beings and hidden until teachers emerged who could understand them.[39] Another explanation was that the original hearers did not understand the content of these talks but transmitted them anyway for later generations better equipped to comprehend them.[40] The claim was prevalent that certain teachings were revealed only to a select few. Many Mahāyāna commentators went to great lengths to reconcile the teachings of the Hīnayāna with those of the Mahāyāna by a careful reworking of the story of the Buddha's life in which every teaching ever attributed to the him was understood to be given to particular disciples on various levels of spiritual attainment. In these scenarios, less spiritually developed people were given teachings of the Hīnayāna, while bodhisattvas and other nearly-enlightened beings received the higher teachings of the Mahāyāna.

The text which is perhaps the most replete with explanations of novel Mahāyāna doctrines and practices is the *Lotus Sūtra*. The rhetoric of the *Lotus* is suggestive of the polemical context in which these doctrines and practices developed. It directly addresses the contradictions between its Mahāyāna teachings and those of the Nikāyas, much like the Christian Church explained its relationship to Judaism, by claiming supercession. It presents three specific types of people on the Buddhist path – the *śrāvaka*, who hears the words of the Buddha; the *pratyekabuddha*, who attains salvation through his own efforts and without a teacher; and the bodhisattva, who renounces his own entry into nirvāṇa until all sentient beings are saved. After warning that this teaching would be quite disturbing to both human beings and gods, the Buddha explains that all of the teachings held by those on these three paths are merely skillful means (*upāya*) that he employed to lead them all to the one true vehicle to Buddhahood, the Mahāyāna. The teachings held by the three archetypal figures on the path were given because the śrāvakas and pratyekabuddhas were capable of understanding only limited truths, such as the doctrine of causes and conditions, and of attaining freedom from rebirth and suffering in the quiescence of nirvāṇa. In the most famous parable of the *Lotus*, these doctrines are likened to promises told to children in order to lure them out of a burning house.[41] At one time, says the Buddha, these inferior teachings may have been necessary, but now the time has come to reveal the full extent of the Dharma in the teachings of the *Lotus*. The claim, then, that the Hīnayāna teachings were merely skillful means to prepare disciples to receive the higher truth of the Mahāyāna explained the discrepancies between the two, while at the same time asserting the superiority of the new teachings.

The theme of secrecy was also an important factor in explaining novel texts and contradictory doctrines. The arising of additions to the Dharma and the discrepancies between sūtras were sometimes explained by the claim that the Buddha communicated secret Mahāyāna teachings to certain people, at times even in the midst of giving a Hīnayāna teaching. The most complex examples of this claim occurred outside India, for example in the Chinese systems of doctrinal classification (*p'an chaio*). Perhaps the most elaborate of such systems was that of the great Chinese thinker Chih-i. According to Chih-i, the Buddha taught different sūtras to people with different levels understanding and spiritual development, intuiting who was ready to hear advanced teachings and who could only appreciate limited teachings. After teaching the *Avataṃsaka Sūtra* immediately preceding his enlightenment, he then moderated his approach, proceeding from the more digestible Hīnayāna teachings through to the *Vimalakirtinirdeśa*, the *Śūnyavāda* teachings, and others, until finally he revealed the perfect expression of the Dharma, the *Lotus Sūtra*. Most interesting is Chih-i's notion of the secret methods by which the Buddha communicated all these divergent doctrines to different people, according to their level of understanding. The "secret indeterminate" teachings were those in which the Buddha said the same thing in such a manner that different listeners, each unaware of the other, heard the teachings in a different way, thus came away remembering completely different discourses. In other cases, the Buddha spoke secretly to separate individuals, each of whom thought that he alone was the exclusive recipient of the message; but in fact, others were present, magically concealed from each other so that, again, they came away with contradictory teachings. In the "express indeterminate" teachings, Chih-i asserts that the Buddha said the same thing, but different people – this time all present and aware of each other – heard distinctly different sermons; thus, again, each came away with different doctrines. All of these explanations served, first, to explain the wide variety of seemingly conflicting doctrines all claiming to be the words of the Buddha; second, to impose a hierarchical structure on the various doctrines with the teachings of one's own school on top; and third, to try and determine the highest teaching, that which was closest to representing the Buddha's own enlightenment.

What is important about Chih-i's attempt to understand the great diversity of teachings all claiming to be the words of the Buddha, is that it epitomizes the way in which, even after the Mahāyāna attained dominance in China, the Great Vehicle struggled both to subvert and reconcile itself to more orthodox Buddhist doctrine and practice. Although it reached its most elaborate forms in China, this effort began with the early Mahāyāna in India. Virtually every school of Buddhism in India had its own version of which doctrines had definitive meaning (*nītārtha*) and which had merely provisional meaning (*neyārtha*), and since there were no univocally accepted standards for deciding such matters, each school drew this distinction based on its own doctrinal suppositions. The organization of doctrines based on the notion that some were merely skillful means indicates the strong need felt by Mahāyānists to legitimate their novel teachings, while maintaining a connection of lineage with Śākyamuni. It is noteworthy that, while the orthodox schools often criticized the Mahāyāna as being inauthentic, the Mahāyānists never questioned the legitimacy of the Pāli sūtras. The effort to authenticate the Mahāyāna sūtras was aimed at explaining how the Buddha actually gave doctrines that contradicted each other – how a unity of thought and intention could be understood to lie beneath the apparent discrepancies between the large and small vehicles. The rhetorical devices used to establish legitimacy in the Mahāyāna were always a hermeneutic of inclusion – albeit an inclusion that was also a subversion, for while the Hīnayāna sūtras were considered authentic, they were relegated to being merely provisional.

Visionary Literature and Grounds for Legitimacy

Having suggested the significance of writing and various strategies of legitimation for the emerging Mahāyāna movement in South Asia, I now return to our passage from the *Gaṇḍavyūha*, and to the question of the pronounced difference in literary style between the Pāli sūtras and many of the Mahāyāna sūtras. Recall the stark contrast between the sparse style of the Pāli sūtras and the lush visionary images of the *Gaṇḍavyūha*. While the *Gaṇḍavyūha* is one of the more effusive examples of such literary style in Buddhist writings, it is not alone among Mahāyāna sūtras in presenting dazzling scenes attendant upon the Buddha's preparing to deliver a discourse. Many such sūtras begin in similar, though sometimes toned-down, ways. It is tempting to point to the "magical" and visionary elements in Mahāyāna literature, intertwined as they often are with devotional themes, as evidence that the movement began among the laity and that these features were products of the popular religious imagination and capitulation to "cultic" practices. But while the laicizing tendencies of the Mahāyāna were certainly important to the development of many novel features of these texts, the works themselves were obviously written by an educated elite thoroughly familiar with all facets of Buddhist doctrine and practice. Furthermore, in addition to the nourishing of the popular desire for salvific figures, there is embedded in these lavish presentations highly polemical rhetoric designed to both explain the emergence of previously unknown sūtras and to establish them as superior to the orthodox forms of Buddhism. Thus, the visionary elements of Mahāyāna sūtras, in addition to weaving an aesthetically rich and fascinating fabric of symbolic imagery that would nourish the Buddhist imagination up to the present day, made a unique contribution to the afore-mentioned strategies of legitimation.

The *Gaṇḍavyūha* makes these polemical strategies quite clear. Continuing with the passage presented at the beginning of this study, we find that after the extensive description of the transfigured Jeta Grove and the wonders attending the arrival of the otherworldly bodhisattvas, the narrator points out that the śrāvakas who were present, such as Śariputra, Mahākāśyapa, Subhūti, and others who are the frequent interlocutors of the Buddha in the sūtras, were quite oblivious to the entire miraculous scene. The reason they did not see it is because, among other defects, they "lacked the roots of goodness conducive to the vision of the transfiguration of all buddhas . . . and did not have the purity of the eye of knowledge."[42] Furthermore, they did not have the "power of vision" to see these things because they were of the vehicle of the śrāvakas, who had neither the "developed bodhisattvas' range of vision" nor the "eye of the bodhisattvas."[43] Part of the significance of these elaborate visionary depictions, then, is to establish a kind of spiritual hierarchy with those who merely heard the words of the Buddha, the śrāvakas, on the bottom, and those bodhisattvas who saw the true transfigured state of the Buddha and his surroundings, on top. The fact that the bodhisattvas are depicted as seeing the vision, while the śrāvakas remain oblivious, is at once an assertion of the value of seeing over hearing and of the Mahāyāna over the Hīnayāna.

While the *Gaṇḍavyūha* is the text that makes this strategy most obvious, other Mahāyāna sūtras employ similar devices, often involving visions of the higher bodies of the Buddha. The *Lotus Sūtra* is one of the early Mahāyāna texts that lays the groundwork for the importance of having visions of the Buddha insofar as it explicitly claims that the Buddha is actually a transcendent being.[44] This theme is taken up in the sūtra when the Buddha discusses the countless numbers of beings that he has led to Buddhahood in his past lives. In a rare moment of doubt and confusion, Maitreya broaches the subject of how the Buddha could have led to enlightenment these many beings in countless ages past if Gautama had himself only attained enlightenment in this lifetime and only relatively recently. The answer is a bombshell. The stories of the Buddha's life, his leaving the household, his achieving awakening under the bodhi tree, and his warning that he would soon be gone, were themselves all merely *upāya*, skillful means to lead less developed beings toward the higher teachings of the Great Vehicle. In fact, he reports, he attained enlightenment innumerable eons ago and has been teaching the Dharma in this and countless other world-systems for incalculable ages. The reason he teaches certain beings that the appearance of a Buddha in a world is rare and that he will soon be gone forever is so that they will practice the Dharma with vigor and be diligent in striving for awakening. But in reality, he says, he is always present and never perishes, is unlimited by time and space, and is able to manifest in the world whenever he is needed.[45]

The notions of the transcendence of the Buddha and the fictitiousness of the received stories of his life were powerful tools in the struggle of the Mahāyāna for legitimacy. First, these ideas de-emphasized the "historical" Śākyamuni and presented many of the core elements of orthodox Buddhism as irrelevant. Second, they gave an additional rationale for the emergence of new sūtras and doctrines. The idea that the Buddha had not, in fact, passed into nirvāṇa, forever beyond the reach of sentient beings, but, rather, continued to teach on an as-needed basis could serve, in combination with the doctrine of *upāya*, as a explanation for the introduction of new teachings. Paul Williams points out a tradition in some Mahāyāna literature in which the origins of certain Mahāyāna sūtras were associated not with the historical Buddha *per se*, but with the visionary experience and inspiration by the supermundane Buddha or buddhas who exist in pure lands. He offers a passage from the *Pratyutpanna Sūtra* that gives instructions for visualizing the Buddha Amitāyus in his pure land teaching the Dharma, and in which the meditator is actually given teachings by this buddha:

> ... While remaining in this very world-system that bodhisattva sees the Lord, the Tathāgata Amitāyus; and conceiving himself to be in that world-system he also hears the Dharma. Having heard their exposition he accepts, masters and retains those Dharmas. He worships, venerates, honours and reveres the Lord ... Amitāyus. After he has emerged from that *samādhi* [meditative absorption] that bodhisattva also expounds widely to others those Dharmas as he has heard, retained and mastered them.[46]

It is possible, then, that some Mahāyāna sūtras were the result of what the author considered a direct visionary revelation of the Dharma from a transcendent source, one that at once augmented and surpassed the teachings in the Pāli cannon.

The idea of supermundane buddhas and the significance of seeing their transcendent form deflected the importance of having heard the words of Gautama when he was in Jeta Grove. While hearing the words of the Buddha was the basis for authenticity and legitimacy in the orthodox traditions, it became less important – if not associated with a handicap – in some Mahāyāna sūtras: in the *Gaṇḍavyūha*, having heard a discourse from the finite form of the Śākyamuni in an ordinary park merely showed the hearer's limitations, that is, his inability to see the higher form of the Buddha and his pure land which is co-extensive with the ordinary world.

Thus, in contradistinction to the ordinary settings of early sūtras in which a group of simple monks gather in a park to hear the Buddha give a talk, many Mahāyāna sūtras begin by depicting the Buddha revealing himself in his enjoyment body (*sāṃbhogika-kāya*). In another Perfection of Wisdom text, the *Pañcaviṃśatisā-hasrikā*, for example, before giving his talk the Buddha's body suddenly becomes radiant, and rays of light emit from his "divine eye," his toes, legs, ankles, thighs, hips, navel, arms, fingers, ears, nostrils, teeth, eyes, and hair pores. This light illumines all the multiple world-systems in the triple cosmos. Only after an extensive description of the resplendence of the Buddha's form and the attendant miraculous events, does he actually begin his sermon.[47] This preliminary visual display is one of the primary means of attempting to establish the legitimacy of the Mahāyāna sūtra – perhaps more so than the dubious claim of the narrator to have heard the sūtra from Śākyamuni. The idea of the transcendent Buddha allowed a reversal of value with regard to the spoken word. The fact that the monks who committed the Pāli sūtras to memory claimed to have heard the teachings of the Buddha as a man in a specific place and time was the seal of authenticity in the Pāli sūtras, but is presented as a sign of limitation in the *Lotus* and other Mahāyāna sūtras. If the Buddha were actually a transcendent being, and the ability to see his higher form was contingent upon one's spiritual development, then hearing him preach in the voice of a man in an ordinary body at a typical place and time, as depicted in the Pāli sūtras, was simply an indication of the limited capacities of the hearer.

These elaborate introductions are intended to establish the transcendent source of the teachings contained in the sūtras and serve to relativize the comparatively prosaic Pāli accounts. This also had an important effect on the notion of place and space. While Mahāyāna sūtras continued invariably to begin according to standard form – with the narrator claiming to have heard the dialogue in a particular historical place and time, thus preserving the legitimacy and connection to received tradition and lineage conferred by the phrase, "*evaṃ mayā śrutam* ..." – the presentation of the transcendent form of the Buddha in his pure land served to mitigate the importance of any particular time or place. The tendency of the Mahāyāna sūtras, then, was to dis-embed the teachings from Jeta Grove and re-embed them in a transcendent realm. The Mahāyāna attempted to transfer the basis of legitimacy from the spoken word of Śākyamuni to the vision of the transcendent Buddha, which rendered the specificity of the places that the Buddha spoke during his lifetime less relevant. The transfiguration of Jeta Grove suggests that the locale in which the *Gaṇḍavyūha* was given was not really Jeta Grove at all, but a kind of placeless place in which the wonders of the Buddha and his world were revealed. The displacement of the Buddha's teaching parallels the displacement of sacred spaces occasioned by the cults of the book. Both tended to de-emphasize the particularities of time of place associated with the Buddha's life in favor of creating the ideal of a universal sacred space that was at once everywhere and yet nowhere in particular.[48] The image of the ground turning into a transparent diamond in the cited passage from the *Gaṇḍavyūha* is a most powerful symbol of this displacement – rather than the hills, trees and other landmarks of Jeta Grove that must have been familiar to the disciples who lived in the vicinity or had visited the place on pilgrimage, the land becomes a uniform, crystalline diamond extending in all directions. Such a landscape allows for no distinction or particularity and thus symbolizes the universality and undifferentiation of all spaces – a condition that many Mahāyāna sūtras claim is true from a higher point of view. It reflects, thus, the Perfection of Wisdom texts' assertion that perfect wisdom is undifferentiated, placeless (*adeśa*), and without locality (*apradeśa*), like space itself.[49]

Conclusion

This consideration of the literary styles of different sūtras opens up a number of issues involving the development, sustenance, and establishment of the Mahāyāna. Writing allowed its heterodox teachings to survive and instituted forms of sūtra worship that would serve to expand the movement, not only through spreading its doctrines but by consecration of places. The development of writing also shifted access to and organization of knowledge from an exclusively oral/aural mode to one that emphasized visuality, and this allowed for greater analysis and commentary, as well as dissent. The Mahāyāna's embracing of the shift from oral/aural to literate/visual also challenged the authority of the orthodox traditions in a number of ways, the most vivid example being the use of visionary literature to establish authority and supersession. Examining what was at stake in the conflicting claims between the Mahāyāna and the more orthodox schools helps to elucidate the concrete concerns that constituted the conditions under which these Mahāyāna sūtras were produced. All of this suggests some of the social and historical factors that contributed to the intense visual imagery of some Mahāyāna sūtras and that made a highly visual orientation well-suited to the Mahāyāna.

We should be careful not to oversimplify or overstate the point here. It is not that Mahāyāna sūtras were exclusively focused on vision and Pāli sūtras on hearing and recitation. In fact, some of the resources for the visionary material in the Mahāyāna are found in the Pāli texts in a more subtle form, and these early texts also contain many ocular metaphors, such as the frequent pairing of knowledge and vision. Conversely, traditions of recitation and mnemonic devices are not absent from Mahāyāna sūtras, and some extol the virtues of those who are able to recite long texts from memory. The point is, first, that the Mahāyāna tended to emphasize vision to a greater extent than the orthodox traditions, who emphasized hearing; and second, that these respective orientations were specifically involved with each tradition's claims to authority and legitimacy.

It would also be inadequate to claim that the sole function of and reason for visionary literature in the Mahāyāna was to serve as a strategy of legitimation. As was mentioned, some non-Buddhist Indian literature contemporary with these sūtras was of a similar visionary style, and in many ways these sūtras reflect a pan-Indic visionary trend in literature beginning in the first couple centuries before and after the beginning of the common era. The strategic use of visionary themes does not fully "explain," much less "explain away," the visual emphasis in the Mahāyāna or the philosophical themes involving the devaluation of language and concepts. However, the polemical uses of such literature should not be overlooked, for they shed light on the historical and social context in which the Mahāyāna emerged. They should be seen as providing some of the necessary, but not sufficient, conditions for the arising of certain features of Mahāyāna discourse. Nor do these considerations need necessarily mitigate the impact and religious significance of this extraordinary visionary literature and the visionary experiences they depict – it does suggest, however, that even the most otherworldly visions are often intertwined with this-worldly concerns.

CHAPTER FOUR

Realms of the Senses: Buddha Fields and Fields of Vision in the Gaṇḍavyūha Sūtra

> Any seeing of an object by me is instantaneously reiterated among all those objects in the world which are apprehended as co-existent. . . . The completed object is translucent, being shot through from all sides by an infinite number of present scrutinies which intersect in its depths leaving nothing hidden.
>
> Maurice Merleau-Ponty[1]

> Come, I will show you the unimpeded realm.
>
> Maitreya to Sudhana in the *Gaṇḍavyūha*[2]

So far our discussion of vision in the Mahāyāna has focused primarily on seeing as a metaphor for unmediated knowing and the apprehension of what is normatively considered the unconstructed, non-conceptual truth. We have also discussed some of the rhetorical and social functions of visionary literature such as the *Gaṇḍavyūha Sūtra*. Now we take up more thematically the constructive aspects of vision in the Mahāyāna using the *Gaṇḍavyūha* and its imagery as the primary case study.

What I am calling the *constructive* aspects of vision – as opposed to the "deconstructive" efforts to dismantle conceptual structures, an approach characteristic of the Perfection of Wisdom – includes the ways in which vision and visionary imagery become means of presenting the Dharma and representing Buddhist views of reality in a positive sense, rather than the negational critiques found in much Mādhyamika and Perfection of Wisdom literature. I suggested in chapter 1 that the paradoxical dialectic in the Perfection of Wisdom Sūtras, with its tension between presence and absence or positivity and negativity, played itself out in many different forms, each emphasizing one side or the other but still maintaining the basic underlying structure. The emptiness discourses emphasized the negative side, ultimately rejecting positive portrayals of reality and affirming a non-conceptual vision that finally "sees" the highest truth by seeing no inherently existing things at all. The *Gaṇḍavyūha*, with its rich imagery, focuses on more positive presentations of reality, but magnified and transfigured so that the ordinary world seems but a colorless after-image of the lustrous mythical worlds it presents. While the emptiness discourses attempt to cut off ordinary thinking through negation of all conceptual constructs, the *Gaṇḍavyūha* attempts to disrupt ordinary thought and perception by multiplying construct upon construct, creating a dense tapestry of images that defy the most basic parameters of ordinary reality. Despite the difference in approach, however, we shall see that the paradoxical dialectic is also implicit in this text as a structuring principle, as is emptiness philosophy.

Other texts could be used to discuss the constructive visionary elements of Indian Mahāyāna Buddhism – most obviously the Pure Land texts. The large *Sukhāvatīvyūha Sūtra*, for instance, is another Indian text from about the first or second century C.E. that presents some of the visionary themes we will be discussing in this chapter. Other sūtras, such as the *Suvarṇabhāṣottama Sūtra* and even the larger Perfection of Wisdom texts also contain such themes. The *Gaṇḍavyūha* makes the most interesting study in this context, however, for a number of reasons. First, it is perhaps the most developed expression of the visionary tendencies in Mahāyāna Buddhism, not only because it contains a wealth of visual imagery rife with symbolic meaning, but also because it self-consciously embraces imaginative and projective vision as an integral part of Buddhist practice. Second, while a considerable amount of scholarly work has been done on the Pure Land texts that also embrace this projective vision, comparatively little work has been done on the *Gaṇḍavyūha* in its South (and possibly Central) Asian context.[3] Third, the *Gaṇḍavyūha* contains some unique appropriations of concepts and rhetorical structures that we have dealt with earlier, thus affording an opportunity to study concept formation and conceptual change and development within the visual paradigm of Mahāyāna Buddhism. Thus, in addition to analyzing the imagery of the text, we will follow some of the concepts and metaphors already discussed in previous chapters as they are realized in unique ways in this sūtra.

Historical Context of the *Gaṇḍavyūha*

Relatively little is known about the *Gaṇḍavyūha* in its early historical context in India. By the time of its translation into Chinese by Bodhibhadra in the early fifth century, it had been incorporated into the *Avataṃsaka Sūtra*, an immense text that is actually a collection of a number of sūtras. The *Gaṇḍavyūha* and the *Daśabhūmika Sūtra*, another text within the *Avataṃsaka* collection, circulated in India as separate texts before this incorporation.[4] The *Gaṇḍavyūha* itself was composed between the first and early third centuries. Hajime Nakamura contends that it was written during the flourishing of Buddhism in the Kuṣāṇa dynasty, where so much of the visual art of Buddhism arose and thrived.[5] The location of its initial composition was likely in Southern India, where most of the story takes place; however, the *Gaṇḍavyūha* and the *Avataṃsaka* as a whole were important in northern India and Central Asia, and portions of the extant versions were likely composed and augmented there. When the latter was originally brought to China, it was from Khotan rather than India, and later portions of the text refer to Kashgar and even China.[6] Thus, it is a composite product of the cosmopolitan, multicultural milieu of South and Central Asia in the early centuries of the common era.

The extent of the *Gaṇḍavyūha*'s influence in the Indian cultural sphere is unclear. There is relatively little surviving commentary from India on the text in comparison to that on works such as the Perfection of Wisdom. Nevertheless, it was undoubtedly part of the Buddhist curriculum in the great Buddhist universities and was widely read by Indian scholars, as it is referred to in a number of prominent commentarial texts including the *Mahāprajñāpāramitopadeśaśāstra*, Śantideva's *Śikṣasamuccaya* and *Bodhicaryāvatāra*, Kamalaśīla's first *Bhāvanākrama*, and Bhāvaviveka's *Madhyamakahṛdayakārikās*.[7] It occupies a prominent place in the Nepalese canon as one of the nine *Vaipulya* texts. It made its greatest impact in East Asia, where the *Avataṃsaka* became the basis for the Hua-yen school in China and the Kegon in Japan. The *Gaṇḍavyūha* was evidently important during the Buddhist period in Indonesia, as extensive scenes from it are represented on the great stūpa at Barabuḍur.[8]

While the Perfection of Wisdom texts gave rise to the Madhyamaka, and the Yogācāra school derives its primary inspiration from the *Lankāvatāra Sūtra* and the *Saṃdhinirmocana Sūtra*, we know of no school or movement in South or Central Asia based primarily on the *Gaṇḍavyūha* or the related sūtras in the *Avataṃsaka*. Nor does the text obviously promote one school's views over another, but rather, combines doctrines common to both Madhyamaka and Yogācāra and contains, as well, strong elements of Pure Land thought, practice, and imagery.

Visionary Literature and Thaumaturgy in India

The *Gaṇḍavyūha* and similar Buddhist texts are not alone in India in their visionary orientation. In fact, India was experiencing during the time of their composition a wave of devotionalism that was inseparable from such visionary themes. Perhaps the most famous example is the *Bhagavad Gītā*, which emphasizes devotion to Kṛṣṇa and contains the great vision in which Arjuna is, by Kṛṣṇa's lending him a "divine eye," allowed to see Kṛṣṇa's cosmic form containing many mouths and eyes, garlands, and ornaments, and possessing infinite radiance.[9] This vision closely parallels some in the *Gaṇḍavyūha*, especially those of the bodies of buddhas and bodhisattvas containing within them infinite worlds and emitting rays of light that illuminate the cosmos. Devotion and worship (*bhakti*) in India have always been closely associated with vision and visualization as a way of simulating the appearance of a deity. Seeing and being seen by a deity, the practice of *darśan*, is even today one of the primary forms of worship in India. Thus the creative simulation of a deity, in wood and stone or in the imagination, is an essential part of Indian religious practice, as we shall explore further in the next chapter. Suffice to say at this point that the emergence of many early Mahāyāna sūtras and the rise of a visionary emphasis in Buddhism was likely part of a wider flowering of devotionalism and visionary movements in India, as is suggested by the proliferation of visionary literature and devotional art and the growth of image worship and visualization practices around this time. This visionary/devotional tendency would have profound and lasting effects on Indian religion, as is attested to by the ubiquity of the devotion to Viṣṇu, Śiva, and the Goddess, as well as the worship of images being the dominant religious expression continuing up to this day.

Another factor helpful in understanding the imagery of the *Gaṇḍavyūha* is the presence of thaumaturgy in ancient India.

A frequent simile in Mahāyāna Buddhism is that all dharmas are like magical creations (*māyopamanirmāṇa*) or illusions, a reference to magicians who were believed to be capable of creating magical appearances of things. In the *Gaṇḍavyūha*, this notion is joined with a development in the idea of the bodhisattva as one who is able to manipulate the appearances of the world as a magician manipulates his or her illusory appearances. Thaumaturges were supposed to be capable of manifesting themselves within a small object, manifesting large objects within their own bodies, or multiplying images of objects.[10] The ability to manipulate physical reality by mental power as an incidental result of advanced meditative development was also generally accepted in ancient India. Many Buddhist texts refer, for example, to clairvoyance, telekinesis, thought transference, and bi-location as by-products of the refinement of meditation. Also common is the idea of mind-made bodies (*manomayakāya*); the *Visuddhamagga*, for instance, gives detailed directions on how to make such a body through concentration and visualization, thereby transforming one's appearance into that of a small boy, an elephant, or a manifold military array.[11] Other sources indicate that advanced yogis are able to project these bodies and have them function at remote distances, move with great speed, and travel through solid substances.[12]

In the *Gaṇḍavyūha*, such powers of psychic construction and illusion-making are reinterpreted and fused with Mahāyāna philosophy. If everything lacks inherent existence and has no fixed identity, then the buddhas and bodhisattvas, realizing this, can create any appearance appropriate for the spiritual level of any sentient being. The lack of inherent existence, fused with the image of bodhisattva as dharmic thaumaturge, implies a basic malleability of the world, such that the adept can control appearances so that they all become skillful means (*upāya*) to lead others to awakening. Such powers in the Mahāyāna are given a decisively visionary slant. Luis Gómez notes a number of such miraculous powers of transformation (*ṛddhi*) resulting from meditative concentrations as summarized by Asaṅga:

> [T]hese powers (*ṛddhibala*) are divided into two types – powers of transformation (*pāriṇāmikī ṛddhi*) and powers of creation (*nairmāṇikī ṛddhi*). The first group includes, among others, the power to produce fire and emit rays of light of

> many colors (*jvalana*), the sight of which allays all suffering (*raśmipramokṣa*); the power to produce light that pervades every corner of the universe (*spharaṇa*); the power to make everything visible anywhere in an instant (*vidarśana*); the power to change the form of things (*anyathībhavakaraṇa*); the power to introduce any object, however large, into his own body (*sarvarūpakāyapraveśana*); and the power to appear and disappear anywhere (*āvirbhāvatirobhāva*). In the class of *nairmāṇikī ṛddhi*, the most important subtype is the capacity to create or project bodies (*kāyanirmāṇa*), one of the most important transfigurational faculties (*vikurvaṇa*) in the scheme of the *Gv* [*Gaṇḍavyūha*]. A Buddha or Bodhisattva can create illusory bodies, similar or dissimilar to the creator. ... Still another subtype of the *pāriṇāmikī ṛddhi* class, also called *vikurvaṇa* by the *Gv* is that of producing the vision of all the Buddha-fields of the universe in one limited location (*ārambaṇa*), be this one speck of dust, or a hair pore on the skin of the Bodhisattva.[13]

This is a later systematization of capacities displayed frequently throughout the *Gaṇḍavyūha*, where the ancient thaumaturgic practices are combined with Mahāyāna philosophic ideas to create fantastic visionary episodes. The power to create such extraordinary visions are, in the *Gaṇḍavyūha*, at once illustrations of the emptiness of phenomena, depictions of awakening, and teaching devices.

Buddha-Fields and Images of Kingship

One theme that becomes prominent in a great deal of Mahāyāna literature is that of buddha-fields (*buddhakṣetra*) or pure lands of the sort we encountered in the previous chapter with the transfiguration of the grove in which the Buddha was preaching. The concept of a buddha-field is that of a world-system – one among many in the infinite cosmos – that is constructed or purified by a buddha or advanced bodhisattva during the course of his bodhisattva career, and which serves as a realm for sentient beings to receive his benevolence and benefits. The realm is usually described in the most lavish terms as an ideal world in which there is little if any suffering, and the primary occupation of beings is to receive the teachings and infinite blessings of the presiding buddha.

While the final goal of nirvāṇa is not lost in many texts emphasizing buddha-fields – these realms are generally understood as places for a final rebirth from which it is easy to attain complete awakening – often the goal of rebirth in a buddha-field is implicitly understood as an end in itself.

The most influential texts dealing with these buddha-fields are those devoted to the Buddha Amitābha: the larger and smaller *Sukhāvatīvūha Sūtra* and the *Amitāyurdhyāna Sūtra*. These and other such texts represent the full flowering of devotional Buddhism, the main practices of which are the devotion to "celestial buddhas" and visualization of a buddha in his or her buddha-field. These buddhas are depicted as having sworn long ago not to become fully enlightened until they have fulfilled certain vows. In Amitābha's case, he makes a large number of vows regarding the pure land that he will create: for example, it will be a place where everyone will be endowed with the ability to remember their previous births; there will be no lower realms in which to be reborn; there will be no difference between gods and humans; the light of his own body will be immeasurable; his lifespan will be immeasurable; there will be no pain; the land will grow jewel trees with beautiful ornaments; all beings will easily attain knowledge and meditative concentrations. Presumably, all of these vows are fulfilled over the eons of his career as a bodhisattva, and Amitābha is said now to preside in his pure land containing all these qualities.[14]

The purification or construction of a world-system by the virtuous deeds and the meditative and magical powers of a bodhisattva or buddha, as well as the power of a bodhisattva's vows to affect such a transformation, are important factors in the *Gaṇḍavyūha*. Fantastically arrayed buddha-fields are constantly appearing in the sūtra, and frequent reference is made to the purificatory powers of vows. Another idea, known more commonly from the *Vimalakīrtinirdeśa Sūtra*, also plays an important role: in this sūtra, it is said that a buddha-field is pure to the extent that the mind is pure, and that the impurities of the world depend on the impurities of mind. The implication is that, while the pure lands may be far away, to one with a pure mind even the ordinary defiled world is itself a pure land. Thus, as we saw in the previous chapter, people deemed to have higher spiritual development perceived the transfiguration of Jeta Grove at the beginning of the *Gaṇḍavyūha*, while those with remedial understanding perceived the ordinary world. This text makes the further suggestion that all pure lands, indeed all of space and time, are present in *this* world, even in the smallest speck of dust.

One aspect of the emphasis on pure lands is the connection of Buddhism and the concept of Buddhas to kingship. In a purified buddha-field such as Amitābha's pure land, a buddha rather than a king presides over the land as its spiritual guide and object of devotion, having transformed the realm into a utopia. The pure land is presumably free from all crime, suffering, and the need for administration and defense; therefore, as the creator and spiritual leader of the realm, the buddha, although he or she is not described as a monarch in the literature, implicitly assumes the place of royalty. That these celestial buddhas were strongly associated with royalty is clear from the imagery in descriptions and artistic depictions of buddhas in their buddha-fields. For example, in the opening scene of the *Gaṇḍavyūha*, Śākyamuni Buddha is dwelling in a multi-storied palace or tower (*kūṭāgāra*) that then expands to encompass the universe as the surrounding area is transformed into a luxuriant pure land. Many images associated with royalty are present in this transfigured landscape. In sharp contrast to the humble surroundings of the Pāli sutras, the Buddha now appears in the midst of immense buildings with arches, turrets, sculptures, pools, balconies – buildings that could only have been modeled on an ancient royal palace.[15] The palace, in fact, becomes a prominent symbol in Buddhist literature, sometimes representing reality itself and sometimes associated with stūpas and shrines (*vihāra*s), as well as the great tower that we shall encounter in the *Gaṇḍavyūha*.[16] The many bodhisattvas and disciples in the scene now resemble a vast retinue of royal attendants. Behind them, many banners and pennants fly in the wind, symbols of royalty probably imported from Persia and common in ancient and medieval India. Royal images of the Buddha, one of whose many epithets is "Dharma King" (*dharmarāja*), occur in other Mahāyāna sūtras as well, which, along with Buddhist sculpture, commonly depict the Buddha on a throne and with royal accouterments.

The association of ruler and buddha, of course, goes back to the earliest stages of Buddhism. Gautama was of the *kṣatriya* class, the warriors who most often functioned as rulers in Indian history. In the legend of the Buddha, a soothsayer predicts that he can become either a world ruler (*cakravārtin*) or a religious leader, implying that the personal characteristics needed for one are also essential for the other. Moreover, certain features of Buddhist practice and organization seem to have been modeled on royal practices; for instance, consecration rituals (*abhiṣeka*) for the saṅgha were fashioned after annointment ceremonies for kings. This association of divinity and royalty drew on the widespread ideal in ancient India of divine kingship, the presence of which is indicated by the complicated ceremonies and sacrifices whereby kings were symbolically identified with Indra or Prajāpati and thus made divine, or at the very least, divinely appointed.[17]

The concept of the world ruler or universal emperor figures into an increasing amount of Buddhist literature as the Mahāyāna gains prominence. It's importance in ancient India and in Buddhist circles was no doubt enhanced by Aśoka's far-reaching rule of India, a reign that furthered Buddhism and gave it royal sanction. Aśoka came to be the symbol of the wise and benevolent Buddhist king who, although he conquered much of India by force, then renounced violence and spent a great deal of effort promoting the Dharma throughout his kingdom. Greek, Persian, and perhaps Chinese influences brought by the Kuṣāṇas may have further strengthened the notion of kings as divine or semi-divine. Kings from these areas who ruled in South and Central Asia adopted titles echoing the Greek notion of "savior" and *rājātirāja*, "king of kings," from Persian concepts of kingship, as well as *devaputra*, "son of the gods," a title taken by the Kuṣāṇa rulers, perhaps under the influence of the Chinese "son of heaven."[18] The *Suvarṇabhāsottama Sūtra* offers an account of the divinity of kings, affirming that the good ruler is a divine son who has descended from the gods to the mortal realm to set up a just rule.[19] While earlier Buddhism apparently did not promote the idea of the divinity of kings,[20] the concept must have gained considerable cultural currency among Buddhists during the rule of the Kuṣāṇas and other Buddhist-friendly regimes in South and Central Asia.

It is probably no coincidence that images of the Buddha as a ruler of an idealized utopia proliferate in Buddhist literature during the periods of imperialism and social unrest following the Mauryan era. On one hand, many Mahāyāna sūtras were produced during this time of successive invasions and fragmentations of the Indian subcontinent, and a widespread fear of political and social anarchy signaling the end of the era and the destruction of the world is discernable in this literature. Such fears no doubt created the desire for a good king, a "world-protector" who would rule the land in a just and fair manner. Further, the political structure in India and Central Asia early in the common era, with its wide-ranging monarchies engulfing huge areas, some of which were Buddhist or Buddhist-supporting, was favorable to the ascendancy of doctrines and imagery exhaulting royalty and drawing correlations between kings and buddhas who were masters of vast realms. While the texts emphasizing buddha-fields do not explicitly conflate buddha and king, the buddha of a pure land functions as a kind of surrogate king in a utopia where mundane administration is no longer needed and the primary activity of the inhabitants is spiritual practice. Moreover, this model surely was a factor in the legitimation of the great Buddhist kingdoms outside India. The Tibetan system of rule by the Dalai Lamas operated on this ideal of a divine ruler presiding over a buddha-field. Similarly, the Chinese rulers drew heavily on images of buddha or bodhisattva as emperor and exploited it to their advantage.

One final point regarding the emphasis on buddha-fields with regard to the *Gaṇḍavyūha* is that it provided a way for thinking of awakening in terms of a *place* or *domain* rather than an abstract and intangible state of consciousness – a significant move toward the positive portrayal of buddhahood in concrete, visual terms. In this context, the results of a buddha's or bodhisattva's deeds are manifest in his or her enjoyment body (*sāṃbhogikakāya*), the resplendent body full of light that results from the accumulation of meritorious karma. The idea of a buddha-field develops along similar lines, in some texts as the result of a buddha's purifying deeds over countless eons, in others as a sudden, miraculous transformation of the land resulting from the meditative concentrations and transformative powers of a buddha. Either way the buddha's virtue and spiritual power establishes a *domain* of awakening – a place only visible by having the obstructions of mental afflictions removed from one's eyes, and a visible manifestation of awakening as a kingdom in which a buddha serves as benevolent ruler.

In previous chapters we have observed that emptiness and awakening are often symbolized in emptiness discourses as having "having no place or location." This may seem antithetical to the representation of ultimate truth as a domain or land. As we shall see, however, the function of such symbolism in the *Gaṇḍavyūha* follows along lines quite similar to that in the emptiness discourses. Rather than the displacement of all concepts through the critique of inherent existence, the *Gaṇḍavyūha* displaces visible objects in space and time through its repeating images of the interpenetration of all things, thus reiterating in visual imagery the de-essentializing of all phenomena, just as the emptiness discourses de-essentialized all concepts and "beings." The utopian "domain" of the *Gaṇḍavyūha*, therefore, becomes a transparent no-place, unimpeded by fixed boundaries, yet where visible objects maintain conventional forms.

Elements of the Narrative

A. K. Warder calls the *Gaṇḍavyūha* a "literary masterpiece" and a "highly imaginative religious novel." While his assessment of the text as the "most readable of Mahāyāna sūtras"[21] might be questioned by anyone encountering its dense wording, complex imagery, and length, it does in fact contain the most organized and cohesive plot structure of any extant Mahāyāna sūtra. It is a story of religious quest, although the narrative structure does not contain many of what are sometimes considered standard elements of this genre. In fact, it is in many ways quite unlike other more familiar tales of spiritual quest. There is no crisis, no time of darkness from out of which emerges a transformed hero, no monumental difficulties to overcome, no tests of physical or spiritual strength. The supposedly universal stages of a typical heroic narrative proposed by Joseph Campbell are nowhere to be found.[22] Instead, the plot is cyclical, with each chapter mirroring the others in its basic form. Although cyclical, the story does have linear movement in that each chapter represents a stage in the bodhisattva path, and the hero attains full awakening by the end after coming full-circle and returning to the teacher who originally inspired him on the quest. Rather than overcoming monsters or dark nights of the soul, he encounters a series of beneficent teachers, each of whom take him further in his career as a bodhisattva by sharing their practices and specific attainments with him.

We have discussed, at the beginning of the previous chapter, the first scenes of the story, in which the Buddha's meditative concentration evoking a vast, dazzling display which draws bodhisattvas from various worlds in the ten directions. The Buddha Śākyamuni recedes after this and plays virtually no further role in the sūtra except to return briefly at the end and give his approval to what has been said by its main teachers. Instead, the narrative follows one of the celestial bodhisattvas who comes to this world, Mañjuśrī, the bodhisattva of wisdom, as he leaves the Buddha's presence at Śrāvasti for South India. There he meets the hero of the story, Sudhana, the son of a guild leader. Inspired by Mañjuśrī's teaching, Sudhana follows his advice to go in search of spiritual mentors (*kalyāṇamitra*, literally "good friends") and receive teachings from them, a quest which comprises the rest of the text and takes him to fifty-two bodhisattvas. To each he asks to be taught the way or practices of the bodhisattvas (*bodhisattvacaryā*). Each bodhisattva teaches Sudhana about his or her particular practice and the liberation (*vimokṣa*) particular to that practice, but almost all, until the last two, plead ignorance regarding the most profound way of the bodhisattva and send him on to the next teacher. Each visit is a dramatization or a symbolically charged visionary representation of a specific Buddhist teaching. Sudhana's visits to these bodhisattvas takes him on a pilgrimage all over India, receiving teachings from bodhisattvas of striking variety. A distinct emphasis on the laity is present, as many of the bodhisattvas are householders, merchants, sailors, perfumers, women, and even youths. Many of the trades and crafts of ordinary people are highly praised and included in some of the scenes of buddha-fields alongside the more supernal imagery. Conversely, there is a decided de-emphasis on monastic Buddhism – only a handful of the teachers are monks or nuns.

While a story of a pilgrim traveling around India in search of practices might presumably be a wonderful source for trying to understand what people were actually doing "on the ground" in ancient India, the *Gaṇḍavyūha*'s value does not lie primarily in determining such practices, although it is not devoid of information on them. The activities and realizations of the characters in the text are stylized archetypes of Buddhist principles, and their descriptions are teeming with hyperbole and symbolism. The purpose of the text is far from that of the straightforward, practical manuals of meditation practices found in Buddhist traditions; rather, it is a collection of visionary episodes dramatically illustrating Buddhist ideals – an advertisement for the marvels and ecstatic rewards of the bodhisattva path. It was most likely aimed at educated laypeople and religious specialists, those with the time, patience, and facility to absorb its unusual style and imagery. Yet it also contains devotional elements that could have had a broad appeal. Its complex imagery and difficult language likely kept it from a wide audience, yet it drew extensively on popular tradition and devotional cults as well as abstruse Mahāyāna philosophy. It is, like many Buddhists sūtras, an amalgam of the popular and elite – indeed to an extent that it invites suspicion of a hard and fast distinction between these two categories.

The first bodhisattva that Sudhana visits, Meghaśrī, serves as a typical example of his encounters with bodhisattva teachers. Sudhana approaches Meghaśrī, pays the respects due a prominent teacher, tells him of his desire to achieve full awakening, and asks him how one should practice the way of the bodhisattva that leads to perfect enlightenment. Meghaśrī commends him for his aspiration and tells him of the particular ability he has achieved: through cultivating devotion and observational power, he has developed the capacity to see the innumerable Buddhas in the ten directions and in countless world-systems. He gives an evocative description of some of the magnificent sights he sees, but claims to be ignorant of the even richer depths of those who know the way of the bodhisattva. Thus he sends Sudhana on to another teacher.[23]

This pattern is repeated with each teacher, some telling Sudhana of relatively simply practices and attainments, but many sweeping him up in their own experience, often affording Sudhana extraordinary visions that overwhelm him with their grandeur. For example, upon his first glimpse of the "night goddess" Pramuditanayanajagadvirocanā, he sees rays of light emanating from her body revealing far-off worlds and a multitude of projections showing the bodies of all different kind of sentient beings performing sacred and virtuous acts. He sees, as well, her past lives as a bodhisattva and her many acts of generosity and wisdom. Although she seems to embody every conceivable characteristic of a fully enlightened buddha, she too sends Sudhana on to another teacher, claiming that she does not know the way of the bodhisattva that Sudhana seeks.[24]

Among Sudhana's other benefactors is Sāgaramegha, who meditated on the ocean for twelve years and then was granted a vision of the Buddha. The teaching the Buddha gave him was called the "arrangement of dharmas within the universal eye" (*samanta-netradharmaprayāya*), by which Sāgaramegha can discern all the different planes of all world systems. Another bodhisattva, Supratiṣṭhita, whose special form of knowledge is called "having non-obstruction as foremost" (*asaṅgamukha*), is aware of the thoughts of all sentient beings, is capable of pervading all buddha-fields, and can travel unhindered through solid objects and over great distances. Paralleling this attainment, another bodhisattva named Muktaka, with his ability for "unobstructed manifestation" (*asaṅgavyūha*), sees great distances and can perceive anything he desires (usually buddhas or buddha-lands) no matter how far away. Prabhūtā, a female lay devotee who gives an inexhaustible supply of food from her jar, illustrates the virtue of giving (*dāna*). Śilpābhijña pronounces syllables, each of which open specific doors of transcendent wisdom. By pronouncing *A*, for instance, he enters into a "door of perfect wisdom" called "undivided realm" (*asaṃbhinnaviṣaya*), and by pronouncing *Ra*, one called "distinguishing infinite levels" (*anantatālalasaṃbheda*).[25]

Some of the interesting and surprising characters that serve as Sudhana's teachers include some apparently non-Buddhist ascetics: Jayoṣmāyatana, a *ṛṣi* cultivating the endurance of heat while seated between four large bonfires, and Bhiṣmottaranirghoṣa, a ragged ascetic with matted hair, seated on an antelope skin in a straw hut at the base of a tree. The popular bodhisattva of compassion, Avalokiteśvara, makes an appearance as Sudhana's twenty-eighth teacher. A layman named Indriyeśvara, who is adept at writing, mathematics, arts, crafts, sciences, and a wide variety of other areas of knowledge, has the ability to count out infinite numbers by means of advanced mathematical techniques used by bodhisattvas to count the multitudes of worlds, the innumerable sentient beings within those worlds, and ultimately "everything in the ten directions." A number of "perfumers" are included among the bodhisattvas, as well as a goldsmith. All of those involved in the seemingly mundane professions are depicted as using their trade-specific knowledge as a spiritual practice, thus emphasizing the continuity between the ordinary and the sacred.

No less than twenty of the fifty-two bodhisattvas Sudhana visits are female, establishing the *Gaṇḍavyūha* as one of the very few, and perhaps the earliest, of the pre-Tantric Buddhist texts with women in prominent positions of spiritual authority. In one scene, a nun sits teaching disciples in a park setting just like the Buddha in the sūtras. There is a healer woman and even a number of young girls, among them Maitrāyaṇī, who has attained wisdom from contemplating the "arrangement of the totality" (*samantavyūha*). Vasumitra, a prostitute from the land of Durgā, teaches men dispassion by first arousing passion, sometimes by means of "kisses and embraces." The mother of Gautama Buddha appears in the role of the archetypal mother of all bodhisattvas in all times and places. A female bodhisattva called Ananyagāmī has the ability to speed forth in all directions and go immense distances with each moment of awareness. A series of night goddesses teach Sudhana their practices, including one who is able to see all Buddhas of the past, present, and future, and another whose body seems to appear everywhere simultaneously.

References to light and vision are interwoven into the narrative in a great variety of ways. Many of the bodhisattvas have names and practices directly relating to vision or light, such as Sūryavikramasamantapratibhāsa (Infinite Light Like the Sun) and Samantajñānaprabhāsa (Light of Infinite Knowledge).[26] In one of a number of lists containing the names of bodhisattvas, fifty-seven refer directly to light or vision and many others refer to fire and other symbols associated with light or vision.[27] The ability of Meghaśrī, the first bodhisattva Sudhana visits, and whose attainment involves the ability to see countless Buddhas, illustrates another visual theme that runs throughout the *Gaṇḍavyūha* and a stock component of the many visions in the text – the multiplication of Buddha images throughout the cosmos, sometimes seen by means of the expanded powers of vision granted by the bodhisattvas and sometimes as projections from their bodies, from the pores of their skin or between their eyes. One interesting variation on this that does, in fact, provide a window onto actual practices at the time of the text's composition is the practice and attainment of the bodhisattva Veṣṭhila, a householder with a buddha shrine in his home. He relates a story of an incident that happened when he opened the door to his shrine and suddenly beheld a vision of all the successive buddhas, past and future, of this world-system and all world-systems. Now when he opens the door to the shrine he is able to enter into the thoughts and teachings of all these buddhas. "In a single moment of awareness, I see and comprehend a hundred buddhas; in the next moment of awareness I see and comprehend a thousand buddhas, and in innumerable moments of awareness I comprehend as many buddhas as atoms in untold buddha-lands."[28] Veṣṭhila's story suggests the presence of Buddhist home shrine devotion early in the common era. Another bodhisattva, a night goddess named Samantasattvatramojahśrī, is able to see all worlds in all directions at once and manifests herself in these worlds, thereby being seen by all sentient beings who are ready to being guided. A laywoman,

Bhadrottamā, teaches and practices a form of meditation allowing the practitioner to discern the fact that phenomena have no foundation, a realization that produces a transformation of all the sense faculties so that each sense perceives all-knowledge with respect to its sphere of apprehension.

While the emphasis on visions in the *Gaṇḍavyūha* overpowers references to other senses, the text presents a lush fabric of sounds and scents as well. Frequently the visions are accompanied by wondrous fragrances and sweet music. The relationship between sound or speech and vision follows along the lines of our previous discussion, with vision taking precedence over the other senses, but here in novel ways. Some of the references to verbal knowledge include mention of hearing verbal teachings from the buddhas and bodhisattvas as well as occasional praise of speech and language in service of the Dharma; for example, one bodhisattva is a linguist who has attained "light through eloquent sayings" and knows the languages of all the many different beings in the universe so that he can teach all of them in their own tongue.[29] Another teacher, a goddess whose special form of understanding is the "entry into the profound transformations of beautiful sounds," is able to prevent use of duplicitous, confused talk. The way she gets this understanding, however, is by a vision of the dharma-realm (*dharmadhātu*), characterized as a "vision of vast knowledge."[30] When verbal knowledge is specifically mentioned, therefore, it is often presented as a component of a great vision. Teachings are heard, but within the context of a vision which first reveals the teachers' practices and attainments.

Another way the text relates vision to sound and speech is through synesthesia, the phenomenon of sensory cross-over, such that one seems to "hear visions" or "see sounds." Passages that cross sensory boundaries are fairly frequent in the *Gaṇḍavyūha*. The night goddess Samantasattvatrāṇojaḥśrī, who faces in all directions, relates a story in which a Buddha is predicted to emerge in the future as "a ray of *light* called '*sound* of the appearance (*vidarśan*, literally "sight") of the inconceivable realm of the Buddhas'."[31] Other senses are crossed as well. One goddess whose mind is "tireless in seeing all Buddhas" gives a long list of the visions she sees, including seeing "various clouds of fragrant light-rays."[32] David Chidester contends that synesthesia in imaginative religious literature is often a way of representing a breaking through of ordinary structures of perception, transcending the separation of the senses and combining these usual separate aspects of experience into a unity of sensory experience prior to their division.[33]

The most climactic visions occur toward the end of the story when Sudhana visits Maitreya and Samantabhadra. Upon encountering Maitreya, the buddha of the future, Sudhana finds himself before the immense "tower of the adornments of Vairocana." Throughout the *Gaṇḍavyūha*, as well as the *Avataṃsaka* in its entirety, Vairocana[34] rather than Śākyamuni, often occupies the place of supreme buddha, though remaining a silent figure in the background, never uttering a word through the entire lengthy text. The tower represents the *Dharmadhātu*, the realm of suchness (*tathatā*) wherein all things interpenetrate unimpededly, and the microcosm and macrocosm become co-extensive. As Sudhana gazes at the tower, he realizes:

> this is the abode of those who dwell in full awakening, in the state of the unity of the *Dharmadhātu* . . ., the abode of those who dwell in the state of the entering of one eon in all eons and all eons in one eon, where one land is not distinct from all lands and all lands from one land, where one dharma is unopposed to all dharmas and all dharmas are unopposed by one dharma, where one being is not different from all beings and all beings are not different from one being, where one Buddha is not separate from all Buddhas and all Buddhas not separate from one Buddha, where all meanings enter into one moment, where [one] goes to all lands with the arising of a single thought.[35]

Maitreya leads Sudhana through the door into the tower, and within Sudhana sees that it is immeasurably vast, filling all of space, and adorned with the lavish scenery that is by now a common motif in the *Gaṇḍavyūha*: jewels, banners, flowers, and immense mansions with archways, mirrors, turrets, chambers, sculptures, lush vegetation, singing birds, and lotus ponds. He also sees hundreds of thousands of other similar towers, symmetrically arrayed in all directions, "each similar to the others, [yet] not confused or merging with each other, and with each reflecting the appearance of the others while remaining in its own place."[36] Experiencing great bliss, Sudhana bows reverently and at that moment, "by the power of Maitreya," sees himself in all of the towers. Then he sees Maitreya's entire career as a bodhisattva with different episodes and lifetimes visible in each of the towers. Among them he then sees one tower in the center, larger than the rest, and in it he beholds a billion-world universe, within which are one hundred million sets of four continents; within each he sees Maitreya enacting the career of a bodhisattva. On the walls of the towers, within each piece in the vast mosaic patterns covering the surface, he sees similar scenes, and each scene reflects the whole while the whole is reflected in each scene. Just as he perceives infinite spatial depths, he sees into vast stretches of time, both past and future, and seems to experience countless eons in just a few moments. Then, with a snap of his finger, Maitreya makes the entire spectacle disappear and makes a rather striking claim, combining the doctrine of emptiness with the granting of near god-like powers to the bodhisattvas: "This is the nature of things; all elements of existence are characterized by malleability (*aviṣṭhapana*) and are controlled by the knowledge of the bodhisattvas; thus, they are by nature not fully real, but are like illusions, dreams, reflections."[37]

Maitreya then tells Sudhana to return to Mañjuśrī and ask him again about the way of the bodhisattva. Later, Mañjuśrī appears to Sudhana and blesses him, apparently preparing the ground for the final vision, that of the bodhisattva Samantabhadra. After a number of preliminary signs and displays of light, Sudhana, in a state of profound concentration and with all his energy and senses directed toward the vision of Samantabhadra, sees the great bodhisattva seated on a lotus in front of Vairocana Buddha. As in the display of the Buddha Śākyamuni that begins the text, light rays emanate from Samantabhadra's body illuminating all the worlds throughout the cosmos, bringing ecstasy to all those present. Fragrant trees, aromatic powders, flowers, ornaments, jewels, images of celestial beings, bodhisattvas, and buddha-fields, all "as numerous as atoms in all buddha-fields" emanate from his pores. Upon contemplation of Samantabhadra's body, Sudhana sees within it untold billions of buddha-fields in all their detail, with rivers, oceans, jewel mountains, continents, villages, forests, and various realms of the different orders of life. He also sees the succession of all of these worlds simultaneously in the endless past and infinite future eons, each world being distinct and unconfused with the others.[38]

Upon seeing this vision, Sudhana attains "ten states of perfect knowledge," and, upon Samantabhadra's laying his hand on his head, attains even deeper forms of awakening and sees, in the countless world-systems now visible to him, images of the scene in his own world, that is, of countless Samantabhadras laying hands on countless Sudhanas. In the final phase of Sudhana's encounter with the great bodhisattva, he enters into the worlds within Samantabhadra's body, an episode worth quoting at length in order to give a flavor of the unique prose and imagery of the text.

> Then, Sudhana, son of a guild-leader, contemplating the body of the bodhisattva Samantabhadra, saw in each pore untold multitudes of buddha-fields, each filled with countless buddhas. And in each of the buddha-fields, he saw the buddhas surrounded by assemblies of bodhisattvas. He saw all of these multitudes of lands situated and arranged in various ways, in various patterns, with multiple manifestations, mountain ranges, clouds in the sky, various buddhas arising, and various proclamations of the wheel of Dharma. And just as he saw in one pore, he saw in every pore, in all of the marks [of a superior person], in the limbs and parts of Samantabhadra's body. In each he saw multitudes of worlds, and from them emerged clouds of created buddha-bodies, as many as the number of atoms in all buddha-fields, pervading all worlds in the ten directions and bringing developing beings to full awakening.
>
> Then Sudhana, guided by the words and teachings of the bodhisattva Samantabhadra, entered into all the worlds within Samantabhadra's body and cultivated beings there toward maturity. ... As he entered one buddha-field with qualities as many as atoms in untold buddha-fields within Samantabhadra, so with each moment of awareness he entered more such buddha-fields; and as in one pore, so it was in all pores. In each moment of awareness he proceeded further among worlds as countless as atoms in untold buddha-fields, going into worlds of endless eons – and still he did not come to an end. ... He moved through one buddha-field in an eon. He moved through another in as many eons as atoms in untold buddha-fields without moving from that field. In each moment of awareness he cultivated beings toward full awakening. Thus he continued until he achieved equality with Samantabhadra in his practices and vows, and with all tathāgatas in their pervasion of all

> buddha-fields, in their fulfillment of practices, in their full awakening, visionary transformations, and visions, in their turning of the wheel of Dharma, in their purity of knowledge, in their voice and speech, in their level of awakening, in their great friendliness and compassion, and in the inconceivable enlightening transformation of the bodhisattvas.[39]

Thus Sudhana, in his journey through the cosmos within Samantabhadra's body and by his enacting countless practices and deeds on that journey, attains the way of the bodhisattvas and becomes completely awakened.

Vision and Doctrine

George Tanabe points out that although many Mahāyāna sūtras contain abundant visionary episodes, the vast majority of modern scholars of Buddhism deal only with philosophy and doctrine and have been "reluctant to examine [these] visions *as visions* rather than as ideas."[40] With the *Gaṇḍavyūha* and the other sūtras within the *Avataṃsaka* corpus, it is apparent that a significant part of the subject matter of some Mahāyāna sūtras consists not of ideas, *per se*, but of visions. The *Avataṃsaka* is, as Tanabe points out, "not just a report of undigested visions, but a sophisticated work that blends fantastic visions with interpretative discussions about them."[41] Scholarly interpretation, in ancient and medieval Asia as well as in the modern world, has often tended to reduce such visions to doctrine rather than dealing with them first as visions. In trying to understand the significance of the visions in the *Gaṇḍavyūha*, we would do well to try to avoid either reducing them to doctrine on the one hand, or ignoring their relationship with doctrine and interpreting them as representations of free-floating, spontaneous mystical experiences, on the other. Despite the fact that the *Gaṇḍavyūha* is, in effect, a long succession of visions, and that a great deal of the text involves the quest for such visions, all of these many visionary episodes are intimately related to specific points of Buddhist doctrine. They are not, however, simply visual representations of such ideas, dispensable once those ideas are understood. Each vision in the text is a highly structured, imaginative evocation of ideas, ideals, and values of Mahāyāna Buddhism in the early common era. Thus, our challenge is to understand them *as visions*, yet still within their relationship to doctrine, as well as the wider context of Indian Buddhist practice and culture.

The first step toward understanding the relationship between ideas and images in the *Gaṇḍavyūha* is to briefly return to its literary genre, which is constituted by a radicalization of visionary tendencies present in most Mahāyāna sūtras. Many of these sūtras depict initial scenes of the Buddha entering a state of meditative concentration and an otherworldly vision arising from this state, which is seen by all or most of the audience. In the many scenes of Sudhana's visits with bodhisattvas, the *Gaṇḍavyūha* emphasizes these kinds of meditation-induced visions to such a great extent that it, along with the rest of the *Avataṃsaka*, may be understood to represent a distinct Buddhist literary genre that we could call "symbolic fantasy." This genre creates fantastic worlds that are grounded in Buddhist principles and constructs images that are symbolic, narrative embodiments of those principles. In this respect, it bears some resemblance to modern science fiction, which starts from scientific principles, discoveries, and hypotheses and then imagines possible worlds based on them. Science fiction invents worlds that are scientifically plausible in principle but are not actualized because of current technological limitations.[42] Buddhist symbolic fantasy takes the principles, stories, and values of Buddhist thought and practice and imagines the experience of beings who have developed the human technologies of meditation and self-cultivation, as understood in the tradition, to their fullest capacity – technologies considered capable of not only transforming the person but also his or her entire world.

How then can we understand more specifically the relationship of visions and images to ideas in this kind of literature? Certainly, there is no one paradigm that will cover all such relationships in all Buddhist texts, but there are certain patterns that recur frequently enough to suggest the kind of logic that is operative. One pattern is the returning of metaphors prevalent in Buddhist thought to their more concrete meanings, thereby making them amenable to being made into symbolic images. Take, for example, a passage in the *Samādhirāja Sūtra* that nicely illustrates the transition from metaphor to visual symbol, in this case the familiar metaphor of *light*. In this sūtra, the Buddha expounds a form of meditative concentration (*samādhi*) called "manifestation of the sameness of the essential nature of all dharmas." He explains that the one characteristic necessary for acquiring an undefiled mind is that of sameness or evenness (*sama*) of mind toward all beings.[43] This teaching incorporates the earlier teachings of equanimity (*upekṣa*) as an attitude or disposition as well as the Mahāyāna understanding of all elements of existence being the same in their basic nature. After the Buddha gives a litany of attitudes and practices entailed in this *samādhi*, a number of events occur: many in the audience achieve various degrees of understanding and awakening, the earth quakes, and finally:

> a boundless light flooded the world and the whole world system with its gods and Māras and Brahmas, with its śramaṇas and brahmans. All living beings were suffused with that light. And the sun and moon, though powerful, mighty and strong, seemed not to shine at all. Even the pitch-dark spaces between worlds, even they were suffused by that light, and the beings who had been reborn there suddenly became aware of each other, saying, "What! Could it be that another being has also been reborn here!" And so it was down to the great Avica Hell.[44]

We have discussed the importance of light as a metaphor for knowledge, and now we see an illustration of how this metaphor is actualized as a literary image and a religious symbol. Light flooding the world is a common image in Mahāyāna sūtras, and in this particular case, the event of light suffusing and penetrating all corners of the world, from the highest realms in which the gods live to the lowest hell-realms equally, is a concrete symbol for the very doctrine of the sameness of all dharmas that is propounded by the Buddha just previous to the light event. The Buddha preaches an attitude of equanimity towards all beings and an understanding of the sameness of the nature of all dharmas, then the light manifests as a symbol of this very attitude and understanding, permeating the highest and lowest worlds equally without any partiality or discrimination. This example suggests that symbolic visual imagery in Mahāyāna is an attempt to evoke a sensual presentation homologous with a cognitive concept. Assuming this model of the relationship between ideas and images in Mahāyāna texts, let us now examine the way in which some of the images in the *Gaṇḍavyūha* evoke such a presentation of one of the key structuring elements of Mahāyāna thought, the paradoxical dialectic that we explored in chapter one.

Dialectics of Words and Dialectics of Vision

The *Gaṇḍavyūha* almost certainly has some connection to the textual traditions we have discussed in earlier chapters; that is, what we have been calling emptiness discourses, consisting mainly of the early Perfection of Wisdom and Mādhyamika literature. In some ways, the sparse dialectics of say the *Vajracchedika* or the *Madhyamakakārikās* may seem to have little to do with the lush imagery of the *Gaṇḍavyūha*, even though both most likely arose in the same geographical area and around the same time. Nevertheless, a number of scholars, both ancient and modern, have pointed out that, despite the great differences in literary style, emptiness philosophy is implicit in the *Gaṇḍavyūha*, a point that need not be extensively reiterated here. Rather, I want to explore a more specific connection between the two, one more germane to our subject of the roles of vision and visual imagery in the Mahāyāna – the relationship between some of the recurring images in the *Gaṇḍavyūha* and the rhetorical pattern of the paradoxical dialectic in the early emptiness discourses.

The emptiness discourses explored the boundaries of language, generating paradoxes that, when understood, could be rendered intelligibly without violating the rule of non-contradiction, as we have seen. Nevertheless, this rational understanding is difficult; moreover, the doctrine of emptiness indicates that any linguistic understanding still falls short of the truth in the highest sense – that truth that the dialectic attempted to "show" but could not "say." We have seen that the dialectic is itself an implicit critique of the capacities of language and conceptual, dualistic thinking, and further, that visual metaphors are often employed to indicate the mode of understanding that occurs upon the clearing away of delusive conceptions. Given these factors, it should not be surprising if forms of discourse arose that attempted to represent this awakened understanding not primarily in conceptual terms but rather in *images* – and this is precisely what the *Gaṇḍavyūha* attempts to do through its recurring images of the interpenetration of the one and the many.

Because the dialectic *appears* to violate the basic logical rule of non-contradiction, it invites the reader to imagine a solution to the paradox, and one way that human beings work out such solutions is by visualization. In a very general sense, the visual representation of an apparent contradiction can serve to make it more intelligible

– to defuse the tension between the contradicting terms by placing them, or more precisely, some symbolization of them, side by side in visual space. This placing in the visual space of the imagination, with both sides of the paradox present in that space, is more amenable to imagining the solution to the paradox as a "both/and," rather than an "either/or," relationship. Visual representation of a paradox also invites the noticing of resemblance and may thereby suggest harmony and complementarity rather than stark contradiction.

The ways in which the *Gaṇḍavyūha* recapitulates the logical form of the paradoxical dialectic in this visual space of the imagination is more complicated than the symbolization of the sameness of all dharmas that we have noted in the *Samādhirāja*, but is still identifiable in the illustrations of interpenetration. One of the most widely noted themes in the *Gaṇḍavyūha* is the notion that all things interpenetrate; that is, each thing contains all things and all things contain each thing, such that the entire universe is present in each particular phenomenon. Yet what is often called the "doctrine" of interpenetration in the later theoretical formulations of Hua-yen Buddhism in China is not an item of theoretical discourse in the *Gaṇḍavyūha* (and the *Avataṃsaka* as a whole) at all. The doctrine of interpenetration is, in fact, a later set of elaborations on *images* found throughout the *Avataṃsaka*. These images are repeated throughout the *Gaṇḍavyūha*, present to some extent in virtually all of Sudhana's visions. In the opening passages, for example, the image of the entire history of all universes and their infinite numbers of living beings become visible in each of the Buddha's hair-pores, and his body is seen to pervade all worlds.[45] The image of all buddha-fields contained within one atom is repeated throughout. The eye of wisdom is said to see all objects in the cosmos as a whole, as well as all objects contained in each individual object. Images of interpenetration are perhaps best illustrated by the final two climactic visions in which Sudhana beholds the entire cosmos with all its infinite particulars within the body of Samantabhadra. Here the whole is seen as contained in the part. Also in this vision, the great bodhisattva blesses him, placing his hand on Sudhana's head, and Sudhana sees identical scenes of himself being blessed by Samantabhadra in all the world-systems of the universe. Here the part is recapitulated throughout the whole. Sudhana also sees in Samantabhadra's cosmic body the succession of all worlds in the past and future, and experiences eons of living in all these worlds in a single instant. While the previous two examples have to do which the mutual interpenetration of the large and small in *space*, this example illustrates the same pattern with respect to long and short durations of *time* – all of time is experienced as present within a moment, and within a moment Sudhana sees all of time. Countless other examples in the text could be given illustrating this same basic pattern of all things contained in one thing and one thing present or reflected in all things. Perhaps the best-known illustration of this pattern is Hau-yen master Fa-tsang's simile of Indra's jewel net, which stretches out infinitely in all directions and has a reflecting jewel at each juncture so that each jewel both reflects and is reflected by every other jewel. This relationship represents the relationship between all things in the cosmos and is construed, in Hua-yen thought, as mutual identity and causality.[46]

We have examined precedents for some of the imagery in the *Gaṇḍavyūha*, such as the illusion-producing abilities of thaumaturges and the imagery of royalty superimposed on that of buddhahood. But why this sudden proliferation of imagery repeating in countless ways the rather idiosyncratic theme of the interpenetration of the part and the whole? To explore this issue further, let us re-visit our discussion of the paradoxical dialectic as a way of providing one of the keys to understanding the particular character of this imagery.

Recall that the basic form of the paradoxical dialectic consists of three terms: A, ~A, and "A." The first term represents the ordinary conceptual appropriation of the world; it is characterized by thinking in binary oppositions, a dualism that falsely discriminates each thing in the lived world as a separate and independent entity. The second term negates the first and entails the doctrine of emptiness, which declares all these discriminations and the entities thus apprehended to be lacking this inherent existence, and instead to be mutually dependent. Given this understanding, the first term is then re-asserted in a qualified sense, indicating the re-affirmation of conventional phenomena and of life in the conventionally constituted lifeworld without the delusion and attachment entailed in falsely ascribing inherent existence to phenomena. This third move, in effect, holds the first two opposites together in a kind of paradox that I claimed earlier serves as a recurrent pattern embedded in a great deal of Mahāyāna thought and practice throughout history.

It is precisely this structure in the paradoxical dialectic that informs the recurrent imagistic pattern of the interpenetration of part and whole in the *Gaṇḍavyūha*, but not so much in a verbal as a visual mode. The pattern of visual imagery in the *Gaṇḍavyūha*, therefore, can be understood as a transposition of this dialectical pattern from words to images in the imagination – images that constitute a *visual paradox*. We can see this paradox, for example, in the image of the Buddha's body, first as a finite appearance in space and time, then as pervading all worlds while at the same time containing all worlds within it. In many such images, the text is careful to point out that this is not an obliteration of all distinction nor an absorption into an undifferentiated unity. Rather, within this confluence of the great and small, container and contained, part and whole, each thing iremains distinct and unconfused.[47] Were it not for this, we could understand this coextensiveness along the lines of the merging of all things in Brahman or Prākṛti, but the images instead depict the holding together of two contradictory images in a paradoxical tension, like that of the dialectic. The holding together of things in their distinct forms, on one hand, and the representation of things as transparent, with their boundaries erased so that all things pervade each other, on the other hand, is a visible representation of the paradox of emptiness, of the coextensiveness of saṃsāra and nirvāṇa. The two truths are now recast as two *realms* – the *lokadhātu*, the ordinary world, and the *Dharmadhātu*. Never in the *Gaṇḍavyūha* is awakening represented as the dissolution or ultimate transcendence of the phenomenal world; instead, the *Dharmadhātu* is the ordinary world presented as the interpenetration of all worlds and all things in all worlds, each of which maintains its conventional identity, yet contains and is reflected in all other conventional identities.

It is tempting to think that this mythical space wherein all things interpenetrate, the *Dharmadhātu*, is presented in the text as an ultimate reality or metaphysical absolute. In one sense this is true: the interpenetration of things, the transparency of their boundaries, and their ability to defy the laws of common sense are visual representations of the emptiness of inherent identity, which is according to the Mahāyāna the true nature of things. Yet, in the emptiness discourses, emptiness too is empty of inherent existence; similarly, the mythic space of the *Dharmadhātu* is a projection of the bodhisattvas, who can make the entire scene disappear with a finger-snap, as Maitreya does with the tower. According to Maitreya, the reality of the situation is that the universe itself, the vast visual projections and well as the ordinary world, is upheld by the bodhisattvas as a mental projection or conventional construction, just as in the Perfection of Wisdom the world has only a conventional existence.[48]

The movement of the "dialectic of images," then, could be construed as (A) the presentation of one object in finite space and time, for example, the body of the Buddha, (~A) the negation of that object as a fixed, individual entity by its multiplication throughout the cosmos and its simultaneous containment of the cosmos, ("A") the assertion of all objects as conventional projections maintained for the training of sentient beings for awakening.

Concretization of Metaphor

I have argued that the basic quest of the protagonist in the *Gaṇḍavyūha* is for visions and that these visions are synonymous with awakening (or steps toward awakening). I have also discussed in chapter 2 the importance of vision as a central metaphor for knowing in Buddhist thought. Additionally, I have interpreted some of the visions in Buddhist literature as a returning of prevalent metaphors to their more concrete meanings so that they can be made visible as textual imagery, as in the image of light in the *Samādhirāja*. This is one literary device that shifts vision from being a metaphor for the unmediated apprehension of the highest truth to vision in the sense of the "visionary" as we find it in the *Gaṇḍavyūha*. This concretization of other knowledge metaphors discussed earlier is also present in this text, for example:

KNOWING IS SEEING
KNOWLEDGE IS LIGHT
KNOWING IS ENTERING A REALM
KNOWING IS PENETRATION
KNOWLEDGE IS (LIKE) SPACE

In a way similar to its transposition of the logical form of the paradoxical dialectic into a dialectic of visibilities, the *Gaṇḍavyūha* renders some of these key metaphors in visual imagery, representing the process of awakening by concretizing these metaphors, returning them to their more literal meanings so that they can serve as symbolic images of this process and, thereby, taking them "beyond" theoretical discourse into the realm of the visible. The most frequent of these metaphors are those relating to entering and seeing.

While earlier texts metaphorically referred to understanding truth as "entering into truth," or "penetrating the truth," the *Gaṇḍavyūha* concretizes these metaphors by depicting images of various "enterings." The previously mentioned emphasis on buddha-fields and world-systems sets up a visual environment of the imagination within which the metaphors of seeing and entering can be realized. The entering into certain realms is, next to seeing bodhisattvas and experiencing their visions, the most frequent symbol in this text for realizing profound truths. Take, for example, Sudhana's entry into Maitreya's tower. Here the metaphor TRUTH IS ENTERING INTO A REALM is reinvested with concrete meaning.[49] In invoking this metaphor, the text also invokes the other visual and spatial metaphors that are systematically related to this one. Thus the tower, representing the highest truth or ultimate reality, is first presented as a visible object located in space and time, then as a realm to be entered into, as Sudhana opens the door and enters what Maitreya calls "the unobstructed realm" or "realm of unimpeded knowledge" (*asaṅgajñānagocara*), the *Dharmadhātu*. Upon his entering this space, he sees that it contains all spaces and all worlds, and that all worlds likewise contain this space. Entry into the realm of the Dharma is entering all realms, and moreover, *seeing* all realms. Likewise, the unlimited accessibility of all realms, either by seeing them or being able to go to them instantly, is a concretizing of the metaphor of non-obstruction. The recurrent images of interpenetration are also a radicalization of the theme of penetration present in so many Buddhist texts. A similar dramatization of visual and spatial metaphor occurs with the vision of Samantabhadra. The two events that constitute Sudhana's awakening are his seeing of the entire universe within Samantabhadra's body and his entering into his body, thereby entering, penetrating, and permeating the entire universe and becoming equivalent with Samantabhadra and, by implication, the cosmos itself.

Of course, the most prevalent metaphor that is realized in the images of the sūtra is our primary metaphor, KNOWING IS SEEING. One of the literary functions of the images of the interpenetration of all worlds is to render all worlds and all particulars in all worlds *visible*. The lights that radiate from the buddhas and bodhisattvas in the *Gaṇḍavyūha* reveal a profusion of things, beings, and events, providing a stunning array of particulars in its extensive lists of the objects of sight within its magical fields of vision; then these things are turned into reflectors of all other things in the cosmos, rendering each particular visible many times over. In this way the visibility of one thing becomes the visibility of everything, just as the emptiness of one thing reveals the emptiness of all things. In the *Gaṇḍavyūha*, then, visibility is the sensory analogue to emptiness. The transparency of all boundaries between things, allowing for their mutual pervasion, is a visual representation of the lack of inherent existence in all things. Just as the realization of this emptiness of fixed identity is tantamount to all-knowledge in the Perfection of Wisdom texts, the transparency and reflectivity of all things in the *Gaṇḍavyūha* is tantamount to the unimpeded visibility of all things. The images of interpenetration and mutual reflection serve to lay bare all surfaces within the cosmos, thereby constituting the ultimate actualization of the metaphor KNOWING IS SEEING.

The fact that the *Gaṇḍavyūha* is largely a narrative of visionary events presented in visual space makes it an ideal environment for the dramatization of the above metaphors involving seeing, entering, and space. The places that Sudhana moves through in his pilgrimage fluctuate from the ordinary landscape of India, with its identifiable and widely known sites, to mythic spaces which open up in the presence of the bodhisattvas he encounters. These are the places that, while occurring within a specific location in "ordinary" space, serve as doorway to spaces in which the most basic lived understanding of space and time dissolve. Here the boundaries between things, the logical relationship between container and contained, and between large and small are circumvented. The mythic spaces, then, represent a "confluence of spaces" (*ākāśadhātuparyayasāna*)[50] suggestive of the universal, infinite space so often used as a symbol for awakening in Buddhism. Yet, this confluence does not obliterate particular spaces, just as the complete interpenetration of objects does not obliterate each object's distinctness, for the ordinary places in India through which Sudhana travels remain, as does the distinctness of the world-systems he sees.

Finally, the rendering of Buddhist themes in visual imagery and the transposition of doctrine into images provides a way for the text to represent time in spatial terms. I have pointed out that a frequent aspect of Sudhana's visions in the *Gaṇḍavyūha* is his seeing of past, present, and future laid out before him as if in visual space. A number of his teachers lay claim to the ability to "see" the three times, and Sudhana, in his vision of the tower, for example, sees the entire career of Maitreya contained within the space of the tower. In chapter 2, we noted that the representation of dharmas as situated in space rather than coming and going in continual flux is a way in some Mahāyāna texts of symbolically nullifying the inexorable momentum of temporality and its devastating effects. This spatialization of time displays past, present, and future as if they were contemporaneous realms in space. Such a subordination of time to space, along with the frequent suggestions of the awakened ones' ability to enter any and all spaces, is a way for the *Gaṇḍavyūha* to illustrate the symbolic transcendence of time. The spatialization of time as a recurring theme in the text is a radicalization of tendencies already present in early Mahāyāna and pre-Mahāyāna texts, in this case the tendency to find ways of representing temporality in such a way as to render it impotent.

This discussion of the concretization of metaphor assumes that not only are metaphors constitutive of doctrine, a point made in chapter 2, but that they are also generative – that is, they generate new ways of envisioning reality and, in the case of Sudhana's tale, contribute to the new literary forms and imagery. Certainly the prevalence of visual and spatial metaphors do not alone provide the sufficient conditions for this new genre – we have already noted other factors, such as strategies of legitimation and pan-Indian visionary devotionalism – but they do provide some of the necessary contributing factors. Without the predominance of such metaphors in the Buddhist and Indian traditions, and without the dialectics of emptiness as a prevalent rhetorical motif in the Mahāyāna, the *Gaṇḍavyūha* would be a very different text.

The generativity of metaphors through their narrative concretization and the transposition of verbal dialectic into a dialectic of images shows the potentially wide-ranging results of subtle, and sometimes not so subtle, semantic shifts in the operative vocabulary of an epistemic system. Whether the rendering of knowledge metaphors into visual imagery was a conscious choice of the authors of the *Gaṇḍavyūha*, or if it just seemed "natural" given their immersion in that epistemic milieu, the conversion of these terms into visibilities had lasting effects on Buddhist philosophy, art, and practice. Many of the prominent themes of the emptiness discourses are, in the visionary literature, further developed in the visual field of the imagination and in turn reflected back into the cognitive realm in somewhat different forms. For example, in the *Avataṃsaka* the lack of inherent existence is illustrated visually by the interpenetration of all things, their physical boundaries becoming transparent so that each thing flows into all things while still retaining its own conventional form; this imagery then becomes the basis for extensive theoretical and cosmological reflection in the Hua-yen school in China. The presentation of the interpenetration of things – which, again, was at first presented as *imagery* rather than doctrine – gets reflected back to the cognitive level as an idea to be elaborated upon, explained, and interpreted. In this case the images were reconstituted back into the realm dominated by abstract concepts in the highly complex doctrinal formulations of Fa-tsang, Chih-yen, Tu Shun, and other Hua-yen scholars who contributed to this school of Buddhism. Thus, if the visions of the *Gaṇḍavyūha* and *Avataṃsaka* were in part radical attempts to evoke a visionary experience beyond the grips of conceptual systems, nevertheless, they ironically became themselves the material for the building of an elaborate conceptual system.

All of this suggests that the development of diverse interpretations of doctrine and the semantic changes that key concepts in a system of knowledge go through can be related in part to an emphasis on particular sensory modalities. The conversion of ideas into images and then back again will not necessarily yield the original idea. Rather, such conversions are semantic mechanisms productive of meaning, mechanisms which generate new ways of understanding a given theme. Just as a novel metaphor affords a new way of understanding something, evoking a network of concepts that both reveal certain possible meanings and conceal others, images can similarly light up a web of meanings, suggesting associations and resemblences that, when translated back into theoretical reflection, constitute the logic of a new philosophical position. With regard to Buddhism, the increasing emphasis on vision in the Mahāyāna played a formative role in the development of new doctrinal positions insofar as it entailed attempts to envision key ideas and metaphors and to illustrate them in visionary episodes – attempts that produced shifts in the significance and meaning of such ideas and metaphors. In the next chapter, we will explore some of the ways in which the metaphors and images we have been addressing, as well as the transposition of concepts into images, would be ritualized in meditation and devotional practices.

CHAPTER FIVE

The Optics of Buddhist Meditation and Devotion

Perhaps in no other area of Buddhist culture is the reliance on the visual more evident than in certain meditation and devotional practices. Vision and visualization occupy such a prominent place in Buddhist meditation that even the most cursory examination of the role of vision in Buddhism would be remiss if it did not address this issue as it relates to such practices. Indeed, it is in this realm of practice that some of the most interesting actualizations of the ocular metaphors and concepts that we have been exploring occur. We have seen how visual and spatial metaphors ground the Mahāyāna Buddhist epistemic system and how these metaphors are realized in the literary imagination. An examination of certain meditation and visualization practices shows how these same visual metaphors and visual dispositions are played out in the realm of practice – more specifically, the metaphors that were *concretized* in certain sūtras also became *ritualized* in certain practices. If, in South Asian Buddhism, the quest for awakening was often symbolized as a quest for a vision of truth, and if this truth were ordinarily obscured by obstructions to such a vision, then some forms of meditation were considered to be ways of removing the obstructions and enhancing the "visual" capacities. This all makes perfect sense in terms of the metaphorical and conceptual underpinnings of the Buddhist epistemic system; yet, as we have seen in the previous two chapters, metaphors can slip into actualizations in such a way that the line between the metaphorical and literal becomes blurred. Since the vocabulary of knowledge and awakening was to a great extent tied in with the visual, in that the paradigmatic act of knowing was symbolized by seeing, it is not surprising that the techniques developed for facilitating such knowing were often visually-oriented as well. Such techniques consisted not only of attempts to clear away false constructions, but also included procedures to *create* different visual constructions – images of alternative realities and sacred beings that could be actualized in the meditator's imagination through creating and maintaining mental images of them.

Although the quest for grand visions of such alternative realities like those found in the *Gaṇḍavyūha* is not as much a part of the pre-Mahāyāna traditions, the seeds of techniques for cultivating such visions were present from the earliest stages of Buddhist practice. Even in practices largely designed to counteract attachment to sensual experience, the cultivation of the visual imagination was an essential part of early Buddhist meditation. This chapter first surveys some of the visually based devotional and meditation practices that have been prominent in Buddhist traditions, then examines perhaps the epitome of the visionary tendencies in Indian Buddhism, Tantric visualization practices, showing how such practices form a continuity of imagery and structure with the visionary sūtras we have examined thus far.

Vision and Visualization in Early and Non-Mahāyāna Meditation

The vocabulary of Buddhist meditation is largely homologous with the vocabulary of knowledge, thus it is configured to a great extent along the lines of the visual-spatial terminology already discussed. The foundational layers of Buddhist meditation emphasize the cultivation of quiescence (*śamathā*) and observational analysis aimed at insight (*vipaśyanā*) into the nature of mind and world through the contemplation of Buddhist teachings such as impermanence, *duḥkha*, and the twelve-fold chain of causation. Such techniques are said to allow for the arising of "knowledge and vision" (*jñāna* and *darśana*) through the elimination of obstructions (*nivaraṇa*) and the employment various "aids to penetration" (*nirvedhabhāgīya*).[1] These are closely connected to the model of knowing we have been discussing, one that represents knowledge and its object as seer and seen. On this model, meditation is designed to clear away obstructions to vision such as greed, ill-will, sloth, listlessness, restlessness, worry, and skeptical doubting.[2]

Much of Buddhist meditation is designed to cultivate calm, detachment, and tranquillity, and to reduce the level of engagement of the senses and conceptual thinking with objects in the world. Paul Griffiths, following Mircea Eliade, calls this the cultivation of "enstatic" states of consciousness. "Enstasy," (from the Greek *en-stasis* meaning "standing within") the opposite of "ecstasy" (standing outside), is a term he uses "to denote techniques designed to withdraw the practitioner from contacts with the external world, to establish autonomy and ultimately to empty consciousness of all content."[3] While many Buddhist meditation practices aim at such an end, certainly not all of Buddhist meditation is an attempt to reduce the contents of consciousness to a minimum. Meditative techniques that use the visual imagination are intertwined with enstatic techniques, and these often employ visualizations that are designed to fill the mind with rich and colorful content. Even visualizations developed in the orthodox schools contain the rudiments of what later in the Mahāyāna and Vajrayāna could be conceived as ecstatic, rather than enstatic, meditations.

Meditation and Mental Imagery

Practitioners of Buddhist meditation have long been concerned with the arising and controlling of mental images. While some forms of meditation sought simply to observe mental images and other cognitive phenomena, others consciously trained the visual imagination to control and manipulate mental imagery through visualization exercises. Some forms of visualization are not designed to develop the faculties of visualization *per se*, but use these faculties as part of contemplations designed to enhance the understanding and personal realization of certain Buddhist teachings. Among some of the more memorable of these are the "meditations on the horrible," in which practitioners see, either in the cremation grounds or in the imagination, decaying corpses. Practitioners are invited to contemplate corpses in various states of decomposition – swollen, blueish and festering, gnawed by animals, bloody, reduced to a skeleton held together by tendons, and reduced to a skeleton scattered about. The meditator is to keep in mind that this is likewise the fate of his own body, thinking: "This body too is of the same nature, it will be like that, it is not exempt from that fate."[4] Such practices are designed to impress upon the meditator the doctrine of impermanence, as well as counteract lust that may be distracting to the practice of the Dharma.

This is just one of the more striking practices designed to structure perception and emotion in terms of Buddhist doctrine. Others include the cultivation of friendliness, compassion, kindness, and equanimity. In one well-known practice, the meditator cultivates a basic sense of regard for her own well-being, then envisions before her a person who is very dear to her, a person to whom she is indifferent, and a person to whom she has ill-will. Then she extends the sense of regard for her own well-being first toward the friend, then toward the one to whom she is indifferent, then to her enemy, and finally to all beings in the universe. All of these require the exercise of imagination and visualization in order to bring forth the subject of contemplation.

While being able to sustain a mental image is helpful to these exercises, other practices were more definitively oriented towards the cultivation of the ability to maintain images through visualization. An example of an earlier visualization practice in Buddhism is one in which the meditator starts out gazing at a material object (*kasina*), then attempts to reproduce the object in the imagination. One such practice, the "earth *kasina*" is a meditation on a plain clay disc. The practitioner gazes at the disc, focusing on it with full concentration and trying to eliminate from awareness all other thoughts and stimuli. After using the material support for long enough that he can maintain a steady mental image of the disc, he then meditates on that image, eliminating any of the small flaws and imperfections present in the physical object. When the image of the object can be maintained clearly over a long period of time, it is extended in all directions until it fills the entire universe. This is just one of the ways in which Buddhists attempted to work with the "visual consciousness," one of the six forms of sense consciousness. The process of gazing at an external object, internalizing the image, then manipulating it in various ways seems to have as part of its aim the freeing of visual consciousness from being determined by external forms, and the training of the imagination to be able to see whatever one desires. Even in this practice we see the rudiments of later deity visualizations, as well as suggestions of the thaumaturgic powers of transformation so prevalent in the *Gaṇḍavyūha*.

Vision and Devotion

Dharma, Buddha, Stūpa, and Saint

The subject of visualization and devotion must begin at least with the earliest phases of Buddhist history, perhaps with the death of the Buddha himself. It is at this point that the saṅgha was faced with the problem of the Buddha's absence – a problem that had at once emotional, institutional, doctrinal, and praxiological import. Although it is common in Western scholarship to represent the Buddhist community in the first few centuries after the Buddha's death as devoid of tendencies toward "deification" of the Buddha, there clearly was ambivalence quite early on the question of whether the Buddha was to be an object of worship. Much of the non-Mahāyāna Buddhist literature presents a picture of the monastic community that rejects the idea of the Buddha as a continuing presence in the world. In the *Mahāparinirvāṇa Sūtra* and the *Vinaya*, the Buddha is gone forever after his death (*parinirvāṇa*), even though the Dharma lives on. For the more conservative traditions of early Buddhism, there is no point in praying to him, making offerings to him, or worshipping him. The Theravāda literature discourages monks and nuns from making ritual offerings (*pūja*s) to the Buddha, although they allow it for laypeople, interpreting it as an aspect of self-discipline and a form of giving (*dāna*) and demonstrating non-attachment to possessions.[5] The Pāli canonical tradition is quite unambiguous about the fact that upon the Buddha's entering into final nirvāṇa he is gone from the world and no longer accessible to human beings.[6] Honoring the memory of the Buddha was acceptable, but the focus should now be on the Dharma, which in canonical sources was the guide appointed by the Buddha himself on his deathbed. Such a focus on the Dharma is illustrated in the *Saṅgīta Sutta*, in which Śāriputra, recalling disputation among another group of monks regarding what the Buddha taught – disputation proceeding the death of the wise and authoritative head monk, perhaps suggestive of the Buddha himself – proposes to another assembly of monks that they chant together a synopsis of the Buddha's essential teachings so that they will be remembered and not become objects of dispute.[7] This focus on the Dharma is the basis for the early distinction between the physical body of the Buddha (*rūpakāya*), which was no longer present, and the body of the Dharma (*dharmakāya*), the collection of teachings which would serve as the saṅgha's guide after the Buddha's death.[8] Emphasis on the body of Dharma, rather than the Buddha's personality as Śākyamuni, was part of the dissuasion against making him into an object of worship.

Despite orthodox admonitions, however, other practices, probably from the earliest stages of Buddhism, focused less on the Dharma than on the Buddha himself as a continuing living presence. With such practices we are again faced with the tension between presence and absence that pervades the Buddhist tradition – in this case the tension between the Buddha as absent teacher and immanent savior. Perhaps the earliest and most widespread form of practice that implicitly assumed the continuing presence and influence of the Buddha was the veneration of stūpas. While some may have regarded stūpas as memorials worthy of great respect, but not worship, many believed in the continuing power of the Buddha in the stūpa.[9] Stūpas were often understood as embodiments of the Buddha himself or of other Buddhist saints thus enshrined, and ritual behavior toward them was in many respects quite like behavior toward those considered living buddhas or other Indian saints. Devotees prostrated before them, uttered salutations to them, made offerings of food and gifts, circumambulated them, prayed to them, and decorated them with flowers, garlands, banners, and parasols.[10] That such decoration should seem familiar to us by now from descriptions of pure lands is not coincidental. In fact, Hirakawa argues that in at least one case, that of the smaller *Sukhāvatīvyūha Sūtra*, the pure land is modeled after the stūpa and largely replaced it in later devotional movements. Sukhāvati, he claims, "is an idealized image of a huge Buddha *stūpa*."[11] Also significant is the fact that the stūpa was identified with the physical body of the Buddha, and the relics it contains were considered to be the remaining life-force, which is still potent and able to function as a source of blessings and beneficent power.[12] Moreover, stūpa worship was not confined to those devoted to the Buddha Śākyamuni. Gregory Schopen argues that the relic cult of Gautama is only one well-known example of widespread cults and practices devoted to various Buddhist saints.[13] Reginald Ray suggests that such cults of Buddhist saints, who were seen to be living embodiments of enlightenment and who were at least symbolically identified with the Buddha, were present from the earliest periods of Buddhism.[14]

Recollection of the Buddha and Visualization Sūtras

Another way that the saṅgha responded to the Buddha's absence is by the practice of the "recollection of the Buddha" (*buddhānusmṛti*), in which a practitioner would systematically recall the excellent qualities of the Buddha, his virtues, conduct, and character as an example for inspiration. This was practiced in some form by virtually all schools. In Buddhaghoṣa's instructions on the recollection of the Buddha, he asserts that the results of the practice, in addition to complete confidence, mindfulness, understanding, and merit, are that the practitioner "comes to feel as if he were living in the Master's presence. And his body . . . becomes as worthy of veneration as a shrine room. His mind tends toward the plane of the Buddhas."[15] This too could be understood as simply an imaginative exercise that is both comforting and inspiring, and not transgressive of the orthodox position on the post-*parinirvāṇa* status of the Buddha. Nevertheless, such activities were precedents for practices designed specifically to evoke not only the memory and example of a buddha, but also his living presence.

Practices designed to more purposefully evoke this presence also fell under the category of *Buddhānusmṛti*, but in addition to (and sometimes instead of) recollection of the Buddha's moral and spiritual character, they often emphasized the excellence of his *physical appearance* and that of his surroundings. These practices were not confined to recollection of Gautama, but often concentrated on buddhas of other world-systems, particularly Amitābha and Akśobhya, as well as bodhisattvas such as Maitreya, Avalokiteśvara, Tārā, and Mañjuśrī. These are the visualization practices that I have already mentioned in connection with the flourishing of visionary imagery in the early common era, such as those in the *Sukhāvatīvyūha*s. Such texts share with the *Gaṇḍavyūha* the often stunning imagery of buddhas in their buddha-fields along with extensive descriptions of the buddha's resplendent appearance and superb physical attributes. But these texts function differently than the *Gaṇḍavyūha* in that they are not only descriptions of such beings and their realms but also manuals on how to access them by bringing forth their presence in meditative concentrations, making them directly available to the devotee, who will thereby worship, receive teachings, and eventually be reborn in the particular buddha's pure land. While the purpose of *Sukhāvatīvyūha*s is to obtain a vision of Amitābha at death and a subsequent rebirth in his pure land, other sūtras devoted to Amitābha, such as the *Pratyutpannabuddhasaṃmukhāvasthitasamādhi Sūtra*[16] (hereafter, *Ptratyutpanna*), a second century Indian text, and the *Amitāyurdhyāna Sūtra* (*Kuan Wu-liang-shou Fo ching*),[17] a fifth century text composed in either North India or Central Asia and embellished in China, are concerned with obtaining such a vision in this very life.

In the *Pratyutpanna*, the meditator is instructed to go to a secluded place, face in the direction of one's chosen Buddha, and envision the Buddha directly in front of him or her:

> [A] bodhisattva ... when he has gone alone to a secluded place and seated himself, after concentrating on the Tathāgata, Arhat, Samyaksaṃbuddha Amitāyus in accordance with what he has heard, then faultless in the mass of the precepts and undistracted in mindfulness [*smṛti*] should he concentrate for one day and night, for two, three, four, five, six, or seven days and nights. If he concentrates on the Tathāgata Amitāyus with undistracted thought for seven days and nights, then ... he shall see the Lord by day, then in a dream while sleeping the face of the Lord, the Tathāgata Amitayus, will appear.[18]

> [H]ow is this *samādhi* of the bodhisattvas, mahāsattvas to be developed? Bhadrapāla, just as, for example, I at present am sitting before you and teaching the Dharma, in the same way, Bhadrapāla, the bodhisattva should also fix his mind on those Tathāgatas, Arhats, Samyaksaṃbuddhas as sitting on the Buddha-throne and teaching the Dharma. He should fix his mind on the Tathāgata as being endowed with the best of all modes [*sarvākāravaropeta*], fair in appearance, beautiful, pleasing to look upon, and endowed with perfect development of body.[19]

Having obtained a vision of the Buddha, the text goes on to say, the practitioner can then worship and receive teachings from him.

In the larger *Sukhāvatīvyūha*, those who visualize Amitābha in his pure land and follow the moral precepts will increase in faith and meritorious roots, and will, upon death, see Amitābha standing before them, and this buddha will then lead them directly to rebirth in his pure land. The clarity and substantiality of the vision depends on the degree of faith and the degree to which one has successfully been able to perform the rather complex visualization of Amitābha in his pure land. Those with the strongest faith will see the actual Amitābha when they die. Even those, however, whose faith and ability to perform such visualizations are limited, will have less vivid visions of Amitābha and will still be reborn in the pure land.[20] In the smaller *Sukhāvatīvyūha*, an aspirant can attain such a rebirth merely by invoking the name of Amitābha, a practice appealing to those who did not have the time and training to master complex visualizations.

Many texts focusing on pure lands give detailed instructions to the meditator on exactly how to visualize a buddha and buddha-field. The *Amitāyurdhyāna* emphasizes not just rebirth in Amitābha's pure land, but also having visions of him in the present life. In this text, the Buddha gives instructions to an unjustly imprisoned queen who wants to be reborn in a land free of troubles. The Buddha explains that the queen is unenlightened, that her spiritual powers are weak and obscured because she has not yet attained the divine eye, so he will teach her special techniques to enable her to "see afar."[21] He then teaches her a series of visualizations to attain a vision of, and rebirth in, Amitābha's buddha-field. The stages, summarized here by Williams, are successive meditations on various images:

> (i) on the setting sun in the west; (ii) on pure, still, limpid water, then visualized as ice, then as crystal, and then gradually visualized as the Pure Land itself; (iii) this visualization of the ground is fixed in the mind unwaveringly; and then are added (iv) the trees; (v) the lakes; (vi) the palaces; (vii) the lotus throne of Amitābha; (viii) with Amitābha upon it, and to the life of the Buddha Avalokiteśvara, while to the right is Boddhisattva Mahāsthāmaprāpta; (xi) then one contemplates the form of Amitābha; (x) then the form of Avalokiteśvara; (xi) and then the form of Mahāsthāmaprāpta; (xii) one prays for rebirth in Sukhāvatī, and visualizes completely, in detail with a fixed mind, oneself born on a lotus in the Pure Land; and finally (xiii) one visualizes before one Amitābha and the two bodhisattvas in front.[22]

Evoking a deity through visualization establishes a definitive connection between the eye and the presence of the deity, a connection that is clear from other forms of devotion as well, particularly those of shrine and icon worship. Because of the similarities between visualization and image worship, to which we will now turn, we can see visualization practices as a part of the more general phenomenon of image worship in India.

Image Worship and Darśan

We have addressed the phenomenon of stūpa worship, perhaps the oldest form of devotion toward human-made objects representing the Buddha and his power, as well as the veneration of sūtras in the Mahāyāna, a practice structured along lines similar to stūpa worship. Buddhist image worship, including veneration of icons made of stone and wood, as well as images in the imagination, shares its basic ritual and liturgical patterns with these earlier forms of devotion. A symbolic unity exists between the various objects of veneration in Buddhist devotion – the stūpa, the sūtra (in the Mahāyāna), and the anthropomorphic image all are means by which the devotee can access the power and blessings of the buddhas. Stūpa worship provided the prototypes for these practices, which were then applied to sūtra worship, image worship, and devotion to celestial buddhas and bodhisattvas.

Aniconic symbols such as the stūpa apparently sufficed for much of the veneration of the Buddha in the early centuries after the his death, but icon veneration soon became the norm in both Mahāyāna and non-Mahāyāna Buddhism.[23] The *Ratnaguna*, probably the earliest Perfection of Wisdom sūtra, contains indications of iconic image worship in its allusion to the practice, still current in Buddhist countries, of painting the eyes on an iconic image, a final consecrational act that brings the image to life.

> How could those countless numbers of people born blind, not proficient in the path, and without a guide find the entrance to the city? Without wisdom the five perfections have no eyes, and those without a guide cannot reach awakening.
>
> When they have grasped wisdom, they obtain an eye and receive that name [perfection]. They are like a painting complete except for the eyes; only when the eyes are completed does one receive merit.[24]

If Conze and Nakamura are correct in dating this sūtra to the first or second century before the common era, then image worship evidently was common enough for readers in that time to understand this reference. It is certain that the practice was well-established by the first or second century of the common era, as the *Gaṇḍavyūha* and other texts mention shrines in the home and in public spaces, and many images were being produced in India and Central Asia. Whatever the reasons for the early aversion to making anthropomorphic images of buddhas, they were overcome by the irresistible trend of *association between image and presence* that appears to have been pervasive in North India and Central Asia beginning early in the common era, both in Buddhist and other traditions. We may see veneration of images of the Buddha as an extension of the focus on the Buddha that was previously expressed in stūpa worship – a focus that considered the Buddha to be present in these objects of veneration. While ritual and devotion involving images did not completely replace stūpa veneration and other kinds of aniconic worship, they undoubtedly proved to be a very powerful and compelling form of practice for the visually oriented South Asians.

In order to fully appreciate the power of the iconic image in Indian Buddhism, it is important again to understand the significance that ritual seeing has had in India, perhaps since before the time of the Buddha. The act of "seeing" (again, designated by the ubiquitous term, *darśana*; more commonly known today in the Hindi: *darśan*) any embodiment of a holy person or deity – be it a stūpa, sūtra, image, or the holy person him- or herself, is a salient feature of devotion in India. Seeing and being seen by a holy person are highly significant acts in India, as Diana Eck's book on the subject has pointed out.[25] More than ordinary seeing, the sight of such a person is considered to be an inherent blessing, and an exchange of glances is one of the primary means by which a devotee can participate in a saint's power and charisma. *Darśan* is often presented in Indian literature as a profound and intimate exchange whereby the devotee receives the holy person's transforming power and spiritual energy. Lawrence Babb makes some points about *darśan* in Hindu traditions that are hermenuetically productive when applied to Buddhist traditions as well:

> In the Hindu world "seeing" is clearly not conceived as a passive product of sensory data originating in the outer world, but rather seems to be imagined as an extrusive and

> acquisitive "seeing flow" that emanates from the inner person, outward through the eyes, to engage directly with objects seen, and to bring something of those objects back to the seer. One comes into contact with, and in a sense becomes, what one sees. ... Under the right circumstances, then, seeing and being seen by a deity is valuable because it permits the devotee to gain special access to the powers of a superior being.
>
> But I think even more is involved than this. If seeing itself is carried outward as flow, then what the gazing devotee is receiving, at least by implication, is an actual exteriorized visual awareness, one that is superior to his own. This means that quite apart from its more general benefit-bestowing characteristics, darshan [*darśan*] has important potential soteriological implications, for by interacting visually with a superior being one is, in effect, taking into oneself a superior *way* of seeing, and thus a superior way of knowing. Given the premises of this system, this makes available to the devotee the symbolic basis for an apprehension of himself as transformed. Since he himself is an object of his lord's seeing, by mingling this seeing with his own he can participate in a new way of seeing, and thus a new way of knowing.[26]

This certainly seems to be the presumption behind the visions occurring in the presence of buddhas and bodhisattvas in the *Gaṇḍavyūha* and other sūtras: the visionary episodes are ways for the audience (and thereby the reader of the sūtra) to see the world as the buddha or bodhisattva sees it. The transformed space of the vision, illumined by light pouring forth from between the awakened one's eyes, is the visual field of the buddha or bodhisattva, to which those seeing the buddha have access if they are spiritually attuned.

Numerous passages in Buddhist literature indicate that seeing in this particular sense was highly significant to Buddhist devotional attitudes, and this specialized sense of devotional seeing occurs within the context of a more general attitude toward sight – even aside from the philosophic attitudes we have discussed – that tends to understand the act of seeing to be revelatory. This is clear from some of the most prominent Buddhist narratives in which key events are structured around acts of seeing that produce an instantaneous realization or transformation. In the *Buddhacarita*,

Aśvaghoṣa's life of the Buddha, the young Gautama ventures out of the palace and views the "four sights" – an old man, a sick man, a corpse, and a renunciate – and, after a lifetime of sheltered naivete, realizes the full impact of old age, sickness, death, and the possibility of overcoming them. After his awakening, the *śramaṇa*s with whom he once studied are struck by his appearance and become his followers.[27] Beings from throughout the world-system, including gods, come to view the Buddha at key points in his life, and at his death many gather to see him one last time. In the *Mahāparinibbāna Sutta*, the Buddha on his deathbed commands his disciple Upamāna to stand away from him. When asked why, the Buddha replies that the countless deities from the ten world-systems have gathered to see the him, and have their view obstructed. They complain:

> We have come a long way to see the Tathāgata. It is rare for a Tathāgata, a fully-enlightened Buddha, to arise in the world, and tonight in the last watch the Tathāgata will attain final Nibbāna, and this mighty monk is standing in front of the Lord, preventing us from getting a last glimpse of the Tathāgata![28]

In the Sanskrit *Parinirvāṇa* Sūtra, the Buddha, just before dying, strips off his robe and says to those gathered:

> Monks, gaze now upon the body of the Tathāgata! Examine the body of the Tathāgata! For the sight of a completely enlightened Buddha is as rare an event as the blossoming of the udumbara tree. And monks, do not break into lamentation when I am gone, for all karmically constituted things are subject to passing away.[29]

The significance of seeing the Buddha seems to have increased with the passage of time, as Buddhist and other South Asian traditions came more and more under the sway of the visual. Illustrating this historical trend, Kevin Trainor points out an early and later story about a monk, Vakkali, who was very emotionally attached to the sight of the Buddha. In the *Saṃyutta Nikāya*, with its canonical emphasis on the Dharma over the physical body of the Buddha, Gautama scolds Vakkali for his attachment to his physical form, saying: "Enough Vakkali; what good is this putrid body to you? The one, Vakkali, who sees the Dhamma sees me; the one who sees me sees the Dhamma."[30] However, a later story about Vakkali, told in a commentary to the *Dhammapāda*, presents his reverence for the Buddha's appearance in a different light. In this tale, he is despondent when the Buddha forbids him to accompany him during the rainy season retreat. Vakkali is so disturbed by his being deprived of the sight of the Buddha that he resolves to kill himself. The Buddha, who knows suicide will prevent Vakkali from attaining liberation, appears to him in a radiant image and speaks comfortingly to him, which leads to Vakkali attaining the status of an arhat and acquiring extraordinary powers (*ṛddhi*s).[31] Thus in the early version, seeing the Buddha is a hindrance; in the later, a means of salvation.

Mahāyāna or Mahāyāna-influenced texts often stress the physical perfection and beauty of buddhas. In the *Divyāvadāna*, a king sends artists to sketch a picture of the Buddha, but the artists are unable to paint the picture because they are so transfixed with his appearance and cannot stop gazing at him.[32] While in some literature, the sight of a Buddha is considered auspicious, in certain Mahāyāna texts this sight rivals, and even surpasses in importance, the hearing of a Buddha's teachings. For example, in the *Gaṇḍavyūha*:

> The word of a Buddha is hard to come by even in a billion eons; How much more so the sight of a Buddha, which ends all craving. . . .
>
> Those who have seen the Buddha, the supreme man, are certain of awakening. . . .[33]
>
> All obstructions are removed when a Buddha is seen,
> Increasing the immeasurable virtue whereby awakening will be attained.
>
> The sight of a Buddha severs all the doubts of sentient being
> And fulfills all purposes, mundane and transcendent.[34]

Not only Buddha Śākyamuni, but also later Buddhist figures were held in high enough esteem that they became objects of such veneration, being seen as participants in the sacrality epitomized by Śākyamuni. As Reginald Ray points out, figures like Mahākāśyapa, Upagupta, various arhats, pratyekabuddhas, and forest saints all became focal points for devotion, some having stūpas dedicated to them and narratives told and written about them presenting accounts of their lives on the model of Śākyamuni's. Again, many of these figures were evidently taken to be the functional equivalents of the Buddha. In the story of king Aśoka, the *Aśokarājāvadāna*, the ruler visits Upagupta, a saint who in Aśoka's estimation fulfills the Buddha's role in the world and is declared to be "like the master." The text indicates that taking *darśan* from Upagupta can, among other benefits, lead to rebirth in a heaven and to obtaining the same benefits of the Buddha's Dharma.[35] In another episode, Aśoka asks an elder monk if there is anyone still alive who has seen the Buddha during his lifetime. The monk replies that Piṇḍola, a great saint known for his extraordinary longevity, has. Aśoka becomes very excited and desires to see this saint. Looking into the sky, he then sees Piṇḍola miraculously appear, surrounded by thousands of arhats. Ray relates the rest of the episode:

> Then the king kneels before the elder, declaring his great joy and remarking, 'by looking at you, I can, even today, see the *tathāgata*. You show yourself out of compassion'. . . . Aśoka then asks Piṇḍola a crucial question: has he, in fact, actually seen the Buddha with his own eyes? Piṇḍola replies that he has: 'Indeed, I saw him many times – that great incomparable Sage'. Thus, through the medium of seeing, there is a link of unbroken continuity of transmission between the Buddha himself and Aśoka: Piṇḍola has seen the Buddha, Aśoka has seen Piṇḍola, and thus Aśoka has seen the Buddha, again affirming Piṇḍola's assimilation to the Buddha.[36]

This story suggests the equivalence, through the medium of vision, of the Buddha and the Buddhist saint. Also noteworthy are the elements of similarity in both of these stories to visualization practices. Taking *darśan* with Upagupta can lead to rebirth in heaven, a result similar to seeing Amitābha in his pure land, and the manner in which Piṇḍola appears to Aśoka is much like the kind of vision that visualization practices are intended to illicit.

We have, then, a number of symbolic equivalences between Buddha, stūpa, scripture, saint, and image. This in no way implies that all Buddhists agreed on what specifically qualified as a sacred reality identified with the Buddha – in fact, evidence suggests ample disagreement, with some rejecting stūpa worship, others rejecting visualization practices, and others rejecting sūtra worship. Nevertheless, the principle remained for most Indian Buddhists of various traditions, that the sacred reality of the Buddha could be present in the world through such symbols, and that devotees could access this reality, its blessings, and its sacred power.

Significantly, the form of worship that established prominence over all others was icon worship – the kind of veneration in which the image can return the devotee's gaze. One of the common phrases found in both visualization instructions and descriptions of spontaneous visions is "directly in front of"; Amitābha appears directly in front of his worshipper when he is finally granted a vision, and a meditator is instructed to visualize the deity directly in front, fully accessible for the sacred exchange of gazes. In India, the gods do not conceal themselves; we would be hard pressed to find stories in which a modest god only allows a prophet to catch a glimpse of his back, as in Moses's vision of God. Visibility is the precondition for the primary means of access to sacred symbols and beings – the direct encounter with the presence of the Buddha and the truth he represents through *darśan*. While, in the elite philosophical traditions, an invisible reality always lurks in the background – the absent Buddha, emptiness, *nirguṇa* Brahman – for the most of the religious of India, visibility has been the *sine qua non* of their practice.

Visualization practices such as those we have discussed so far have their roots in earlier ritual and devotional practices focused on the Buddha, such as the recollection of the Buddha and shrine/image worship. Visualization is a logical extension of such practices, a way of creating an internal shrine that is not separate, non-dual, from the mind of the practitioner and relies on no external support. If the presence or power of a Buddha could be present to a devotee in a painted or sculpted image, how much more present could he be if the image were within his or her own mind? Such practices also indicate a supposition about the power of vision and visual resemblance – that of a strong connection between image and presence. The visual image "resonates" with, and becomes an extension of, the actual deity when the image is empowered by consecration.

The importance of the embodied image, the ambivalence among some monastics about worship of physical forms, and the attempt to harmonize the worship of images with sophisticated Buddhist philosophy invited a great deal of speculation regarding the nature of the body of the Buddha. A discussion of one formative treatment of this topic, Asaṅga's formulation of the three-body doctrine, should suffice to indicate the issues of concern to those who took seriously both devotion and philosophy.

Asaṅga on the Buddha's Bodies

The prominence in the Mahāyāna of the various devotional movements centered around worship of particular buddhas in their pure lands likely caused tension within the Buddhist communities in South and Central Asia. First, the existence of cults devoted to different buddhas was one of a number of factors we have already mentioned that deflected attention away from Śākyamuni Buddha. This no doubt disturbed those who considered it essential that Śākyamuni remain the central figure. Second, some Buddhists were probably worried that allegiance to different buddhas was splintering the Dharma into many small sects and movements, drawing attention away from what they considered the more essential teachings. Another issue, one probably more of concern to the most educated scholar-monks but still having wider repercussions for the Buddhist community as a whole, was that devotion in general could undermine the philosophical cornerstone of the Mahāyāna, the doctrine of emptiness. Worship of a being or image that is not inherently existent (although no less so than anything or anyone else) must have posed some unique problems to those involved in such worship while still maintaining the philosophy of emptiness, a situation which was probably the norm among educated monastic Buddhists. It is with these issues in mind that Asaṅga, the great fourth-century Yogācāra scholar, addressed this issue in the context of the Yogācāra doctrine of the three bodies of the Buddha (*trikāya*).

One function of the three body theory was the unification of the diverse buddhas who were objects of worship into one based on the Buddha Śākyamuni. According to this theory, a buddha has three different aspects, called bodies (*kāya*). The "manifestation" or "transformation" body (*nairmāṇikakāya*) is the physical body, limited in time and space and present in the world as a human being. In most Mahāyāna accounts, this is a kind of conjured manifestation of the buddha for the benefit of those who cannot apprehend the higher aspects. It corresponds to the earlier form-body (*rūpakāya*), but now understood as an illusory appearance, a form of skillful means (*upāya*) to appeal to those of lesser understanding. The enjoyment body (*saṃbhogikakāya*) is the resplendent body, full of light and adornments, produced by and enjoying the fruits of eons of meritorious karma. This, according to Asaṅga, is the body that those who visualize buddhas in their pure lands see. Finally, the dharma-body (*dharmakāya*) is the transcendent aspect of the buddha which fully embodies all the characteristics of enlightenment and is identified with emptiness, the ultimate nature of the universe.[37] The dharmakāya, according to Asaṅga, is the basis for the other bodies, which are manifestations of the dharmakāya. Furthermore, all buddhas are unified in the dharmakāya. Asaṅga and his commentators characterize all of the various buddhas in their pure lands who were objects of devotional cults as enjoyment bodies that are manifestations of the one dharmakāya. The enjoyment body is manifested in all world-systems as the various buddhas of these systems. This notion brings some legitimation to the visualizing of, and devotion to, buddhas of diverse realms, since they are all manifestations of the same dharmakāya, which is emptiness, ultimate reality itself.[38]

Moreover, since these buddhas are all manifestations of the dharmakāya, they are empty of inherent existence; therefore, the visualized bodies should not be understood as having a fully objective existence or as the true object of devotion in and of themselves. All buddhas in their buddha-fields are in the end constructs of purified consciousness whose real purpose is to refer to the higher truth of emptiness. In this schema, then, the myriad practices for visualizing and worshipping buddhas are both given some justification and at the same time subsumed under the doctrine of emptiness and the primacy of the dharmakāya.[39] The three body theory was an effort to maintain the doctrine of emptiness in the face of the devotional movements prevalent in the Mahāyāna without destroying the benefits and efficacy of such worship.

Asaṅga's writings on visualization of the enjoyment body reveal some of the tensions that had arisen in the Mahāyāna between reification and veneration of buddhas and the insistence on upholding the doctrine of emptiness, tensions also illustrated by the apparent competition between devotees of stūpas and devotees of Perfection of Wisdom texts. Asaṅga's formulation of the three-body doctrine is another instance, this one specifically related to visualization practice, of the tensions intrinsic to the doctrine of emptiness – tensions between presence and absence, being and non-being – and of the difficulty in avoiding the reification of phenomena, in this case, objects of devotion. These tensions represent, in one respect, the different needs of different practitioners; many Buddhists were no doubt concerned primarily with security, protection, hope, and salvation for themselves and their families, and likely had no investment in the intricacies of emptiness philosophy, especially when it had the potential to compromise their principal concerns for blessings in this world and the next. The potential conflict between devotion and emptiness was more pronounced among the educated elite Mahāyānists who wanted to make emptiness compatible with the benefits and security that devotion offered. Devotion and worship of buddhas and bodhisattvas was by no means confined to "popular" Buddhism, but was prevalent in the monastic and scholarly communities as well. That it was difficult for ordinary practitioners not to take the beings who were objects of their devotion as inherently substantial is not surprising; the striking thing in the context of the history of religions in general is the unique form of devotional attitudes set up by the attempt to maintain both worship and the philosophy of emptiness, i.e., the worship of images that are self-consciously understood to have no inherent existence. This is one of the prominent features of Tantric *sādhana*, one of the most elaborate forms of ritualized visualization meditations, and an arena for the playing out of tensions between presence and absence that we have been discussing.

Tantric Visualization Practices

Among the practices of evoking deities[40] in Buddhism, Tantric visualizations (*sādhana*s) are the most complex. New factors come into play with the elaborate envisioning rituals of Tantric practitioners, only a few of which we can address within the limited context of this discussion. A great deal of excellent research has come out within the last few decades that sheds a light on the purposes and nature of Tantric practice in both Hinduism and Buddhism, and a number of books now exist that detail the intricacies of these complex systems of thought, ritual, and symbolism. My purpose in examining Tantric visualization here is not to add any substantial amount of new material to this research, but to examine the practice in light of our discussion of the roles of vision in Mahāyāna Buddhism. To this end, I will concentrate only on some of the salient features of typical Tantric sādhanas, rather than getting into a lengthy discussion of the intricacies of Vajrayāna Buddhism, a discussion which would warrant far more than just part of a chapter.

Buddhist Tantric practices are based on Tantras, scriptural texts that are concerned with the ritual evocation of deities, the practice of meditation, and acquisition of special powers. To select one feature fundamental to Tantric texts and practices would probably be futile, for their range of subject matter is wide. Most, however, do contain certain identifiable features shared by most Tantras, notwithstanding the characteristic difficulty scholars have had in defining Tantra, both as a kind of text and as a movement. Most recent scholarship, faced with the multifaceted nature of what is called Tantra, has adopted a "family resemblance" understanding of its most common characteristics. On this notion, no one characteristic is necessary to define a text, group, or practice as Tantric; rather the inclusion of a number of descriptive features constitutes a text, group, or phenomenon as Tantric. One recent list of such features of Tantric Buddhism suggested by Stephen Hodge serves as a helpful indicator of what qualifies as Tantric:

1 Tantric Buddhism offers an alternative path to Enlightenment in addition to the standard Mahāyāna one.
2 Its teachings are aimed at lay practitioners in particular, rather than monks and nuns.
3 As a consequence of this, it recognizes mundane aims and attainments, and often deals with practices which are more magical in character than spiritual.
4 It teaches special types of meditation (*sādhana*) as the path to realization, aimed at transforming the individual into an embodiment of the divine in this lifetime or after a short span of time.
5 Such kinds of meditation make extensive use of various kinds of maṇḍalas, *mudrās, mantras,* and *dhāraṇīs* as concrete expressions of the nature of reality.
6 The formation of images of the various deities during meditation by means of creative imagination plays a key role in the process of realization. These images may be viewed as being present externally or internally.
7 There is an exuberant proliferation in the number and types of Buddhas and other deities.
8 Great stress is laid upon the importance of the guru and the necessity of receiving the instructions and appropriate initiations for the *sādhanas* from him.

9 Speculations on the nature and power of speech are prominent, especially with regard to the letters of the Sanskrit alphabet.
10 Various customs and rituals, often of non-Buddhist origins, such as the homa rituals, are incorporated and adapted to Buddhist ends.
11 A spiritual physiology is taught as part of the process of transformation.
12 It stresses the importance of the feminine and utilizes various forms of sexual yoga.[41]

Tantric Buddhism can be seen as an outgrowth of a number of different influences combining the visual devotionalism we have been discussing with emptiness philosophy, as well as ritual, liturgical, and symbolic elements drawn from both Buddhist and non-Buddhist sources. As a religious movement, Tantra was well-known by the sixth or seventh century in India, although it most likely existed in some form as a marginal or even underground movement perhaps even centuries before that. Geoffry Samuel suggests that the Tantras "provide a sophisticated reworking of common shamanic procedures," some of which may have existed in India on a folk level for centuries.[42] Although it was eventually accepted to some extent into mainstream Mahāyāna Buddhism, and in fact considered itself a part of the Great Vehicle, it's antinomian tendencies and transgressive practices probably kept it in an ambivalent relationship to more conventional forms of Buddhism. Perhaps the feature that distinguished it the most as a separate "vehicle," the Vajrayāna, was its forbidden practices such as drinking alcohol and engaging in ritual sexual activity. In the Tantric interpretation of the Dharma, these were a logical extension of the non-duality of nirvāṇa and saṃsāra put forth in the Madhyamaka. Tāntrikas (Tantric practitioners) attempted to utilize the things and activities of this world to achieve awakening, making liberal use of them as symbols of various aspects of the Dharma or the Buddha. For example, many Tāntrikas were householders, traders, craftspeople, and so on, who made their everyday work into religious acts through symbolic transformation of these acts. Even the most menial work could be thus transformed: digging a ditch could be imagined as shoveling offerings of gold and incense to the deities as offerings; cleaning dishes could be rendered as a symbolic purification of the mind.

Such imaginative transformation of the world and worldly activity is characteristic of Tantric practice and worldview.

The general principle behind these simple kinds of imaginative transformations reaches its epitome in the often elaborate sādhanas, whereby the practitioners attempt the symbolic transmutation of themselves and their entire world by identifying their body, speech, and mind with those of a chosen buddha. These visualizations operate, in some respects, much like the pure land visualizations we have discussed, employing the visual imagination to create an alternative reality replete with symbolic embodiments of buddhahood. But Tantric sādhanas take visualization practice further in a number of ways. First, in some Tantras, the goal is not just to have a vision of a particular deity, but to actually merge identities with him or her. Second, the Tantras extend and make more elaborate use of the symbolic vocabulary already present to an extent in other Buddhist traditions, a vocabulary that includes abundant use of visual signs, hand gestures (*mudrā*s), and mantras associated with individual buddhas. None of these was unknown in non-Tantric Mahāyāna iconology and visualization practices, but they became more central and elaborate in Tantric practice. A proliferation of iconic symbols was added to those already known in Buddhism, for example the various *mudrā*s of the Buddha such as those signifying turning the wheel of Dharma and protection. To these were added the *vajra* (diamond or thunderbolt), garlands of skulls, animal skins, and many implements often held by multiple hands. The union of opposites that had been a part of Buddhism since the early Perfection of Wisdom sūtras also figures prominently in Tantric symbolism: drawing from Mahāyāna philosophy, unification of wisdom (*prajñā*) and skillful means (*upāya*), saṃsāra and nirvāṇa, as well as male and female, sun and moon, right and left incorporated into Tantric symbolism, along with countless sets of complicated correspondences between specific doctrines, words, Buddhas, natural elements, animals, and so on.[43]

The locus for the development and practical implementation of this symbolism is the maṇḍala. Tantric visualization techniques employ maṇḍalas, which function as the primary images used to restructure the meditator's consciousness. Maṇḍalas are images, often quite complex, representing the buddha-fields in which a given buddha resides. They are not exclusive to Tantra, but they achieved their most intricate development in this movement's iconography and textual descriptions. Tantric maṇḍalas generally include the representation of a palace on a lotus coming out of the sea, a central buddha in the palace, and buddhas and bodhisattvas arranged directionally around it, along with a variety of other scenes that vary from maṇḍala to maṇḍala. We usually think of maṇḍalas as physical objects, but they are also consciously and meticulously created images developed and sustained in the imagination of the meditator.

The practice of visualizing maṇḍalas similarly draws on earlier practices: the meditations on *kasina*s, such as the earth contemplation using a clay disc as support, contains in vastly simpler form some of the same basic patterns as maṇḍala visualizations, including the training of the imagination to hold an image in the mind for long periods of time and expanding it to include the cosmos. Of course, pure land visualization, recollection of the Buddha, and contemplation of the body of the Buddha in non-Tantric Buddhism are important precedents as well. Some have suggested that Tantric visualization draws on ancient pan-Indic elements present on the village level for centuries before the development of Tantra as a distinct and visible movement.

Stages of Tantric Sādhana

Although Tantric sādhanas vary considerably in content, using many different deities as objects of meditation, most show basic structural similarities. The following is an outline of the stages that are often standard in Buddhist sādhanas. The details vary significantly with different sādhanas, and not all these steps are universal. I am drawing primarily from three visualizations of Tārā, a benevolent female deity, found in the *Sādhanamāla*, a later collection of disparate *sādhana*s assimilated in the eleventh century, but containing many practices dating from the earlier phases of Tantric Buddhism.[44]

PRELIMINARY PRACTICES

1 Most sādhanas require some kind of ritual purification of both the meditator and the site of meditation prior to engaging in the practice. This often involves ritual bathing and adorning the site, a private place outdoors, with flowers and incense.

2 Preliminary visualization of the letters corresponding to a number of "seed syllables" associated with the particular deity. These syllables are envisioned producing rays of light.
3 Preceding the main visualization, the practitioner pays homage to the buddhas and bodhisattvas; makes offerings of flowers, incense, etc.
4 Confession of any sins one has committed against any beings in the endless cycles of incarnation.
5 Rejoicing in the merit of all beings; taking refuge in the three jewels: Buddha, Dharma, and Saṅgha; expression of reliance on the path of the Buddha; and appeal for the tathāgatas to remain in the world and continue to teach the Dharma.
6 Dedication of merit gained through this practice to the attainment of full awakening of all beings.
7 Cultivation of the four holy states (*brahmavihāra*): friendliness, compassion, joy, and equanimity.
8 Meditation on the inherent purity and emptiness of all things and of oneself. This inherent purity is synonymous with the emptiness of all things, and it is out of this emptiness, visually represented as an empty space, that one creates the maṇḍala.

MAIN VISUALIZATION

1 Here the meditator visualizes the deity in detail. From a Tārā sādhana:

> Then one should visualize the blessed, holy Tārā proceeding from the yellow seed syllable *tāṃ* situated on the spotless sphere of the moon, which is inside the filaments of a lotus in full flower, in the middle of the moon already visualized in one's heart. One should conceive her as deep green in color, with two arms, a smiling face, endowed with every virtue, and free of all defects, adorned with jewelry of heavenly gold, rubies, pearls, and jewels. Her two breasts are decorated with beautiful garlands, her arms wrapped in bracelets and bangles. ... She is a radiant and seductive figure in the prime of youth, with eyes like a blue autumn lotus, her body dressed in heavenly garments, seated in a half-lotus posture in a circle of light rays as large as a cart-wheel. With her right hand, she makes the sign of granting wishes; in her left she holds a blue lotus

> flower in full bloom. One may cultivate this image of the blessed one as long as one wishes.
>
> Then, the [image of] the blessed one [Tārā] is led away on numerous bundles of light-rays illuminating the triple world. [The rays] issue from the yellow seed syllable *tāṃ*, which is in the filaments of the lotus in the circle of the moon situated in one's heart. Then one sees the blessed one, perfect since beginningless time, as the essence of knowledge (*jñānasattva*), brought forth from empty space. When she has been brought forth and established on the firmament, one should receive her by offering oblation at her feet with scented water and fragrant flowers in a jeweled vase. One should worship her ... with flowers, incense, lamps, food, scents, garlands, perfumes, garments, umbrellas, flags, bells, banners, and so on.[45]

In some Tantras, detailed instructions are given for visualization of far more intricate maṇḍalas. Some have a multi-leveled palace with pillars, banners, and many different kinds of jewels. The *Guhyasamāja* maṇḍala has thirty-two deities, all of which are to be envisioned having precise postures, gestures, colors, and ornaments. Meditators are ideally supposed to be able to maintain a steady image of this intricate map of a world for an extended period of time, as well as manipulate elements within the maṇḍala at different stages in the meditation, including changing its size, sometimes reducing it down to the size of a drop while maintaining its detail, or expanding it to envelope the entire cosmos.

2 After visualizing the deity, the practitioner forms the hand gesture (*mudrā*) appropriate to the deity and pronounces the mantra or syllables associated with that deity.

3 In Tantric *sādhana*s, the culmination of the practice is the identification of the practitioner with the deity. This is the primary thing that distinguishes sādhanas from other kinds of Buddhist visualization practices.

> Then, [the light rays] issuing from the yellow seed-syllable *tāṃ* on the filaments of the blue lotus in the sphere of the moon, rays of unlimited power and range, appropriate to the divine Tārā, illuminate all worlds in the ten directions, removing the suffering caused by poverty and other

> afflictions of beings living in the triple world with showers of countless precious substances for all sentient beings in all worlds, and refreshing them with the nectar of Dharma teachings, such as the teaching of impermanence, no-self, and so on. Having brought various kinds of good into the world, [the practitioner] produces [an image of] Tārā in her cosmic form. . . . Emerging from meditative concentration, the practitioner, having seen the entire universe in the form of Tārā and constructed himself as the blessed one, lives as he pleases.[46]

In other sādhanas, the practitioner achieves the identification with the deity through "entering" the maṇḍala and merging with the deity. Others avoid the initial duality altogether and instruct the practitioner to envision herself from the outset as the deity or by generating herself from the outset "as" the deity.[47] This involves the cultivation of "divine pride" (*māna*), the sense that the practitioner *is* the very deity being envisioned. Such a sense is developed through conscious visualizations of the practitioner dissolving into the maṇḍala or into the deity, of the deity dissolving into the practitioner, or maṇḍala and deity dissolving into the "clear light of emptiness." In the major Tantras, such as the *Kālacakra* and *Guhyasamāja*, both the visualization and identification are very complex, involving envisioning the subtle body and attempting to gain control over the movement of energy, or "winds" (*prāna*), through its channels and *cakra*s, points or "circles" along the central channel of the subtle body at which energy coalesces.[48]

4 The maṇḍala is dissolved back into emptiness through a series of stages.
5 Some sādhanas list the "mundane powers" (*laukikasiddhi*s) that one may accrue from the practice. In the Tārā sādhana above, these include a number of magical powers such as the ability to become invisible, fly, travel instantaneously on the ground, and enter nether regions.

Maṇḍala and Sūtra Imagery

The prototype of the Tantric maṇḍala is clearly found in visionary sūtras such as the *Gaṇḍavyūha*. We have seen how, in that text, the Buddha's dwelling is transformed into a vast pure land. In the

Suvarṇaprabhāsa Sūtra is a more succinct account of such a transformation, the main features of which should now be familiar. This is a vision of a devout bodhisattva named Ruciraketu who, significantly, is practicing recollection of the Buddha when the transformation occurs:

> While Ruciraketu was recollecting the qualities of the Buddha, his house became immense and extensive, made of cat's eye, adorned with numerous divine jewels, and, transformed by the tathāgata, it was filled with fragrance beyond the divine. And in the house there appeared in the four directions, seats made of divine gems. On those seats were divine cushions covered with fine cotton cloth, and on the cushions were divine lotuses adorned with jewels, transformations brought about by the tathāgata. And on those lotuses appeared four blessed buddhas: in the east appeared the tathāgata Akṣobhya; in the south appeared the tathāgata Ratnaketu; in the west appeared the tathāgata Amitayus; in the north appeared the tathāgata Dundabhisvara.
>
> Then, as the great city of Rājagṛha was pervaded with a great light, the great three-fold multiple world system and world systems in the ten directions as numerous as the grains of sand in the Ganges river became pervaded with light. Divine flowers rained down, heavenly musical instruments were heard, and the beings in the great three-fold multiple world system became, by the Buddha's power, possessed of divine bliss.[49]

This and other scenes we have already encountered are highly suggestive of maṇḍalas that became standardized as objects of visualization and artistic representation. These sūtras invariably begin with the Buddha about teach and surrounded by a circle (literally, a maṇḍala, the primary meaning of which is "circle") of disciples, bodhisattvas, and sometimes buddhas of other world systems. Most notable in the scene from the *Suvarṇaprabhāsa* is the geometric configuration in which buddhas take seats in the four directions, just as they are placed in maṇḍalas. In the *Gaṇḍavyūha*, bodhisattvas from the world systems in the ten directions similarly take their places around the Buddha. Attention to these opening visionary passages in Mahāyāna sūtras strongly suggests that they are the models for maṇḍalas ritually constructed for meditation.

In this regard, a maṇḍala becomes a "place" in which the ideal teaching situation presented in a sūtra is recreated – a place where the Buddha is present to be seen and heard teaching the Dharma. Just as a place where a buddha resides either in physical form or in relics, images, or other embodiments is a *tīrtha* – a sacred place conducive to communication between divine and mortal beings – the maṇḍala is a *tīrtha* where the meditator meets a buddha in a symbolic, ritual recreation of the sacred encounter of buddha and disciple. In the maṇḍala, all of the homologies that I have pointed out between stūpa, pure land, icon, and buddha come together as embodiments of enlightenment.

One textual motif that draws together these embodiments and is common in visionary sūtras is that of the dwelling place of a buddha or bodhisattva as palace or three-storied tower (*kūṭāgāra*), a standard feature of the Tantric maṇḍala. Both in the passage above and in the *Gaṇḍavyūha*, the locus of the visionary episode is a house or dwelling where a buddha or bodhisattva is staying. In fact, the episode of Sudhana's encountering Maitreya's tower is a pre-Tantric vision that, together with other elements of the *Gaṇḍavyūha*, contains many of the standard ingredients of the Tantric maṇḍala. It is a visionary episode in which a devotee (Sudhana) first stands outside the tower seeing it from without, then enters it, whereupon the structure expands to cosmic proportions to become a geometrically arrayed pure land. Such expansions of a structure also recall another scene from the *Gaṇḍavyūha* in which a bodhisattva has a home shrine and sees millions of buddhas upon opening its door. In his vision of Samantabhadra, Sudhana is similarly presented with a cosmic image of a buddha whose body he enters and with whom he thereby becomes identified. These episodes all share important features in common with Tantric visualization: the visionary construction of an idealized sacred place, the presence of a palace or tower, a geometrical or directional arrangement of the site, the ritual "seeing" of the place, and the entering into and becoming identified with its living powers or personalities.

The maṇḍala, therefore, can be considered a site of *darśan*, of seeing a buddha, and of the ritual appropriation of a buddha's power. A maṇḍala sets the scene for receiving *darśan* from the visualized deity. This is especially true in the case of sādhanas that generate the deity "in front" of the practitioner. I have suggested, paralleling Babb's assertions about Hindu *darśan*, that the exchange of glances between a buddha and a devotee is a means by which the devotee participates in the vision and knowledge of a buddha by accessing the buddha's own visual field. Again, Babb asserts: "if seeing itself is carried outward as flow, then what the gazing devotee is receiving, at least by implication, is an actual exteriorized visual awareness, one that is superior to his own. . . . [T]his makes available to the devotee the symbolic basis for an apprehension of himself as transformed."[50] This is precisely what is dramatized in some Mahāyāna sūtras' opening scenes depicting the transformation of the landscape through the Buddha's concentration, with light emerging from his forehead illuminating a transfigured world – visions recapitulated again and again in Sudhana's encounters with the bodhisattvas. These visionary episodes are depictions of the world *as seen by buddhas and bodhisattvas*; but, more importantly, the devotee or disciple is granted access to that vision through encountering the awakened being and witnessing his or her externalized vision. In this sense, Tantric sādhanas could be considered ritual enactments of these visionary episodes recounted in the sūtras, episodes that establish the formal structure of encounter with a holy being. Such ritual re-enactments of sūtra narratives allow the practitioner to re-create the ideal teaching situation presented in every sūtra – the direct encounter of buddha and disciple.

But sādhanas are not just devotional or instructional encounters; they are also technologies of self-transformation whereby practitioner is identified with deity. In contrast to pure land visualizations and practices of recollecting the Buddha – whose primary aims are worship, hearing of teachings, and a better rebirth – Tantric sādhanas, while they may include all of these purposes, are meant to allow practitioners to symbolically merge with the deity. This is accomplished in part by the practitioner's sharing in the deity's visionary capacities. The generation of the maṇḍala is a ritual replication of the visionary displays projected by the buddhas and bodhisattvas in Mahāyāna sūtras that allows this sharing. Recall the emphasis in the *Gaṇḍavyūha* on the malleability of the world and the assertion by Maitreya that the entire world-appearance is a manifestation of the advanced bodhisattvas for the benefit of sentient beings as an arena for their awakening. Sudhana is the recipient of these visions, a participant in the vast displays of the bodhisattvas. Through the appropriation of the powers of projection and transformation of appearances, the Tantric practitioner engages in a similar process, generating a world that serves as an arena for awakening and the development of powers. The meditator does on a small scale what the bodhisattvas are said to do on a large scale – create mind-made realities in which awakened beings appear as a matter of course and devotees can see buddhas and become buddhas themselves. Nor is it just the generation phase of Tantric visualizations that find a precedent in the visionary episodes of the sūtras; recall Sudhana's final encounter in which, after contemplating the body of Samantabhadra and seeing that it is itself the entire cosmos, he enters the body and experiences the entire bodhisattva career, attaining awakening by identifying himself with this buddha and thereby with the cosmos and buddhahood. This episode shares precisely the same structure as the Tantric sādhana and is obviously a narrative precedent to both generation and completion stages of this practice.

Not only are maṇḍalas arenas for the development of the powers of creative envisioning, they also suggest the more metaphorical senses of vision as knowledge. Generation of oneself as deity entails both a claiming of a buddha's power to transfigure the world and a claiming of his or her insight into the nature of the world, the nature of emptiness, and the power to behold the entire cosmos, here as a maṇḍala, in one synchronic vision. Again, an important feature of the maṇḍala is its symbolic presentation of the cosmos, including past, present, and future, in a vision of simultaneous presence.

Embodiment and Resemblance

The part played by visual resemblance in this technology of divinization is also important in the understanding of Tantric visualization. There is a notable lack of theoretical consideration in Tantras, or for that matter in other Indian literature, of what makes a deity embody a particular image. Whatever the ambiguous, probably pre-theoretical, assumptions on this matter were, the various forms of iconic ritual and devotional practices suggest that visual resemblance and consecration were the most important factors in compelling a deity to inhabit an image. What, then, is the nature of the affinity between image and deity that allows the former to become the latter? One important point in considering this issue is that in ancient India, and perhaps in the ancient world in general, there existed a more fluid sense of boundaries between things than we are used to in our scientific age. I have mentioned, for example, the families of entities classed together in Tantric literature, classifications that to modern people would likely seem quite arbitrary and unfounded, but nevertheless display their own internal logic. Such resonances and sympathetic relations between things abounding in natural and astrological taxonomies, for instance, were a prevalent part of ancient and medieval world-views. It is within the context of such sympathetic relations that the transformations of images (whether fashioned of stone or mental imagery) into deities must be understood. Such transformations were special cases of exploiting avenues of correspondence and resonance established not by explicit theoretical reflection but by certain pre-reflective attitudes and ways of being in the world.[51] It is not difficult to discern some of the implicit rules by which connections are made between things and deities or saints; that is, by which a particular entity might count as participating in their sacrality. One of the most obvious is that a particular place is associated with the holy figure by virtue of his or her being born there or by some significant episode in his or her life occurring there and thus sacralizing the site – places like the site of the Buddha's awakening at Bodhinath or Rāma's birthplace at Ayodya.

Another important factor establishing affinities between images and deities is visual resemblance. The thing that invites – even compels – the deity to enter its icon is its resemblance to the deity; thus, images are to be rendered carefully in order that they achieve similarity to the received understanding of what the deity looks like.[52] The production of maṇḍalas, either in the imagination or in paint, sand, or stone, proceeds according to exacting rules to assure this similitude. Images must be created with precision and according to time-honored traditions – individual creativity is not the point in the creation of this ritual art. A certain magic is implicit in the correct rendering of a deity or maṇḍala – a magic of resemblance. Resemblance is, among many ancient systems, a powerful constituent in the constructing of knowledge and establishing of practice. In iconic practices, in India as well as elsewhere, the image of a deity, when properly consecrated, evokes the presence of that deity in part through visual resemblance to what is considered the deity's actual forms – forms described in detail in the Tantras. The importance of a precise rendering of deity and his or her surroundings in the construction of maṇḍalas testifies to the implicit connection assumed between image and presence – specifically, the power of the image to evoke the presence of the deity upon consecration of the image. Consecration actualizes the symbolic resonance between image and presence that is only potential in an unconsecrated image.

The Tantric sādhana is an extension of these assumptions operative in the fashioning and consecrating of images. In the case of the Tantric identification of practitioner and deity, though, it is a process of the practitioner consecrating *herself* and making herself into an image of the deity, thereby inviting the presence and power of the deity into the visualized image. Ritual re-envisioning of oneself and consecration of oneself are the mechanisms that reverse the common-sense understanding of the relation of mental imagery to being – that reality is what it is and mental imagery is derivative from this reality. Ritual consecration, along with specific training in visualization and the knowledge of what to visualize, reverses this relationship between image and reality, allowing mental imagery to directly transform reality. Thus, by the transformative powers of visualizing herself as deity, the practitioner herself becomes a living icon, as actuality follows imagery.

The Somaticization of Doctrine

In order for the visualized image to be generated out of and dissolved back into emptiness, a subtle semantic change in the term "emptiness" is necessary. This change occurs along the lines of what we have seen in our previous discussion: that of the transposition of abstract concepts into visual imagery. In this case, the "image" of emptiness becomes the space out of which the maṇḍala arises and into which it dissolves. Or it could be understood as a mental canvas or screen onto which the image is painted or projected. Any of these interpretations require that the notion of emptiness be expanded from its earlier meaning as the lack of inherent existence in phenomena – a notion that carries with it no definitive image – and made to inhabit the realm of the visual imagination, all the while without losing its earlier significance. In such imagery the association of emptiness and space in earlier Buddhist texts becomes a more explicit identification. So too becomes the association of emptiness and light, as the images of the maṇḍala are dissolved into the clear light of emptiness.

This is an extension of the process of concretization of metaphor discussed in chapter 2. A further extension of this concretization found in the traditions of iconic representation and visualization, and especially Tantric thought and symbolism, is the "somaticization" of Buddhist doctrines and themes, i.e., the association and representation of specific doctrines, ideas, and narrative themes with various aspects of the body and its adornments. This phenomenon takes a number of forms in Tantric literature, one of which is the representation of doctrine and ideas as contiguous with somatic processes. For example, the notion of *bodhicitta* in Mahāyāna literature means the aspiration towards enlightenment. To "raise the *bodhicitta*" in this sense means to cultivate this aspiration. In Tantric literature, the original meaning is retained, but the psychological process comes to be seen as contiguous with the raising of a physical substance, semen, through the central channel in the subtle body during sexual yoga practices.

Another aspect of the somaticization of Buddhist themes is the symbolic encoding of doctrines on the bodies of the practitioners and deities that are the object of meditation. Various Buddhist doctrines, themes, symbols, and deities are associated with the navel, heart, throat, and head. Tantric Buddhists also placed considerable emphasis on symbolic gesture employed in a ritual context, both in their own bodily movements and in the *mudrā*s and postures of the deities. The somaticization of Buddhist themes represents an attempt to translate these themes from abstract doctrine into the more immediately accessible language of gesture, symbol, and image. Every visible feature of the deity and his or her surroundings is a sign pointing to a Buddhist teaching. Some standard elements of Tantric iconic representation, for example, are choppers or swords, denoting discernment or insight; the lasso, symbolizing harnessing the mind in meditation; garlands of severed heads around deities, indicating various deluded mental processes that have been overcome; skullcaps with blood of a demon, indicating the transmutation of impure substances into pure.[53]

Through these images, the meditator grasps the meaning of the deity and its symbols in a (comparatively) non-discursive apprehension considered to be a more direct vision unencumbered by verbalization and verbal thinking. This somatic symbolization in the context of visualization practice attempts to circumvent the verbal stage of cognitive processing and to offer a more immediate access to a basic teaching, one contained not in a string of sentences but in a unified gestalt. Indian textual traditions often use ellipses to indicate what the reader is assumed already to know; for example, in referring to the five *skandha*s, a text will simply say "form, etc." The figural inscription of doctrine in the gestures and implements of Buddha images is a kind of visual ellipsis. Once the practitioners are familiar with the basic doctrines implied in the symbols, they can call to mind the implications of the symbol non-discursively through the embodied image.

This transition from verbal to symbolic must be seen in light of the critiques of language that had become standard among the educated Buddhists by the time of the early Tantras. One appeal of iconization and visualization practices to those versed in emptiness philosophy, with its implicit critiques of language, was that the somaticization and concretization of doctrine could be seen as a way of circumventing some of the problems involved with trying to express the Dharma in words. Seeing had a magic that was more immediate than words. It was already indicated in sūtras that the vision of the Buddha, both in the sense of seeing him and seeing what he sees, could grant an immediate, intuitive understanding of the Dharma equal or even superior to merely hearing then it put forth in words. The somaticization of the Dharma in Tantric visualization practice was a way of rendering the fundamental teachings in symbols that practitioners would take into their own bodies, thereby becoming, themselves, visible signs of the Dharma. The doctrines, the verbally articulated structures of thought, the complex systems of interlacing concepts are here embodied, quite literally, in the figures, gestures and implements of the deities. Cognitive language is circumvented and the teachings that once had to be thought through with a great deal of ratiocination, verbalization, and conceptualization are present in images.

It could be argued that mantras are just as important to Tantra as visualization, and therefore the Vajrayāna should not be understood as continuing the Mahāyāna preference for seeing over language. Despite the significance of mantras, though, they do not indicate a shift from an ocularcentric model of knowledge toward a language-centered model, for the suspicion of language in the Mahāyāna is a suspicion primarily of *cognitive* language. Mantras, while they do have cognitive content, are not primarily cognitive utterances but sacred sounds, embodiments of the deities with which they are associated. In this sense they are verbal icons, more like stūpas and maṇḍalas than assertions, explanations, and theories.

The Tantric sādhana brings together different aspects of the epistemological, soteriological, and devotional themes we have been addressing so far. It provides an idealized space for seeing a buddha and entering into the buddha's seeing by appropriating his or her visionary powers. It provides instructions for creating a unified micro-universe, the maṇḍala, in the manner of the creative powers of the buddhas and bodhisattvas in some Mahāyāna sūtras. Further, seeing the maṇḍala, the microcosm, and grasping its entirety in one synchronic vision was an enactment of awakening itself as described in a number of sūtras. Finally, the sādhana, by de-emphasizing cognitive language in favor of visible signs and symbols, attempted to circumvent the limitations of verbalization asserted in Mahāyāna philosophy. In this respect, it is in many ways a culmination of the visual orientation of Mahāyāna and Vajrayāna Buddhism.

CHAPTER SIX

Conclusions and Occlusions

I have argued in this study that many of the discourses and practices of philosophy, mythology, and certain forms of meditation and devotion in South Asian Mahāyāna Buddhism were significantly informed and influenced by a tendency to understand sight as the primary locus for knowledge and religiously significant activity. Further, this privileging of vision often involved a concomitant devaluation of language. I have used a number of case studies to illustrate this thesis. I proposed that the privileging of vision over language in the philosophic discourse of the Mahāyāna entailed the predominance of visual metaphor along with the critique of the delusive capacities of language and conceptual thinking. This devaluation of language and conceptual thinking led to some of the more creative theoretical negotiations with language such as the paradoxical dialectic of the Perfection of Wisdom sūtras, a discursive pattern that would manifest in numerous forms throughout Buddhist literature, imagery, and practice. I argued as well that this privileging of vision over hearing and language was a factor in the development of visionary literature. Further, this style of literature had a polemic function in the strategies of legitimation employed by the Mahāyāna to secure legitimacy for its new sūtras and novel doctrines. The exploration of visual and spatial metaphors for knowledge, such as light, space, entering, penetrating, and of course, seeing, demonstrates the degree to which concepts of knowledge and awakening in Mahāyāna Buddhism are modeled on the operations of the eye and rooted in visual and spatial concepts. These metaphors are brought to life in the vivid imagery of the *Gaṇḍavyūha Sūtra*, where they are concretized as narrative elements in the pilgrimage of Sudhana. Finally, I have explored the ways that vision and visualization played a central role in devotional practices and Tantric meditations, further embedding the Dharma in visual and somatic symbols. I have chosen these particular case studies not only because they illustrate the ocular orientations of South Asian Mahāyāna, but also because they are historically important, not only for India, but in other geographic areas to which Buddhism traveled. The crucial role of visual metaphor, visionary literature, and visualization practices in the history of Buddhism beyond India should be clear to anyone even casually acquainted with the forms that Buddhist traditions have taken in China, Japan, and Tibet.

While all of this may be intrinsically interesting to scholars of Buddhism or South Asian studies, I did not undertake this study with only these relatively circumscribed fields in mind. The relation of knowledge, narrative, and religious practice to the senses and sense metaphors is a subject of inquiry that exceeds these sub-disciplines and is relevant to multiple fields in the humanities and social sciences. While the study of vision and its cultural and religious significance has been relatively neglected in Buddhist and South Asian studies, recent studies of the subject with regard to the West are increasing in volume and sophistication. Yet they have a notable lack of cross-cultural perspective, being almost entirely Eurocentric. Studies indicating the ways in which the senses are interpreted and appropriated in the discourse and practice of various cultures can only broaden the range of investigation into roles of the senses. In this concluding chapter, therefore, I will make some preliminary suggestions on the ways in which such work in Buddhism and Asian traditions might provide material relevant to current discussions on ocularcentrism, while indicating some directions for future research that could prove mutually productive to both contemporary analysis of visuality and historical or philosophical analysis of Buddhism.

Ocularcentrism in European and American Philosophy

The relevance of vision and language and their relation to knowledge and cultural practice is not, of course, limited to Asia and is lively issue in a number of fields in the humanities and social sciences. The roles of language in the construction of knowledge and cultural practice is more a staple of contemporary philosophy, both continental and analytic, than is the study of vision. Indeed, the "linguistic turn" heralded by Richard Rorty, through which philosophers began to examine in earnest the ways in which language structures knowledge, is arguably still the most important development in contemporary philosophy and social thought.[1] Nevertheless the study of the senses, particularly vision, and their contribution to knowledge and cultural practice has increasingly been a topic of consideration. I have mentioned, for instance, the studies of Maurice Merleau-Ponty and Hans Jonas, along with David Chidester's study of vision and hearing in the Augustinian tradition. Some of the ways these authors construe the manner in which vision and hearing each structure and orient consciousness in different ways is worth briefly reiterating here before examining some recent work on ocularcentrism. In their analysis, hearing is associated with time and sequence, while seeing is associated with space. While the ear hears sounds arising and passing away in time, the eye sees things situated in space. Audition discerns events rather than things and registers the flux and discontinuity of temporal sequence. Vision can apprehend more things simultaneously than hearing, unifying them in the present moment. It is capable of apprehending static objects, making them more susceptible to analysis and passive discernment of static patterns.

With these and other considerations in mind, a number of contemporary scholars have interrogated vision, visual metaphor, and visual practice in their constitutive roles in the history of knowledge and culture in Europe and North America. Scholars have debated the degree to which European and European-influenced thought and culture are and have been ocularcentric, but an increasingly strong consensus of contemporary scholars has argued convincingly that many facets and periods of Western culture carry a legacy of reliance on vision as the most important and valuable sense faculty, especially in relation to knowledge. Martin Jay, one of the foremost exponents of the ocularcentric hypothesis, asserts:

> The development of Western philosophy cannot be understood ... without attending to its habitual dependence on visual metaphors of one sort or another. From the shadows playing on the wall of Plato's cave and Augustine's praise of the divine light to Descartes's ideas available to a "steadfast mental gaze" and the Enlightenment's faith in the data of our

> senses, the ocularcentric underpinnings of our philosophical tradition have been undeniably pervasive. Whether in terms of speculation, observation, or revelatory illumination, Western philosophy has tended to accept without question the traditional sensual hierarchy. And if Rorty's argument about the "mirror of nature" is right, modern Western thinkers in particular have built their theories of knowledge even more resolutely on a visual foundation.[2]

David Michael Levin similarly argues that the turn toward philosophical studies of language in this century have prompted philosophers and social thinkers to examine the ways in which vision has dominated philosophy, producing a "hegemony of vision" that has been "invisibly constructing models and paradigms of vision within the framework of diverse epistemological, metaphysical, ethical, and political programs."[3] Levin draws together evidence that the history of Western philosophy has been that of a largely "vision-generated epistemology," the primary vocabulary of which is drawn from ocular metaphors. This hegemony of vision is not, he suggests, merely a matter for the abstruse ruminations of scholars, but has significant cultural implications in the modern world. Summarizing some of the wide-ranging implications of discussions regarding ocularcentrism, he notes:

> There is thus an important debate taking place within philosophy regarding the role of vision and the discourse of vision in the very construction of philosophical thought. This debate is actually part of a larger cultural debate over the hegemony and character of vision in the contemporary world. In question are the nature and role of vision, and the functions and effects of the discourses of vision in the formation of individual identity, the constitution of social relations, the cultural genealogy of stereotypes, the administrative power of the state, the visibility and accountability of governmental agents and agencies, the human relationship to nature and use of the environment, and the construction of discursive sites, of places and spaces, in the public sphere.[4]

Much of this interrogation of vision has not been favorable to what was once, as Jonas points out, considered the "noblest of the senses." This is a large and complex subject, but a few salient examples of critiques of ocularcentrism (some of which admittedly were offered before the neologism existed) are sufficient to indicate the basic trend.

Critics of the predominantly visual orientation of Western thought have offered a number of pointed critiques of the limitations and dangers of ocularcentrism. Some of these critiques are a part of the many critical commentaries on the European Enlightenment that abound in recent scholarship. The gist of most is that ocularcentrism in the Western Enlightenment tradition involves a distancing of the subject as seer from the object and a reductive objectification of the seen. Sight, its critics claim, is the sense activity that perceives at a distance and tends to neglect temporality; therefore, it is prone to give rise to uninvolved, spectatorial modes of knowledge in which the separate subject views the world as a collection of static objects. Also involved in this paradigm is an over-emphasis on space, the medium of vision, and the relative neglect of time, the medium of sound.

Such an orientation, according to Jay, informed Cartesian dualism and the ambitious but futile Enlightenment project of achieving a "view from nowhere" – pure objectivity. Cartesian metaphysics set up what Jay and others have characterized as a "hegemonic scopic regime" that dominated European intellectual life until the nineteenth century. For Descartes, like our Indian Buddhist thinkers, visual perception is a central metaphor for knowledge, although Descartes, construing knowledge quite differently, understood it as the correspondence of an object to a mental image or representation. Ideas, for Descartes, are images in the mind's eye. For Voltaire, as well, an idea is defined as "an image that paints itself in my brain. ... The most abstract ideas are the consequences of all the objects I've perceived. ... I've an idea only because I have images in my head."[5] Modern epistemology, rooted in this specular metaphor of seeing ideas in the mind, is based on the notion of knowing the world as the mental representation of corresponding external objects. Also formative in this stance is the linking of light with reason and the ascertainment of Descartes' famous "clear and distinct ideas." The objections to Cartesian dualism, the correspondence theory of knowledge, his enthronement of reason, and his theory of representations are well-documented and need no more than brief mention here. What is important to our inquiry is that the fount of modern ocularcentrism, although derived in part from Greek ideas that we have already noted, is the Cartesian understanding of mind and world.[6]

Henri Bergson, carrying out perhaps the first explicit attack on vision-based metaphysics, critiqued this kind of epistemology for its neglect of temporality, action, and audition in favor of spatiality, passive viewing, and representation. Bergson was critical of the tendency of visual thinking to abstract images and pictures from the concrete flow of experience. Such atemporal abstractions, he asserted, belie the true character of reality as a continuous temporal flow. Moreover, the scientific attempt to predict on the basis of causal patterns constitutes an unjustified attempt to spatialize time, to chart a map of the future.[7] Clocks and other time-measuring devices that depict time as preceding in standard, homogeneous units represented spatially are removed from the immediate, concrete, and heterogeneous temporality of immediate experience. Bergson's representation of the eye as an instrument that "freezes" things into static abstraction, neglecting temporality in favor of spatiality, would be a continuing theme in later critiques of vision. So too would his critique of the Cartesian understanding of thinking as representation, an activity that Bergson viewed not as access to reality, but removal from it.

Michel Foucault has undertaken some of the most detailed and well-known contemporary analyses of Western visuality, claiming that Western culture has shifted periodically between privileging sight and hearing. One such shift, he argues in *The Order of Things*, was part of the transition from the *episteme* of the Renaissance to that of the "Classical Age" (the seventeenth and eighteenth centuries). In the former epoch, words and things were bound together in an implicit unity. In this "*episteme* of resemblance," nature is understood as a divine text authored by God, full of signs and symbols to be read by humanity. An intrinsic connection, a similitude or resemblance between words and things, then, is a part of the divine ordering of nature.[8]

According to Foucault, in the Classical Age exemplified by Descartes and Francis Bacon, this unity of word and thing was ruptured. With the shift from an *episteme* of resemblance to the classical *episteme* of representation, words came to be understood as representations of things, functioning to classify, describe, and measure objects in the world. The split between subject and object is implicit in the separation of words and things; word and thought were no longer direct revelations of nature's script, but subjective representations mediating an objective world. Construed by Descartes and others as a realm of objects visible to the eye of reason, the world became the visible realm to be described and classified, "leav[ing] sight with an almost exclusive privilege."[9] Increasing reliance on, and faith in, visual evidence was one of the marks of the emerging scientific era. Francis Bacon had asserted: "I admit nothing but on the faith of the eyes."[10] This implied, as well, a dissociation of hearing and seeing, previously entwined in the similitude of words and things, now relegated to separate realms and functions.[11]

Chidester interprets this move from Renaissance to Classical *episteme* as shattering the synesthetic unity of the senses that characterized the Augustinian world, in which seeing and hearing shared a unified symbolic horizon. What was left was

> the pendulum-swing alterations between a visual pole preoccupied with a spatial order in which continuous taxonomies could be established and a verbal pole concerned with arranging discontinuous elements in temporal sequences of origin, transformation, development, evolution, and progress. Seeing and hearing, therefore, became autonomous options for organizing knowledge, no longer two coordinates of a unified perceptual sensibility.[12]

For Foucault, the predominance of one sensory orientation over another was not a merely academic matter; it had vast implications for the constitution of fields of knowledge and the configurations of culture as a whole. Foucault's most vivid illustrations of the domination of vision were the spectacle of the corpse on the operating table laid out for analysis and the panopticon – the first representing the cold "medical gaze" of rationalistic science and experimentation trying to understand life by studying the dead, and the second, the all-surveying eye of domination and social control.[13] Implicit in all of Foucault's treatments of the visual in Western philosophies and institutions is the critique of the contemplative, disinterested gaze that presumes to float, uninvolved, above the world; of the philosopher who, in Husserl's words, "wants to accomplish pure *theoria*" and "becomes the disinterested spectator, overseer of the world."[14] It is just this *overseeing*, a word connoting power relations as well as neutral observation, that Foucault saw as not only arrogant and futile, but also implicated in relationships of power and domination.

Richard Rorty, in his book *Philosophy and the Mirror of Nature*, has made one of the most influential critiques of vision-based epistemology in the Western philosophical traditions.[15] He claims that modern philosophy has been captive to the ocular metaphor of the mind mirroring the world, the reproducing of a copy inside the mind of what is outside. As with the others we have mentioned, Rorty locates much of the modern impetus for this metaphor in the Cartesian notion that knowledge is modeled on visual perception, the mind inspecting the idea as the eye inspects the image on the retina.[16] This picture, he claims, has given a specific shape to the idea of philosophy as the privileged discourse that assesses the accuracy of these representations and assigns to them their relative value. Rorty identifies this picture of the way the mind works with the misguided attempt to ground philosophical discourse, through reason, on irrefutable foundations and to secure an all-encompassing, neutral, and objective view of the world without regard to multiple or situational perspectives.

The critique of ocularcentrism has had implications for the study of various non-Western cultures as well. Edward Said implicates the "synchronic, essentializing vision" of Western scholars in the colonialist project of appropriating and constructing the "Eastern other."[17] Stephen Tyler, Johannes Fabian, and other anthropologists have offered similar critiques of what they conceive as a dominating, imperialistic anthropological gaze, drawing on myths of the "noble savage" that both subjugate and exoticize the "primitive other."[18]

This socio-politically charged gaze of domination and subjugation also enters into some feminist critiques, such as those of Luce Irigaray, who conceives of the predominance of the visual in Western culture to be characteristic of traditionally male sensibilities. A number of feminist critiques assert that women have traditionally been construed as the passive objects of the "male gaze" that, like the anthropological gaze, at once elevates and alienates, exoticizes and degrades. [19]

The issue of ocularcentrism, then, is an important facet of some of the most prominent themes in recent philosophy, anthropology, and cultural studies. It bears on the questions of foundationalism, epistemology, the construction of knowledge and practice, and on questions of colonialism, imperialism, and chauvinism. All of the recent interrogations of the eye we have mentioned are not without their weak points and flaws; some perhaps exaggerate the evils incurred by the eye, reducing vision to its most problematic aspects. Some, however, offer challenges and insights on the limitations of visual thinking and the ways in which metaphors and habits of thought become determinative, as well as hidden, forces in the constitution of knowledge and practice. Further, they do make a convincing case that the modern Enlightenment tradition, as well as other specific historical periods and places in the West, has been dominated by vision and that this has engendered certain limitations, and even dangers, in the pursuit of knowledge.

I mention these critiques, though, not to evaluate them, but to present some issues involving vision currently of interest to scholars in the humanities and social sciences and to raise the question of their possible relevance to those aspects of Buddhist visuality – or, conversely, the relevance of Buddhism to these critiques. Irigaray makes a statement in this regard that cannot fail to attract our attention. She suggests that the one kind of vision that may escape such a power-driven economy of vision as has been dominant in the West is "the Buddha's gaze at the flower," presumably referring to the famous flower sermon, in which the tathāgata wordlessly holds up a fresh bloom to his audience. This gaze, she contends, is "not a predatory gaze, it is not the lapse of the speculative into the flesh, it is at once material and spiritual contemplation" that provides a nurturing relationship to the world, fostering interpersonal interaction.[20] To examine Buddhist visuality in light of these observations from contemporary Europe and North America is to introduce both the possibility, on the one hand, that Buddhist vision, as Irigaray suggests, may hold the hope of ameliorating some of the discontents of Western vision, or on the other hand, that Buddhist traditions may themselves be subject to these contemporary critiques of ocularcentrism.

The juxtaposition of two traditions that are themselves actually a multiplicity of traditions and that are, despite their being distant cousins in the Indo-European family, quite dissimilar and far apart in space and time, offers many challenges and dangers. On one hand, we could fall into a superficial comparativism that ignores social and historical context and makes blanket generalizations about the nature of vision and its roles in philosophy. We could, on the other hand, assume that cultures so disparate cannot be understood in terms of one another at all; here, asking if Western critiques of ocularcentrism might apply to other cultures and philosophies would make no sense, since they are ultimately incommensurable, each cultural and philosophical context working according its own internal logic. Yet this approach risks a lack of self-reflexivity on the part of the scholar. Without examining, for example, whether such critiques may be relevant to Asian epistemologies, we may unreflectively assume that they do – or don't. Thus in the effort to avoid consciously imposing theoretical categories on cultures in which these categories did not arise, we risk making the same impositions unconsciously.

I raise the question, then, if only in a preliminary way, of whether those aspects of Buddhist visuality that we have explored are either subject to or antidotal to the concerns raised by Western thinkers regarding vision. For if the privileging of a particular sense modality does, in fact, engender specific and predictable forms of knowledge and practice, then this might be true across cultures that share such an orientation, like those of ancient India and modern Europe. On the other hand, if they are different, perhaps Buddhist traditions offer a more satisfactory role for vision in the informing of knowledge and practice. Levin, for example, suggests that Buddhist ideas and practices may facilitate an "opening of vision" in Western thought.[21] Any more than a sketch of some possible directions for such questioning would require, perhaps, another book-length project, so the following is more a prefatory indication of some issues for further research.

Ocularcentrism and Buddhist Traditions

Certain similarities are discernable between modern European and ancient Buddhist philosophy with respect to the features of visual thinking that have been mentioned. Mahāyāna discourse exhibits a decided tendency toward spatial rather than temporal terms, and toward the spatialization of temporality. Space (*ākāśa*) is, as we have seen, one of the most frequently used symbols of reality correctly apprehended – vast and endless, without differentiation, all-inclusive, and prone to static representation. The Buddhist concepts and uses of space are, of course, different than Western ones, but they share some of the same functions, especially that of the spatialization of time. In Buddhist literature, the valorization of space admittedly occurs with the orthodox doctrine of impermanence as a background, and indeed this doctrine often seems at cross-purposes with the spatial representations of synchronic presence of past, present, and future found in so much Mahāyāna literature. As I have suggested, however, the spatialization of time in Buddhist literature is a response to the original horror of temporality expressed in early Buddhism, so the two are not necessarily in contradiction; the spatialization of temporality is, rather, a response to impermanence. The display of past, present, and future simultaneously in the visions of the *Gaṇḍavyūha* or in the contained geometry of the maṇḍala represents a domestication of temporality, a temporality in which the present is no longer surrounded by the dual abyss of past and future and in which time's inexorable forward motion is halted in the "non-arising" of all dharmas. Time is symbolically overcome by representing it as contained within the visual field.

Such spatial representation of temporality is also intimately related to the effort to achieve 'all-knowledge,' (*savajñatā*) which is often symbolized in the Perfection of Wisdom texts with the image of the bodhisattva or buddha standing on a high place surveying the whole universe in all ten directions at once. In addition to seeing in the ten spatial directions, an aspect of awakening is often presented as the "seeing" of all of the past and future lives of all beings stretching through the eons and laid out in one synchronous vision. In Sudana's vision of Maitreya's tower in the *Gaṇḍavyūha*, he sees the past lives of buddhas and bodhisattvas all contained within the tower, as if time were another spatial dimension.[22] In the story of the Buddha's awakening, he sees all of his own past and future lives and then those of all sentient beings. Some of these visions of all time and space synchronically are distinctively Buddhist examples of the ideal of all-inclusive knowledge – the view from nowhere, or perhaps better from a Buddhist perspective, from everywhere – as well as the assimilation of temporality to space and its representation as a visible spatial dimension.

These points regarding space and all-knowledge may suggest that contemporary critiques of foundationalism and of the attempt to establish an all-encompassing, neutral, and atemporal view of unmediated reality – an attempt regarded by most recent scholars as futile and arrogant – apply as well to Mahāyāna philosophy. While this is no doubt a possible critique, significant differences exist between the way these two traditions utilized and conceptualized sight with regard to knowledge, some of which may have allowed the Buddhist traditions of South Asia to avoid some of the problems endemic to modern Western ocularcentrism. Perhaps the most salient feature of Western ocularcentrism is its objectification of the world, its construal of things as fixed empirical objects to be observed by a detached, rational mind. Regarding this issue, we see two directions in Buddhist traditions. On the one hand is the inclination toward detachment from emotional entanglement with phenomena and the observation of the world from an elevated distance. This is evident in early sūtras dealing with non-attachment and the cultivation of neutral attitudes toward pleasure and pain, as well as in images like the one of the all-knowing buddha surveying the world from a high terrace or mountain. Of course, different schools had different views on the limits of knowledge, the earlier traditions being more cautious, while some of the Mahāyāna and Vajrayāna movements embraced extravagant claims of universal knowledge.[23]

On the other hand, however, the exponents of emptiness philosophy, while often embracing the concept of "all-knowledge" (*sarvajñatā*), never construed the subject-object relation as a relationship between unextended and extended substances that were forever separated, as did Descartes. The interdependence of things in Buddhist thought, including "subject" and "object," knower and known, precludes a Cartesian picture of independent things interacting externally in favor of internally related conventional entities or processes, each constituted by the others. The Madhyamaka rejection of substance (*dravya*) can be understood as a rejection of anything like what modern thinkers would call essentialism, foundationalism, and substantialism in favor of the mutually dependent interplay of dharmas. While mirror imagery is present in Buddhist texts, phenomena in the world are not considered fixed things to be mirrored by language or mental representations, and truth cannot be conceived as the correspondence between words and objects. Thus, the efforts of Buddhist philosophy to avert the hypostatization of phenomena made phenomena less amenable to being appropriated as the static objects of a reductive gaze. Mahāyāna emptiness discourses offer an interesting counter-example to the assertion of a necessary connection between concepts of knowledge modeled on seeing and the ontological reification and dualistic representation of phenomena, asserted, for instance by Tyler (see chapter 2), for explicit notions of static being are rejected in these discourses even while they maintain a largely visual and spatial understanding of knowledge.

We also see a decided predilection in some forms of Buddhist practice toward fluidity and transformation by way of interaction, interchange, and integration between the seer and the seen. In many meditation practices, the goal is the apprehension that the sense of a separate self and the object of meditation are both constructions of consciousness and that the two are actually interdependent. In Tantric meditation, this basic structure is carried over into deity visualizations in which the identity of the practitioner is exchanged for the identity of the deity in an acknowledgment of their interdependence and a celebration of their both being ultimately empty of inherent existence. This is far from the distancing and objectifying gaze of the disinterested mind in modern rationalism. It seems, then, that the refusal of most Buddhist schools in India to attempt to ground philosophical discourse in supposed ontological foundations may have averted some of the problems inherent in modern Western ocularcentrism.

Some scholars, in fact, have examined the possibilities in Buddhist thought for redressing some of the problems inherent in the Cartesian view of knowledge, mind, and self. For example, in their book, *The Embodied Mind: Cognitive Science and Human Experience*, Francisco Varela, Evan Thompson, and Eleanor Rosch employ Buddhist categories of thinking in an attempt to bridge the gap that has emerged in Western thinking between scientific reflection and human experience.[24] Drawing widely from sources in the cognitive sciences and continental philosophy, as well as Buddhist thought, these scholars see some forms of Buddhist analysis of mind and world as offering productive ways for contemporary thought to critique the representational model of mind without denying consciousness and experience.

Varela *et al.* also point to the work of Maurice Merleau-Ponty as having potential not only for bridging continental philosophy and the cognitive sciences, but also for bridging Buddhist and American-European thinking on the mind and the senses. Merleau-Ponty proposed a view of embodied vision and consciousness in some ways akin to Buddhist notions in its stressing of the fluidity, interactivity, and interdependence between seer and seen, knower and known. Investigating the pre-reflective lived world of experience prior to the radical severing of subject and object that he claimed was entailed in both rationalism and empiricism, Merleau-Ponty emphasized the complementarity and intersubjectivity of the mutual regard, rather than the mutual distancing implied in the gaze of the disembodied mind or in the suspicious, dehumanizing "Look" (*le regard*) of Jean Paul Sartre's ontology. His attempts to analyze the "pre-objective" world were part of an ontology that involved the "intertwining" of self and world in an "anonymous visibility" preceding bifurcation of self and other. In *The Visible and the Invisible*, he points to this pre-personal awareness in the encounter with another:

> There is no problem of the *alter ego* because it is not *I* who sees, not *he* who sees, because an anonymous visibility inhabits both of us, a vision in general, in virtue of that primordial property that belongs to the flesh, being here and now, of radiating everywhere and forever, being an individual, of being also a dimension and a universal. ...
>
> But what is proper to the visible is ... to be the surface of an inexhaustible depth: this is what makes it able to be open to visions other than our own.[25]

The recent resurgence of interest in Merleau-Ponty, a "rehabilitation" as some have called it, offers the potential for a re-assessment of vision and the senses in modern philosophy and science, as well as an interesting conversation partner with Buddhist thought.

The dangers of this kind of comparativism, however, are well-known in religious studies, including a tendency toward premature totalization of non-Western traditions, for example, which reduces the myriad, complex historical manifestations of Buddhist thought to one normative "Buddhism." The relative novelty of employing Buddhist categories, or any categories not native to Western disciplines, invites either the tendency to dismiss them out of hand or to employ them uncritically and with little understanding of their historical context. With the latter approach, "Buddhism" may seem to be the exotic truth that will rescue the West from its ignorance. Both the unexamined dismissal and the uncritical, ahistorical embracing of "Buddhism" retains the Orientalist inclination to either devalue or exoticize the Other, an inclination still at work either subtly or overtly in much scholarship on Asian traditions. To be successful, a mature comparative consideration must, therefore, avoid premature assimilation of Buddhist ideas, maintaining both critical and historical consciousness while remaining open to informed cross-cultural reflection.[26]

While certain philosophical aspects of Buddhism show possibilities for the benign conjunction of the visual and cognitive, the concrete social, political, and gender ramifications of Buddhist visuality are more difficult to discern. Here we cannot simply rely on straightforward assertions in texts, for we know that what happens "on the ground" does not always reflect what is explicit in doctrine. Nor can we precisely determine the historical effects of Buddhist visuality in the abstract, but only through careful historically-based studies, which are indeed difficult given the ambiguity and scarcity of relevant material. Some scholars, however, have made attempts to explore these areas, for instance, Liz Wilson's study of women in Buddhism, *Charming Cadavers: Horrific Figurations of the Feminine in Indian Buddhist Hagiography.*[27] Wilson explores Buddhist narratives in which women are identified with *saṃsāra*, rebirth, and delusionary enticement, i.e., precisely what is to be transcended in Buddhist practice. The female body becomes, in these narratives, pleasing and desirable yet dangerous and ultimately unfulfilling. Wilson explores meditation practices in which the corpses of women become objects of contemplation along the lines of the "meditations on the horrible" in order that meditators see through this delusion of desirability to the blood, puss, and bone within. According to Wilson, in these narratives the female body becomes an object of the "male gaze" – in this case not the erotic, but the de-eroticizing, detached gaze that overcomes transient, sensual desire. This de-eroticizing devaluation of *saṃsāra*, which is represented by the female body, reverses the subjugation of the (often male) meditator by (female) *saṃsāra*, making him master over his desires. Wilson sees this gaze, these representations of women, and women's internalization of these representations as part of female disempowerment. Although a number of recent works on Buddhism concur with the complicity of the visual in this disempowerment, others challenge the necessity of such a "male gaze" in certain Buddhist cultural contexts, offering more positive assessments of the roles of women in Buddhism.[28]

Interestingly, the traditions that offer the more positive visions of female identity, such as some Tantric traditions, often have their roots in heterodox or folk traditions rather than the established institutions. This gives some indication of the importance of the social location of specific forms of visuality in discerning their functions and effects in a given context. Although very little work has been done in the area of the social and political ramifications of the Buddhist emphasis on vision, Bernard Faure's study of space and place in Chinese religions makes an interesting foray into this area.[29] Drawing from Jonathan Z. Smith's distinction between utopian vision, which values the transcendence of particular places and dwelling in "no place," and the locative vision, which stresses being in a particular place,[30] Faure discusses the relations between Ch'an Buddhist conceptions and uses of space in contrast to those of local traditions. He cites a narrative involving the pacification of a local spirit by Buddhist teachings – teachings that imply an unlocalized vision transcending any specific place. This story, he argues, indicates a dichotomy between two distinct understandings of space: one a universal, homogeneous space representing the Dharma, and the other the pluralistic, differentiated *places* of local traditions. In another example, Faure cites a description of meditation from the fifth Patriarch, Hongren, that describes sitting on a high mountain looking into the distance all around and beholding the infinite *dharmakāya*. Faure notes: "The empty inner space discovered (or produced) by Hongren's contemplation is strikingly different from the densely populated realm of the Daoist body, a microcosm of sacred space where myriads of gods dwell and must be localized, fixed by contemplation to ensure longevity."[31] Further, this dichotomy of universal space and local place is not only indicative of differences between elite and popular or local traditions, but also between "spatial/visual and temporal/auditory metaphors."[32] Ch'an discourse attempted to fly high to get a normative view of the whole from above while local traditions tied their religious vision to specific sites.

We should not assume, however, that elite and popular always unambiguously align themselves with vision and hearing respectively. In India, shifts toward the visual – with regard to both the written word and iconic practice – allowed for greater social inclusivity. The advent of the written scripture in Hinduism broadened access to sacred scriptures beyond the monopoly of the Brahmanical priests. (Of course, to be literate at all likely meant membership in an elite group, but not necessarily a particular caste.) Similarly, written scriptures in Buddhism allowed for greater access to teachings, which were no longer in exclusive possession of the few monastics who specialized in recitation and memorization of the sūtras. The rise of practices involving abundant use of visual imagery in *bhakti* devotional movements in Jainism, Hinduism, and Buddhism was even more of a populist development, one that allowed people of all castes and socio-economic classes access to sacred realities through face-to-face encounter in *darśan* and *pūjā* practices. The dominance of the visual in India, therefore, not only created more socially inclusive modes of religious practice, it was essential to the most widespread popular religious practices in India.

These issues and studies indicate some of the possibilities for exploring the specific historical configurations of the visual in Buddhism and Asian traditions, and suggest that such work could open new and fruitful perspectives on enduring issues in these fields. The tensions revealed by the study of vision represent some of the basic fault lines within and between Buddhist traditions – between ontological presence and absence, plurality and unity, impermanence and permanence, synchronic space and discontinuous time, local and universal, and language and vision. If we try to characterize Buddhist traditions along the lines of Western Enlightenment traditions, as did Stcherbatsky and Murti for example, we must overlook the resolute anti-substantialism of the Madhyamaka, the profound awareness of temporality in the Theravāda, and the fluid interplay between subject and object, and devotee and deity in meditation and devotional practice. But if we characterize them as completely anti-metaphysical along the lines of European postmodernism or American neopragmatism, we ignore the Buddhist search for all-knowledge and the sometimes statizing, spatializing gaze of emptiness.[33] Some of these apparent contradictions come down to differences between Buddhist traditions; others are perhaps only contradictions when viewed through the lens of Western history, philosophy, and cultural practices. Yet, they are also indicative of some of the most basic tensions lying deep within the Buddhist traditions, tensions represented most paradigmatically by the paradoxical dialectic.

The issues raised in this chapter are just a few of many that might be fruitful for further investigation into the area of the relations of knowledge and cultural practice to vision and the senses. Again, conclusive research on any of these subjects would require moving from this general survey of such topics in the abstract to specific cases situated in particular times and places (including, in the case of current constructive Buddhist philosophy, contemporary Europe, America, Japan, etc.). Only then would we be prepared to address more decisively such questions of the concrete historical ramifications of the Buddhist and South Asian emphasis on vision, to what extent such effects occur cross-culturally, and what other social, intellectual, and historical factors combine with ocularcentrism to produce particular philosophical, praxiological, and social formations.

Based on the information I have so far collected, however, I would venture that while different cultures may share a privileging of specific sense capacities in their epistemological orientations, how these orientations function in their cultural contexts may vary considerably due to the many other factors within those contexts. Thus, we should use caution in assuming that ocularcentrism, a term being increasingly applied to Asian cultures, is one single thing carrying the same implications for these cultures as it does for the modern West. In the end, in seems that Buddhist visuality, like that of the Western world, holds the potential for delusion and dominance, but also hope for liberation from delusive intellectual formations and oppressive cognitive and social structures.

Notes

Introduction

1 For a discussion of the various "eyes," see Alex Wayman's "The Buddhist Theory of Vision" in *Buddhist Insight: Essays by Alex Wayman*, edited by George Elder (Delhi: Motilal Banarsidas, 1984), pp. 153–61.

2 For example, see Edward Conze, trans., *The Perfection of Wisdom in Eight Thousand Lines and its Verse Summary* (San Francisco: Four Seasons Foundation, 1973), p. 135.

3 George Lakoff and Mark Johnson, *Metaphors We Live By* (Chicago: University of Chicago Press, 1980).

4 Louis de La Vallée Poussin, ed., *Mūlamadhyamakakārikās de Nāgārjuna avec la Commentaire di Candrakīrti* (Osnabrück: Biblio Verlag, 1970), p. 364.

5 Though scholars are beginning to notice the importance of vision in Buddhism, little has been written on the subject. The only book-length work to date is Malcom David Eckel's fine study of the imprtance of sight in Bhāvaviveka, *To See the Buddha: A Philosopher's Quest for the Meaning of Emptiness* (Princeton: Princeton University Press, 1992). Jacob N. Kinnard's recent *Imaging Wisdom: Seeing and Knowing in the Art of Indian Buddhism* (Surrey: Curzon Press, 1999) addresses the subject in relation to Buddhist art. See also Alex Wayman's "The Buddhist Theory of Vision." Kevin Trainor and Gregory Schopen both suggest the importance of vision to devotional forms of Indian Buddhism. See Trainor's *Relics, Ritual, and Representation in Buddhism: Rematerializing The Sri Lankan Theravāda Tradition* (Cambridge: Cambridge University Press, 1997), and Schopen's, *Bones, Stones, and Buddhist Monks: Collected Papers on Archeology, Epigraphy, and Texts in Monastic Buddhism in India* (Honolulu: University of Hawai'i Press, 1997), pp. 116–17, n. 137. For treatment of vision in Hinduism or in the wider Indian context, see Lawrence A. Babb, "Glancing: Visual Interaction in Hinduism," *Journal of Anthropological Research* 37 (1981), Diana Eck, *Darśan: Seeing the Divine Image in India.* (Chambersburg, Pa.: Anima Books, 1981), Stephen Tyler, "The Vision Quest or What the Mind's Eye Sees," *Journal of Anthropological Research*, 40, 1 (Spring, 1984), pp. 23–39, and Jan Gonda, *Eye and Gaze in the Veda* (Amsterdam-London: North Holland Publishing Company, 1969).

6 Ironically, "enlightenment," the commonly used term for the seminal event in which Gautama became the Buddha, is not a visual metaphor in Sanskrit. The term "*bodhi*" literally means "to awaken," a metaphor that certainly carries relevance to the subject at hand, but not in the way that the rendering of this term as "enlightenment" suggests. *Bodhi* as enlightenment, in fact, has more to do with nineteenth century translators and commentators attempting to draw implicit connections between Buddhism and European Enlightenment philosophy than with the Buddhist sense of the term.

7 "Hīnayāna," or lesser vehicle, is a polemical term used by some Mahāyāna texts to characterize non-Mahāyāna Buddhist groups. When referring to non-Mahāyāna Buddhism, I will use the term Orthodox Buddhism – an admittedly imperfect term among other imperfect options – unless it is referred to specifically in the context of Mahāyāna polemics.

8 See Thorlieff Boman, *Hebrew Thought Compared with Greek* (Philadelphia: Westminster Press, 1954) and Susan A. Handelman, *The Slayers of Moses: The Emergence of Rabbinic Interpretation in Modern Literary Theory* (Albany: State University of New York Press, N. Y. 1987).

9 Tyler, "The Vision Quest or What the Mind's Eye Sees."

10 For a detailed discussion of Western philosophical and cultural attitudes toward vision, see Martin Jay, *Downcast Eyes: The Denigration of Vision in Twentieth-Century French Thought* (Berkeley: University of California Press, 1994) and David Michael Levin, ed., *Sites of Vision: The Discursive Construction of Sight in the History of Philosophy* (Cambridge: MIT Press, 1997).

11 See, for example, Margaret R. Miles, "Image," in Mark C. Taylor, ed., *Critical Terms for Religious Studies* (Chicago: University of Chicago Press, 1998), pp. 160–72.

12 Whether the versions of these texts we now possess truly represent the earliest developments of Mahāyāna is open to question because of the many interpolations in them. Most Buddhist sūtras evolved and changed over time, and the Perfection of Wisdom texts represent this process in an extreme form. Not only were many different Perfection of Wisdom texts produced, from short and succinct summaries of the basic doctrines to extremely long and repetitious tomes, each of these individual texts apparently had a number of different versions as a result of their being added to and embellished over time. For details of the development and different versions of the Perfection of Wisdom literature, see Edward Conze, *The Prajñāpāramitā Literature* (London: Mouton & Co., 1960). For a discussion of the historical significance of the *Aṣṭasāhasrikā*, see Andrew Rawlinson, "The Position of the *Aṣṭasāhasrikā Prajñāpāramitā* in the Development of Early Mahāyāna" in Lewis Lancaster, ed., *Prejñāpāramitā and Related Systems: Studies in Honor of Edward Conze* (Berkeley: University of California Press, 1977), pp. 3–34. Conze argues that the first two chapters of the *Ratnaguṇasaṃcayagāthā* and the chapters 3–28 in the *Aṣṭa* contain the earliest Perfection of Wisdom text, perhaps dating from around 100 B.C.E. See Edward Conze, "The Development of Prajñāpāramitā Thought," in *Thirty Years of Buddhist Studies* (Oxford: Bruno Cassirer, 1967), pp. 123–147. The dating of ancient Sanskrit texts is often difficult, but here we will be dealing with documents and parts of documents that can reasonably be assumed to represent the first few centuries of Mahāyāna thought and practice, beginning between the first century B.C.E. and the first century C.E.

Chapter 1

1 *Aṣṭasāhasrikā Prajñāpāramitā*, ed., P. L. Vaidya (Darbhanga: Mithila Institute, 1960), p. 153 [R 348]. Hereafter cited as *Aṣṭa*. Bracketed numbers refer to page numbers in an earlier edition edited by Rejendralal Mitra (Calcutta: Bibliotheca Indica, 1888) and to which Edward Conze's marginal page numbers correspond in his translation, *Perfection of Wisdom in Eight Thousand Lines*.

2 Donald S. Lopez, Jr., "Interpretation of Mahāyāna Sūtras," in *Buddhist Hermeneutics*, ed. Donald S. Lopez, Jr. (Honolulu: University of Hawaii Press, 1988), pp. 48–49.

3 *Samyutta-Nikāya of the Sutta-Pitaka*, ed. Leon Feer (London: Published for the Pali Text Society by Luzac, 1960–70), p. 39.

4 *Rgs* 1.27, p. 15; 12.10, p. 52.

5 *Advayasiddhi*, ed. Malati J. Shendge (Baroda: Oriental Institute, 1964), pp. 23. Translation by John S. Strong in *The Experience of Buddhism: Sources and Interpretations* (Belmont, CA: Wadsworth, 1995), p. 200.

6 "Early Buddhist," here, is a convenient (and imperfect, as we shall see later) term for Buddhism as presented in the Pāli cannon.

7 To speak of "language" *per se* in this context can, of course, be misleading, since Indic languages have no term that precisely corresponds with the English word. Nevertheless, I will refer to the cluster of concepts in Sanskrit denoting speaking, naming, and cognitive-linguistic activity by the term "language."

8 See *Bṛhadāraṇyaka* I. 4, 7 and III. 2, 12, in Dominic Goodall, ed. *Hindu Scriptures* (Berkeley: University of California Press, 1996), pp. 43–107.

9 The terms "concept," "conceptual thinking," "discursive thought," etc., will be clarified further when we deal with Mahāyāna refinements of these notions. At this point, suffice to say that concepts and discursive thinking are generally translations of "*papañca*" and "*paññatti*" as uderstood in the pre-Mahāyāna literature. For detailed treatment of these terms and others relating to language and concepts in early Buddhism, see A. K. Warder, "The Concept of a Concept," *Journal of Indian Philosophy* 1:2, 1970, pp. 181–196, and Bhikkhu Ñānanda, *Concept and Reality in Early Buddhist Thought* (Ceylon: Buddhist Publication Society, 1971), p. 4.

10 Henry Clarke Warren, *Buddhism in Translations* (Cambridge: Harvard University Press, 1896; reprint, New York: Athuneum, 1984), p. 132.

11 *The Sutta Nipāta*, trans. Dines Anderson and Helmer Smith (London: Pali Text Society, 1913) pp. 156–58.

12 Bhikkhu Ñāṇamoli and Bhikkhu Bodhi trans., *The Middle Length Discourses of the Buddha: a New Translation of the Majjhima Nikāya* (Boston: Wisdom Publications, 1995), pp. 533–36.

13 *Brahmajāla Sutta* 3:32–72. See translation in Maurice Walshe, *Thus Have I Heard: The Long Discourses of the Buddha* (London: Wisdom Publications, 1987), pp. 87–90.

14 See, for instance, Gadjin M. Nagao, *Mādhymamika and Yogacāra: A Study of Mahāyāna Philosophies*, trans., Leslie Kawamura (Albany: State University of New York Press, 1991), p. 41.

15 T. R. V. Murti, *The Central Philosophy of Buddhism* (London: George Allen and Unwin, 1974), pp. 36ff.

16 Jayatilleke, pp. 325–28.
17 *Majjhima Nikāyai* I.487. For translation, see *The Middle Length Discourses*, p. 593.
18 One *can* argue, for instance, on empirical grounds that things are interdependent, but to argue that *everything* is interdependent and has no first cause is just as much a metaphysical statement as arguing for the existence of a first cause based on the intricate functioning of the cosmos, i.e., the argument from design. For an argument that most Buddhist philosophy rejects metaphysics completely and is akin to Empiricism, see David Kalupahana, *A History of Buddhist Philosophy: Continuities and Discontinuities* (Honolulu: University of Hawaii Press, 1992).
19 For a list of epithets of nirvāṇa in the Pāli literature, see Edward Conze, *Buddhist Thought in India* (George Allen & Unwin Ltd., 1962; reprint, Ann Arbor: University of Michigan Press, 1967), p. 73.
20 For more thorough treatments of the Abhidharma and dharma theory, see Th. Stcherbatsky, *The Central Conception of Buddhism and the Meaning of the Word "Dharma"* (Delhi: Motilal Banarsidas, 1970, first printed in 1922; and Herbert V. Guenther, *Philosophy and Psychology in the Abhidharma* (Berkeley: Shambala Press, 1976).
21 *Prajñā-pāramitā-ratna-guṇa-saṃcaya-gāthā*, Akira Yuyama, ed. (Cambridge: Cambridge University Press, 1976).
22 In fact, the idea that dharmas lack inherent existence is not exclusive to the Mahāyāna, but can be found in pre-Mahāyāna texts, especially those of the Mahāsanghikas.
23 *Aṣṭa*, p. 89 [R 177].
24 Ibid., p. 14 [R 29].
25 Ibid., p. 8 [R 15].
26 Ibid., p. 103 [R 207].
27 Ibid., pp. 268–69 [R 278–80].
28 Ibid., p. 23 [R 46].
29 Ibid., p. 148 [R 298].
30 Ibid., p. 158–9 [R 319].
31 *Rgs* 2.3, p. 16–17.
32 Ibid.,10.14, p. 47.
33 *Aṣṭa*, p. 9 [R 18].
34 Ibid., p. 138 [R 278–9].
35 Ibid., p. 13 [R 25–6].
36 Ibid., p. 72 [R 142].
37 Ibid., p. 7 [R 12–13].
38 Ibid., p. 20 [R 19–20].
39 *Suvikrāntavikrāmīparipṛcchā Prajñāpāramitā Sūtra* ed., Ryusho Hikata (Fukuoka: Kyushu University, 1958), p. 4. (Hereafter cited as *Suvikrānta*.)
40 *Aṣṭa*, p. 10 [R 20].
41 Ibid., p. 102 [R 206].
42 Ibid., p. 96 [R 193].
43 Ibid., p. 239 [R 483].
44 *Suvikrānta*, p. 9–10.
45 Ibid.
46 Edward Conze, ed. *Vajracchedikā Prajñāpāramitā* (Rome: Serie Orientale Roma XIII, 1957), p. 38 [5a].

47 This parallels and anticipates Nāgārjuna's *Mūlamadhyamakakākrika*, which negates a litany of philosophical concepts, both Buddhist and non-Buddhist, as understood in terms of inherent existence, but then re-introduces Buddhist teachings in a conventional sense. For further treatment of Nāgārjuna's approach to this issue, see Jay Garfield, *The Fundamental Wisdom of the Middle Way: Nāgārjuna's Mūlamadhyamakakārikā* (New York: Oxford University Press, 1995).

48 See, for example, *Aṣṭa*, p. 8 [R 15].

49 *Suvikrānta*, p. 115.

50 Jay Garfield makes a similar point about Nāgārjuna's dialectical language: "The language must hence be understood, from the ultimate perspective, not as making assertions but rather as ostending – indicating that which cannot be literally asserted without falling into nonsense – as Wittgenstein puts it in the *Tractatus*, showing that which cannot be said." Garfield, p. 213.

51 Eckel, *To See the Buddha* pp. 29–44.

52 Nagao, *Mādhyamika and Yogācāra*. See especially "The Silence of the Buddha and its Madhyamic Interpretation," pp. 35–50, and "What Remains in *Śūnyatā*: a Yogācāra Interpretation of Emptiness," pp. 51–60.

53 Nāgārjuna, *Mūlamadhyamakakārikā*, ch. 24.

54 Quoted in D. T. Suzuki, "A Sense of Zen," *Zen Buddhism: Selected Writings of D. T. Suzuki*, William Barret, ed. (Garden City, N.Y.: Anchor Books, 1956), p. 14.

55 Paul M. Williams, "Some Aspects of Language and Construction in the Madhyamaka," *Journal of Indian Philosophy* 8 (1980), pp. 15–16.

56 *Ch'eng-wei-shih-lun*, 11c, cited in Ibid., p. 15.

57 Williams, "Some Aspects of Language and Construction," p. 15.

58 For example, see *Aṣṭa*, pp. 6, 96 [12, 190].

59 Monier Monier-Williams, *A Sanskrit-English Dictionary* (New Delhi: Marawah Publications, reprint, 1987), p. 674; Franklin Edgerton, *Buddhist Hybrid Sanskrit Grammar and Dictionary*, vol. II., (Motilal Banarsidass, 1993), p. 374.

60 Williams, "Some Aspects of Language and Construction," p. 27.

61 Ibid.

62 Edgerton, *Buddhist Hybrid Sanskrit*, vol. II, p. 380–81.

63 Williams, "Some Aspects of Language and Construction," p. 33.

64 Ibid., p. 32.

65 Ibid., p. 33.

66 Ibid.

67 Bhāvaviveka, *Chang-chen-lun*, Taishō No. 1578, p. 278a; translation, p. 137. Cited in Ibid., p. 31.

68 Jitendra Nath Mohanty, *Reason and Tradition in Indian Thought: An Essay on the Nature of Indian Philosophical Thinking* (Oxford: Clarendon Press, 1992), p. 238.

69 Warder, *Indian Buddhism*, p. 442, citing the *Śrutamayībhūmi*, p. 356 of T 1579, Sanskrit MS in Patna.

70 Vasubhandu's *Vādavidhi*, in Stefan Anacker's *Seven Works of Vasubhandu: the Buddhist Psychological Doctor* (Delhi: Motilal Banarsidas, 1986), p. 40.

71 Dignāga's concise presentation of his theory of perception is found in Masaki Hattori, ed., *Dignāga, On Perception, Being the Pratyakṣapariccheda of Dignāga's Pramāṇasamuccaya* (Cambridge: Harvard University Press, 1968), pp. 24–31.

72 Bimal Krishna Matilal, *Epistemology, Logic, and Grammar in Indian Philosophical Analysis* (Paris: Mouton, 1971), pp. 34–35.
73 Warder, p. 456
74 Surendradnath Dasgupta, *History of Indian Philosophy*, vol. 1 (Delhi: Motilal Banarsidass, 1922), p. 154–55.
75 Warder, p. 457. The *Abhidharma* text referred to is the Sarvāstivāda *Vijñānakāya.*
76 Nāgārjuna, *Vigrahavyayartani*, 30–32. Translated in Frederick Streng, *Emptiness: A Study in Religious Meaning* (Nashville: Abingdon Press, 1967).
77 Eckel, p. 150–51.
78 Critiques of the *rhetoric* of immediacy have also been leveled at this aspect of Buddhism in the Ch'an/Zen schools. See Bernard Faure, *The Rhetoric of Immediacy: A Cultural Critique of Chan/Zen Buddhism* (Princeton: Princeton University Press, 1991).
79 *Bṛhadāraṇyaka Upaniṣad*, 1.4.17. For translation, see *Hindu Scriptures*, p. 52.
80 See *Bṛhadāraṇyaka* 5.14.4 and *Maitri Upaniṣad* 6.10. Cited and discussed in Jayatilleke, p. 59.
81 *Kaṭha Upaniṣad*, 2.3.12, 2.3.9, cited in Jayatilleke, p. 61.
82 Ibid., 1.2.23.
83 Ibid., 1.3.12.
84 *Muṇḍaka Upaniṣad*, 3.1.8.
85 Jayatilleke, p. 61–62.
86 For one of many examples, see a text attributed to Śankara, *Dṛg-dṛśya-viveka*, translated by Swami Nikhilananda in *Dṛg-dṛśya-vivek: An Inquiry into the Nature of the 'Seer' and the 'Seen'* (Mysore: Sri Ramakrishna Ashrama, 1970).

Chapter 2

1 Maurice Merleau-Ponty, *The Primacy of Perception*, trans. Colin Smith (Evanston, Ill: Northwestern University Press, 1964), p. 3.
2 Sigmund Freud, *Civilization and Its Discontents*, trans. James Strachey (New York, 1961), p. 46–47, cited in Jay, *Downcast Eyes*, p. 6.
3 See Beate Allert, ed. *Languages of Visuality: Crossings between Science, Art, Politics, and Literature* (Detroit: Wayne State University Press, 1996) and Hal Foster, ed., *Vision and Visuality* (Seattle: Bay Press, 1988).
4 Eve Sweetser, *From Etymology to Pragmatics: Metaphorical and Cultural Aspects of Semantic Culture* (Cambridge: Cambridge University Press, 1990), p. 32–34. Also see Tyler, "Vision Quest," p. 29.
5 Sweetser, p. 38–39.
6 Ibid., p. 39.
7 Hans Jonas, *The Phenomenon of Life: Toward a Philosophical Biology* (New York: Harper & Row, 1966) p. 147.
8 David Michael Levin, *The Opening of Vision: Nihilism and the Postmodern Situation* (New York: Routledge, 1988), p. 99.
9 Jay, *Downcast Eyes, p.* 24.
10 Ibid., p. 23.
11 Ibid., p. 28.
12 Tyler, p. 23.

13 Ibid., p. 34–35.
14 Sweetser, p. 28–32.
15 Tyler, p. 34–35.
16 Ibid., p. 35.
17 Ibid., p. 35–36.
18 Thorlieff Boman, *Hebrew Thought Compared with Greek* (Philadelphia, 1954) and Susan A. Handelman, *The Slayers of Moses: The Emergence of Rabbinic Interpretation in Modern Literary Theory* (Albany, N. Y. 1987).
19 See, for instance, Jaques Ellul, *The Humiliation of the Word*, trans. Joyce Main Hanks (Grand Rapids, Mich., 1985).
20 José Faur, *Golden Doves with Silver Dots: Semiotics and Textuality in Rabbinic Tradition* (Bloomington: Indian University Press, 1986), p. 29–30; quoted in Elliot R. Wolfson, *Through a Speculum That Shines: Vision and Imagination in Medieval Jewish Mysticism* (Princeton: Princeton University Press, 1994), p. 13. Though he shows that vision and visualization were actually important parts of Medieval Jewish Mysticism, Wolfson is still compelled to acknowledge the "epistemic privileging of hearing over seeing" in Judaism, which he says was characterized by a lack of images and a decided preference for language over vision as the appropriate way to characterize God. Wolfson, p. 14.
21 We should not, incidentally, be led to thinking simplistically that because a culture tends to be ocularcentric we will not find examples of other senses also occupying a prominent place. Visions of light are not uncommon in Hebrew scriptures and visual metaphors crop up in Dravidian languages. The claim is not that these will not exist in a non-ocularcentric culture, nor that hearing, touching, tasting, or smelling will be of no importance. Rather, certain cultures tend to give vision a privileged place in their understanding of knowledge and thinking, and this has significant epistemic, as well as cultural, ramifications including influences on paradigms of knowledge, social practices, literary images, and religious worship.
22 Tyler, p. 36.
23 Ernest H. Gombrich, quoted in Zdravko Radman, *Metaphors: Figures of the Mind* (Dordrecht, The Netherlands: Kluwer Academic Publishers, 1997), p. 151.
24 Andrew Ortony, "Metaphor, Language, and Thought," in *Metaphor and Thought*, ed., Andrew Ortony, 2nd edition (Cambridge: Cambridge University Press, 1993), p. 1.
25 George Lakoff and Mark Johnson, *Metaphors We Live By* (Chicago: University of Chicago Press, 1980), p. 1.
26 Lakoff, "Contemporary Theory of Metaphor," in *Metaphor and Thought*, p. 224.
27 Lakoff and Johnson, p. 7–13.
28 Lakoff, "Contemporary Theory," p. 203.
29 Lakoff and Johnson, p. 4.
30 Lakoff notes that these basic metaphors, such as ARGUMENT IS WAR and others, such as LOVE IS A JOURNEY (distinguished by capital letters) should be understood as mnemonic devices that refer to an entire set of correspondences reflected in the terminology of a particluar concept, i.e., a mapping. In our example, the name of the mapping is ARGUMENT IS WAR, which implies the whole set of conceptual correspondences suggested, for example, arguing is attacking and defending, using strategies, shooting, etc., each of which are metaphoric expressions. Thus,

although there are a number of different metaphoric expressions relating argument to war, there is one metaphor – one unified way of conceptualizing argument – that is realized in a number of linguistic expressions. See Lakoff, "Contemporary Theories," p. 206–9.

31 Lakoff and Johnson, p. 4–5.
32 Richard Boyd, "Metaphor and Theory Change," in *Metaphor and Thought*, p. 486.
33 Ibid.
34 Lakoff, "Contemporary Theories," p. 241–43.
35 *Suttanipāta*, 229, 478. See also Jayatilleke, p. 418 ff.
36 *Rgs* 280–81.
37 Ibid. 172.
38 Ibid. 173
39 Ibid. 304–5.
40 *Aṣṭa*, p. 115 [R 136].
41 Ibid., p. 232 [R 271].
42 *Samādhirāja Sūtra*, in *Studies in the Literature of the Great Vehicle*, p. 55.
43 Ibid., p. 58–59.
44 Candrakīrti *Prasannapadā* 360, in Mervyn Sprung trans., *Lucid Exposition of the Middle Way* (Boulder: Prajña Press, 1972), p. 177.
45 Bhavaviveka *Madhyamakahṛdayakarikā* III, 254, quoted in Eckel, *To See the Buddha*, p.38.
46 Ibid., III, 253–54.
47 *Anguttara Nikāya* IX, 40.
48 Bhāvaviveka, *Madhyamakahṛdayakarikā* 242, 244–45, III. In Eckel, p. 38.
49 Kamalaśīla, "First Bhāvanākrama," in Giuseppe Tucci, ed., *Minor Buddhist Texts*, vol. 2 (Delhi: Motilal Banarsidass, 1986), p. 521–22 (author's translation).
50 For example, in *Samādhirāja Sūtra*, P. L. Vaidya, ed., Buddhist Sanskrit Texts, No. 2 (Dharbhanga: Mithila Institute, 1961), p. 4.
51 Ibid. Also *anupraveśaka* in the *Lankāvatāra Sūtra*, 43.10, "entering into the thought of truth" (citation in Edgerton, *Buddhist Hybrid Sanskrit*, p. 31).
52 *Aṣṭa*, p. 94 [R 187].
53 Ibid., p 146 [R 293].
54 Ibid. p. 196 [R 396].
55 Ibid., p 200 [R 403–4].
56 Ibid., p. 222 [R 449].
57 *Aṅguttara Nikāya* I. 8–10; *Aṣṭa* p. 3 [R 5]; *Suvikrānta* 77a.
58 *Samādhirāja*, *Studies in the Great Vehicle*, p. 53.
59 For example, *Suvikrānta*, p. 9–10. See translation in Edward Conze, *Perfect Wisdom: The Short Prajñāpāramitā Texts* (Devon, England: Buddhist Publishing Group, 1993), p. 6–8.
60 For a Mahāyāna take on intellectual "cutting," see *Suvikrānta*, p. 98–99 (Conze trans. in *Perfect Wisdom*, p. 60–61).
61 Eckel, p. 24, 200n.
62 *Suvikranta*, p. 9–10 (Conze, *Perfect Wisdom*, pp. 6–7).
63 Tucci, *Minor Buddhist Texts*, p. 482.
64 Monier Monier-Williams, *A Sanskrit-English Dictionary*, (New Delhi: Marwah Publications, 1986), p. 906.

65 David Chidester, *Word and Light: Seeing, Hearing, and Religious Discourse* (Urbana and Chicago: University of Illinois Press, 1992), p. 9.
66 Hans Jonas, *The Phenomenon of Life: Toward a Philosophical Biology* (New York: Harper & Row, 1966), p. 144.
67 Ibid., p. 144–45.
68 Chidester, p. 11.
69 Jonas, p. 150.
70 Ibid., p. 151.
71 Conze, *Buddhist Thought in India*, p. 164. See also Vasubhandu, *Abhidharmakośabhāṣyam*, trans. Louis de La Vallée Poussin, Eng trans. Leo M. Pruden (Berkeley: Asian Humanities Press, 1990), Ch. IV, 28.
72 *Abhidharmakośa*, ch I, 5.
73 Buddhagoṣa, *Path of Purification (Visuddhamagga)*, trans., Bhikkhu Ñyāṇamoli (Colombo: A. Semage, 1964), ch. X.
74 Conze, *Buddhist Thought in India*, p. 165.
75 Ibid., p. 164–65.
76 *Rgs*, II., 9–10.
77 Ibid., VIII., 1.
78 Ibid., XVI, 1.
79 *Aṣṭa*, p. 12 [R 24].
80 Ibid., p. 136 [R 273].
81 Ibid., p. 139–140 [R 279–280].
82 Ibid., p. 149–149 [R 297–298].
83 Ibid., p. 230 [R 465].
84 Ibid., p. 150 [R 303].
85 Ibid., p. 218 [R 441].
86 *The Vimalakirti Nirdeśa Sūtra*, trans. Charles Luk (Boston: Shambala, 1990), p. 49–51.

Chapter 3

1 *Salāyatana-vibhaṅga suttam*, in *Majjhima-Nikāya*, ed. Robert Charles (London: Luzac, for the Pali Text Society, 1960), p. 215–22.
2 *Gaṇḍavyūha Sūtra*, ed. P. L. Vaidya, Buddhist Sanskrit Texts, No. 5 (Darbhanga: Mithila Institute, 1960), p. 1. Hereafter cited in notes as *Gv.*
3 Ibid., p. 4–5.
4 See, for instance, Gregory Schopen, "Mahāyāna in Indian Inscriptions," *Indo-Iranian Journal* 21, 1979, 1–19 and Williams, *Mahāyāna Buddhism*, p. 22–25,
5 Translated by Henry. C. Warren in *Buddhism in Translation* (New York: Atheneum, 1984), p. 107.
6 Steven Collins, "Notes on Some Oral Aspects of Pāli Literature," *Indo-Iranian Journal* 35 (1992), p. 121–35.
7 For Example, Collins (Ibid., p. 124) notes the following: *vāceti*, "to make (the pupil) recite;' *uddisati*, "teaches, recites;' *suṇāti*, "listens;' *uggaṇhati*, "grasps in memory;' *adhīyati* and *pariyāpuṇāti*, "learns (by reciting);' *sajjhāyati*, "recites;' and *dhāreti*, "retains (what he has learnt in memory)."
8 Ibid., p. 129.
9 Ibid., p. 128.

10 Ibid., p. 121.
11 Buddha-L, Buddha-l@ulkyvm.louisville.edu, 2–7–96.
12 Richard Gombrich, "How the Mahāyāna Began," in *The Buddhist Forum*, vol. 1, ed.,Tadeusz Skorupski (London: School of Oriental and African Studies. 1990), p. 28.
13 Donald Lopez, "Authority and Orality in the Mahāyāna," *Numen*, Vol. 42, (1995), p. 39.
14 Gombrich, p. 21–30.
15 For a discussion of rules for determining textual authenticity, see Étienne Lamotte, "The Assessment of Textual Interpretation in Buddhism," trans., Sara Boin-Webb, in Donald Lopez, ed., *Buddhist Hermeneutics*, p. 11–28.
16 *Saddharmapuṇḍarīkasūtra*, ed. P. L. Vaidya, Budhist Sanskrit Texts, No. 6 (Darbhanga: Mithila Institute, 1960), p. 265–67.
17 See Ibid., chapters 17,18 and 19 for discussions of merit.
18 Parallel developments exist in Hindu texts of the same period, especially in the Purāṇas and the Mahābhārata. See C. Mackenzie Brown, "Purāṇa as Scripture: From Sound to Image of the Holy Word in the Hindu Tradition," *History of Religions*, 26, 1 (1986), p. 68–86.
19 Kajiyana Yūichi, "Prajñāpāramitā and the Rise of Mahāyāna," in, *Buddhist Spirituality*, ed.,Takeuchi Yoshinori (New York: Crossroad, 1993), p. 143–44.
20 Hirakawa, *History of Indian Buddhism*, p. 270–74.
21 While Hirakawa associates the birth of the Mahāyāna directly with the laity and the stūpa cults, which he claims were almost exclusively the domain of the laity, the laity did not themselves bring about Mahāyāna Buddhism. Rather, the Mahāyāna, or at least its literature, was the product of monks within the established traditions whose understanding of the Dharma was more inclusive of the laity and their practices and perspectives. See Paul Williams, *Mahāyāna Buddhism: the Doctrinal Foundations* (London and New York: Routledge, 1989), p. 20–23.
22 Hirakawa, *History of Indian Buddhism*, p. 274.
23 The term is used in this sense as the state of enlightenment or that which leads to such a state, as well as the text itself.
24 *Aṣṭa*, p. 48 [R 94–95].
25 Ibid., p. 49 [R 96]. The reference to *dharmakāya* is likely a later interpolation; nevertheless, it shows one way in which the cult of the *Prajñāpāramitā* attempted to supercede devotion to relics by playing the terms *śārira* and *kāya* off of each other.
26 Gregory Schopen, "The Phrase '*sa pṛthivīpradeśaā caityabhūto bhavet*' in the *Vajracchedikā*: Notes on the Cult of the Book in the Mahāyāna," *Indo-Iranian Journal* 17 (1975), p. 147–81.
27 Ibid., p. 179.
28 Ibid., p. 178–79.
29 Ibid.
30 *Aṣṭa*, p. 46–7 [R 92–93].
31 Merleau-Ponty, *Phenomenology of Perception*, p. 193.
32 Walter J. Ong, *Orality and Literacy: The Technologizing of the Word* (New York: Methuen, 1982), p. 34. While some of Ong's other generalizations about oral cultures seem disproved by the case of early Buddhism, such as the requirement they they are "agonistically toned," (p. 43) and would never contain

"a vehicle so neutral as a list" (p. 42), the observation regarding mnemetic patterns certainly applies to the Pāli sūtras. For other reservations about Ong with regard to ancient India, see Brown, "Purāṇa as Scripture," p. 82–6.

33 Ong, p. 78.

34 Ibid., p. 85. See also, on the shift from ear to eye, Marshall MacLuhan, *The Gutenberg Galaxy* (Toronto: University of Toronto Press, 1962).

35 Ibid., p. 15.

36 Ibid., p. 78.

37 For examples, see Jack Goody ed., *Literacy in Traditional Societies* (Cambridge: Cambridge University Press, 1968).

38 The other three criteria were that it be the words of a formally constituted Saṅgha, of a small group of elders, or a single learned monk. It should also be in harmony with the other sūtras and the Vinaya.

39 Tāranātha, *Taranatha's Geschichte des Buddhismus in Indien*, trans., Anton Schiefner (Tokyo: Suzuki Gakujutsu Zaidan, 1965), p. 61 ff., cited in A. K. Warder, *Indian Buddhism*, p. 6.

40 Lopez, "Authority and Orality," p. 39.

41 *Saddharmapuṇḍarīkasūtra*, p. 44–50.

42 *Gv*, p. 14

43 Ibid., p. 15.

44 The notion of the Buddha as a transcendent, god-like being, however, is not unknown in pre-Mahāyāna Buddhism. The Mahāsaṃghikas taught the notion of a supermundane Buddha, for instance, in the *Mahāvastu*. See Williams, *Mahāyāna Buddhism*, p. 18.

45 *Saddharmapuṇḍarīkasūtra*, p. 16

46 Paul Williams, *Mahāyāna Buddhism*, p. 30. Translation by P. M. Harrison in "Buddhānusmṛti in the Pratyutpanna-buddha-saṃmukhāvasthita-samādhi-sūtra," *Journal of Indian Philosophy* vol 9 (1978), p. 43.

47 *The Large Sūtra on Perfection Wisdom* (*Pañcaviṃśatisāhasrikā*), trans., Edward Conze (Berkeley: University of California Press, 1975), p. 38–39.

48 Jonathan Z. Smith has commented on similar phenomena in terms of a distinction between 'locative' and 'utopian" understandings of the world in *Map Is Not Territory* (Leiden: E. J. Brill, 1978). For a discussion of this issue in the context of Chinese Buddhism, see Bernard Faure, 'Space and Place in Chinese Religious Traditions,' *History of Religions*, vol. 26, May 1987.

49 See, for instance, *Aṣṭa*, p. 235 [R 476].

Chapter 4

1 Merleau-Ponty, *Phenomenology of Perception*, p. 68–69.

2 *Gv*, p. 379 [C 340]. Bracketed citations are cross-references to page numbers in Thomas Cleary's translation of the *Gv* from the Chinese entitled *Entry into the Realm of Reality: the Text* (Boston & Shaftesbury: Shambhala, 1989). The reader is cautioned, however, that Cleary's translation from the Chinese does not always correspond to the Sanskrit text I have used. All translations are mine from the Sanskrit.

3 See, however, D. T. Suzuki's discussion of the text in *On Indian Mahāyāna Buddhism* (New York, Harper & Row, 1968).

4 Williams, *Mahāyāna Buddhism*, p. 120.
5 Hajime Nakamura, *Indian Buddhism: A Survey with Bibliographical Notes* (Japan: Kufs Publication, 1980), p. 194–97. Also see Luis O. Gómez, *Selected Verses from the Gaṇḍavyūha: Text, Critical Apparatus and Translation*, unpublished doctoral dissertation, Yale, 1967, p. lxviii-lxxv.
6 Williams, *Mahāyāna Buddhism*, p. 121; Eckel, *To See the Buddha.*
7 Gómez, *Selected Verses*, p. xxxiii-xxxvii.
8 See Luis O. Gómez, ed. *Barabuḍur: History and Significance of a Buddhist Monument*. Berkeley Buddhist Studies Series 2 (Berkeley: Asian Humanities Press, 1981).
9 *Bhagavad Gītā*, trans. Franklin Edgerton (Cambridge: Harvard University Press, 1972), Ch. 11.
10 Luis O. Gómez, "The Bodhisattva as Wonder-worker," in Lewis Lancaster, ed. *Prajñāpāramitā and Related Systems: Studies in Honor of Edward Conze* (Berkeley: Berkeley Buddhist Studies Series, 1977), p. 229.
11 *Visuddhamagga*, XII 135–139, p. 443–44.
12 Conze, *Buddhist Thought in India*, p. 183.
13 Gómez, "Bodhisattva as Wonderworker," p 230.
14 For a translation and discussion of Pure Land texts and schools, see Luis O. Gómez trans. *The Land of Bliss: The Paradise of the Buddha of Measureless Light* (Honolulu: University of Hawai'i Press, 1996).
15 Foreign visitors and domestic sources alike attest that Indian kings lived in luxurious palaces with a large retinue of attendants. See A. L. Basham, *The Wonder That Was India* (New York: Grove Press, 1959) p. 91.
16 See Eckel, *To See the Buddha*, p. 17 ff. for a discussion of the symbolism of the palace in Bhāvaviveka.
17 See *Śatapatha Brāhmaṇa*, V, 4, 3, 4; V, 2, 1, 24; V, 2, 2, 5.
18 Basham, p. 85.
19 R. E. Emerick, ed.,*The Sūtra of Golden Light: Being a Translation of the Suvarṇabhāsottamasūtra* (London: Luzac & Co., 1970), p. 58.
20 See *Cakkavattisīhanāda Sutta*, translated in Walshe, *Thus Have I Heard*, p. 395–406.
21 Warder, *Indian Buddhism*, p. 424.
22 See Joseph Campbell, *Hero with a Thousand Faces* (New Jersey: Princeton University Press, 1968).
23 *Gv*, p. 48–50 [C 56–58].
24 Ibid., p. 188–202 [C 175–87].
25 Ibid., p. 353–54 [C 316–17].
26 Ibid., p. 237, 239 [C 219–220].
27 Ibid.
28 Ibid., p. 158 [C 150].
29 Ibid., p 61 [C 67].
30 Ibid., p. 233–42 [C 215–24].
31 Ibid., p. 209 [C 194]; italics mine.
32 Ibid., p. 223 [C 208].
33 Chidester, p. 14–20.
34 Trans. "Illuminator" or "Resplendent," literally, "of the Sun."
35 *Gv*, p. 349–50 [C 330–31].
36 Ibid., p. 408 [C 366].

37 Ibid., p. 415 [C 374].
38 Ibid., p. 424 [C 383].
39 Ibid., p. 427–28 [C 386–87].
40 George J. Tanabe, Jr., *Myōe the Dreamkeeper: Fantasy and Knowledge in Early Kamakura Buddhism* (Cambridge: Harvard University Press, 1992), p. 1.
41 Ibid., p. 11.
42 Science fiction thus defined usually is differentiated from the closely related genre of *fantasy*, which does not necessarily base its created worlds on scientific theory.
43 "The Sūtra of the *King of Samādhis*, in *Studies in the Great Vehicle*, p. 54–55.
44 Ibid., p. 60–61.
45 *Gv* p. 4ff. [C 15ff.].
46 For some translations of Fa-tsang and discussions of the *Gv* and *Avataṃsaka* in the context of Hua-yen philosophy, see Thomas F. Cleary, *Entry Into the Inconceivable* (University of Hawaii Press, 1983); also Francis H. Cook, *Hua-yen Buddhism: the Jewel Net of Indra* (University Park: Pennsylvania State University Press, 1977); Garma C. C. Chang, *The Buddhist Teaching of Totality: The Philosophy of Hua Yen Buddhism* (University Park: Pennsylvania State University Press, 1971).
47 For example, *Gv*, p. 415 [C 374].
48 Ibid.
49 The terms translatable as "realm" that occur frequently in the *Gaṇḍavyūha* are *gocara*, *viṣaya*, and *dhātu*. Reference to entering buddha-fields (*buddha-kṣetra*) is, of course, pervasive as well.
50 *Gv*, p. 27 [C 37].

Chapter 5

1 See chapter 6 of *Abhidharmakośabhāśya* for one systematic presentation. See also the *Visuddhimagga*.
2 *Aṅguttara Nikāya*, IX, 40.
3 Paul J. Griffiths, *On Being Mindless: Buddhist Meditation and the Mind-Body Problem* (La Salle, Illinois: Open Court, 1986), p. 149n.
4 *Satipaṭṭhāna Sutta*, 30, translated in *The Middle Length Discourses of the Buddha: A New Translation of the Majjhima Nikāya*, trans. Bhikkhu Ñāṇamoli, ed., Bhikkhu Bodhi (Boston: Wisdom Publications, 1995), p. 149.
5 Nancy Falk, "Buddhist Pūja," *Encyclopedia of Religions*, ed. Mircea Eliade (New York, 1987).
6 The *Mahāparinirvāṇa Sutra* insists on the Buddha's complete absence after his death. Schopen aruges that the canonical version is a later recension that takes a polemical stand against monks' worship of saints and relics as living presences in the world. See Gregory Schopen, "Monks and the Relic Cult in the Mahāparinibbāna Sutta: An Old Misunderstanding in Regard to Monastic Buddhism," in *From Benares to Beijing: Essays on Buddhism and Chinese Religion in Honour of Jan Yün-Hua*, ed. Gregory Schopen and K. Shinohara (Okville, Ontario: Mosaic Books, 1991), p. 195–96.
7 *Sangīti Sutta* in Walshe, *Thus Have I Heard*, p. 479–510.
8 The word *kāya* can and does refer to the body in the physical sense, but it can also denote any collection of things or qualities. This initial contrasting

of the bodies of the Buddha, then, involves a word-play on the terms *kāya*, the first sense being used for the *rūpakāya* and the second sense for the *dharmakāya*.

9 Akira Hirakawa, "The Rise of Mahāyāna Buddhism and Its Relationship to the Worship of Stūpas," *Memoires of the Research Department of the Toyo Bunkyo* 22 (1963) p. 57–106.

10 It is worth noting that stūpa worship was itself probably a part of a more general phenomenon in ancient India of associating or symbolizing the presence of a deity with mounds of earth, stones, and natural portrusions in the earth. See Diana Eck, *Darśan: Seeing the Divine Image in India* (Chambersburg Pa.: Anima Books, 1981) p. 33–34. Śiavite linga worship is likely another variation on this phenomenon, although it probably proceded the stūpa. Ibid., p. 36.

11 Hirakawa, "Rise of Mahāyāna," p. 92. p. 346–47.

12 Reginald A. Ray, *Buddhist Staints in India: A Study in Buddhist Values and Orientations* (New York: Oxford University Press, 1994), p. 326–27.

13 Gregory Schopen, "An Old Inscription from Amarāvatī and the Cult of the Local Monastic Dead in Indian Buddhist Monasteries," *Journal of the International Association of Buddhist Studies* 14 (1991), p. 300.

14 Ray, *Buddhist Saints*, p. 381–86.

15 *Vissuddhamagga*, p. 230. Quoted in Williams, *Mahāyāna Buddhism*, p. 218.

16 Translation: The meditative concentration of one standing face-to-face with the present buddha. For summary of the text and selected translations, see Paul Harrison, "*Buddhānusmṛti* in the *Pratyutpanna-buddha-saṃmukhāvasthita-samādhi-sūtra*," *Journal of Indian Philosophy* 6 (1978), p. 35–57.

17 This text is no longer extant in Sanskrit, and the Sanskrit title is a reconstruction. Paul Williams suggests the more likely Sanskrit title was *Amitāyurbuddhā-nusmṛti Sūtra*.

18 Harrison, p. 43.

19 Ibid., p. 45.

20 *Sukhāvatīvyūha* 91–94 (larger). See Gomez, *Land of Bliss*, p. 92–93.

21 Inagaki Hisao, trans., *The Three Pure Land Sūtras* (Berkeley: Numata Center for Buddhist Translation and Research, 1995), p. 97.

22 Williams, *Mahāyāna Buddhism*, p. 256; *Three Pure Land Sūtras*, p. 97ff.

23 Paul Mus argues that even early Buddhism should not be considered purely aniconic in the sense that no images existed of the Buddha, since the stūpa itself is identified with the Buddha's body and is thus a representation of the Buddha's "mystical body." See Ray, p. 352–53, n. 7.

24 *Rgs* VII., 1–2, p. 35.

25 Eck, *Darśan.*

26 Lawrence A. Babb, "Glancing: Visual Interaction in Hinduism," *Journal of Anthropological Research* 37 (1981), p. 396–97.

27 *Buddhacarita*, 15.13, 15.15ff, 16.50. For translation, see E. H. Johnson, trans., *The Buddhacarita or Acts of the Buddha*, 2 vols. (Delhi: Oriental Books Reprint Corporation, 1972).

28 *Mahāparinibbāna Sutta* 5.5. Walshe, trans,. in *Thus Have I Heard*, p. 263.

29 *Das Mahāparinirvāṇasūtra*, ed. Ernst Walschmidt, Abhandlungen der deutchen Akademie der Wissenschaften zu Berlin, Philologish-historische Klasse, 1949–50, Berlin: Akademie Verlage, 1950–51), p. 394. Cited in Strong, *Experience of Buddhism*, p. 37.

30 *Saṃyutta Nikāya* 3:120, quoted and translated in Kevin Trainor, *Relics, Ritual, and Representation in Buddhism: Rematerializing the Sri Lankan Theravāda Tradition* (Cambridge: Cambridge University Press, 1997), p. 181.
31 Trainor, p. 182–83.
32 *Divyāvadāna*, E. B. Cowell and R. A. Neil, eds., (Cambridge: Cambridge University Press, 1886), p. 546–49; passage cited and translated in Strong, *Experience of Buddhism*, p. 39–41.
33 *Gv*, p. 23.
34 Ibid., p. 24.
35 Ray, *Buddhist Saints*, p. 127; *Divyāvadāna*, p. 387.
36 Ibid., p. 156; *Divyāvadāna*, p. 400–2.
37 While the first two bodies are corporeal (although the enjoyment body in a more subtle sense) the *dharmakāya*, as described above, obviously cannot be understood as a corporeal body. In Sarvāstivāda thought, the *dharmakāya* was the collection of dharmas, or qualities, that constituted buddhahood. In Theravāda and early Mahāyāna, the term *dharmakāya* came to be understood as the body or collection of Buddhist teachings, the Dharma, and thus identified with the sūtras. In later Mahāyāna thought, such as Asaṅga's, it took on more cosmic implications as signifying the ultimate truth, the *Dharmadhātu*, or emptiness. For a discussion of the development of the concept, see Paul Williams, *Mahāyāna Buddhism*, p. 167–84.
38 See Paul J. Griffiths and John Keenan, et. al. *The Realm of Awakening: Chapter Ten of Asaṅga's Mahāyānasaṅgraha* (New York: Oxford University Press, 1989) p. 49–51.
39 For a more detailed discussion, see John P. Keenan's introduction to *The Realm of Awakening*, p. 36–39.
40 As Tantra recognizes a proliferation of buddhas, bodhisattvas, and saint figures as objects of meditation and devotion, I will use the term "deities" to cover all of them.
41 Stephen Hodge, "Considerations on the Dating and Geographical Origins of the *Mahāvairocanābhisaṃbodhi-sūtra*," in *The Buddhist Forum III*, ed. Tadeusz Skorupski and Ulrich Pagel (London: School of Oriential and African Studies, University of London, 1994), p. 59.
42 Geoffry Samuel, *Civilized Shamans: Buddhism in Tibetan Societies* (Washington: Smithsonian Institution, 1993), p. 238.
43 For examples, see David Snellgrove, *Indo-Tibetan Buddhism: Indian Buddhists and Their Tibetan Successors* (Boston: Shambhala Publications, 1987), 247 ff. and *The Hevajra Tantra: A Critical Study* (London: Oxford University Press, 1959).
44 *Sādhanamāla*, ed. Benoytosh Bhattacharya (Baroda: Oriental Institute, 1968). Some translations of Tārā sādhanas from this text exist: see Conze's *Buddhist Meditation*, p. 133–39; Luis O. Gómez "Two Tantric Meditations: Visualizing the Deity," in *Buddhism in Practice*, ed. Donald S. Lopez, Jr. (Princeton: Princeton University Press, 1995), p. 318–27, and Martin Willson, *In Praise of Tārā: Songs of the Saviouress* (Boston: Wisdom Publications, 1986), p. 337–50.
45 *Sādhanamāla*, p. 208–9.
46 Ibid., p. 206.
47 Tibetans sometimes divide visualizations into "generation in front" and "self-generation." See H. H. the Dalia Lama, Tsong-ka-pa, and Jeffrey Hopkins, *Deity Yoga: In Action and Performance Tantra* (Ithica: Snow Lion Publications, 1981).

48 For more detailed descriptions, see Daniel Cozort, *Highest Yoga Tantra: an Introduction to the Esoteric Buddhism of Tibet* (Ithica: Snow Lion Publications, 1987); Tenzin Gyatso, the Dalai Lama, *The Kalachakra Tantra: Rite of Initiation*, trans. and ed., Jeffrey Hopkins (London: Wisdom Publications, 1985); David L. Snellgrove, *The Hevajra Tantra* (Oxford: Oxford University Press, 1959).

49 *Suvarṇaprabhāsa Sūtra*, ed. S. Bagchi, Buddhist Sanskrit Texts No. 8 (Darbhanga: Mithila Institute, 1967), p. 4–6.

50 Babb, p. 396–97.

51 Moshe Barasch's characterization of the assumption of resemblance between god and image in the ancient Greek world is equally applicable to the Indian world: "The idea of affinity between god and image, then, remains a feeling, an emotional disposition or attitude, rather than an explicitly stated doctrine." Moshe Barasche, *Icon: Studies in the History of an Idea* (New York: New York University Press, 1992), p. 41

52 Questions of how an artist knew what the deity "actually looks like," or what "image" the first such artist worked from are inevitably dead ends. Artists and practitioners undoubtedly worked from received images and descriptions of deities in texts and oral traditions that developed over centuries.

53 For more descriptions of iconic features of Tantric Buddhist deities, see Dipak C. Bhattacharyya, *Studies in Buddhist Iconography*, vols. 1 & 2 (New Delhi: Mahonar Book Service, 1978). For interpretations of the iconic symbols in some maṇḍalas, see Marylin M. Rhie, *Wisdom and Compassion: the Sacred Art of Tibet* (New York: Abrams, 1991). It is noteworthy, too, that much of this imagery taken from Hindu iconography and myth and adapted to Buddhist ideas.

Chapter 6

1 Richard Rorty, ed., *The Linguistic Turn: Recent Essays in Philosophical Method* (Chicago: University of Chicago Press, 1967).

2 Jay, *Downcast Eyes*, p. 186–87.

3 Levin, *Sites of Vision: The Discursive Construction of Sight in the History of Philosophy* (Cambridge: MIT Press, 1997), p. 3.

4 Ibid., p. 7.

5 Voltaire, *Philosophical Dictionary*, ed. and trans. Theodore Besterman (New York: MacMillan, 1910, 1972), p. 236; quoted in Jay, *Downcast Eyes*, p. 83.

6 For the most widely read introduction to Descartes's epistemology, see René Descartes, *Meditations on First Philosophy* (New York: Cambridge University Press 1986). For his specific theories of vision, see "Optics" in *Discourse on Method, Optics, Geometry, and Meteorology* (Indianapolis: Bobbs-Merrill, 1965).

7 Henri Bergson, *Time and Free Will: An Essay on the Immediate Data of Consciousness*, trans. F. L. Pogson (New York, 1960), p. 239.

8 Michel Foucault, *The Order of Things* (New York: Random House, 1973), p. 39.

9 Ibid., p. 132.

10 Francis Bacon, *The Great Instauration* in *The Works of Francis Bacon*, James Spedding et al., eds., 14 vols. (London, 1857–1864), vol. 4, p. 30. Cited in Jay, *Downcast Eyes*, p. 64.

11 Foucault, *Order of Things*, p. 43.
12 Chidester, *Word and Light*, p. 134.
13 Michel Foucault, *The Birth of the Clinic: An Archaeology of Medical Perception*, trans. Alan Sheridan (New York: Vintage, 1973), and *Discipline and Punish: The Birth of the Prison*, trans. Alan Sheridan (New York: Vintage, 1979), p. 195–230.
14 Edmund Husserl, *Phenomenology and the Crisis of Philosophy*, trans. Quentin Lauer, (New York: Harper & Row, 1962), p. 172.
15 Richard Rorty, *Philosophy and the Mirror of Nature* (Princeton: Princeton University Press, 1979).
16 Ibid., p. 45.
17 Edward W. Said, *Orientalism* (New York: Vintage, 1979), p. 239ff.
18 Tyler, "The Vision Quest in the West"; Johannes Fabian, *Time and the Other: How Anthropology Makes Its Object* (New York: Columbia University Press, 1983).
19 Luce Irigaray, *Speculum of the Other Woman*, trans. Gillian G. Gill (Ithica: Cornell University Press, 1985). For an analysis of Irigaray's notions on the relation between ocularcentrism and feminism, see Jay, *Downcast Eyes*, p. 523–42.
20 Irigaray, p. 362.
21 Levin, *The Opening of Vision*, especially p. 471–84.
22 *Gv*, p. 420 ff. [C 379ff.].
23 For a survey of these views, see Padmanabh S. Jaini, "On the *Sarvajñatvā* (Omniscience) of Mahāvira and the Buddha," in L. Cousins, A. Kunst, and K. R. Norman, eds., *Buddhist Studies in Honour of I. B. Horner* (Boston: D. Reidel, 1974).
24 Francisco Varela, Evan Thompson, and Eleanor Rosch, *The Embodied Mind: Cognitive Science and Human Experience* (Cambridge: MIT Press, 1991).
25 Maurice Merleau-Ponty, *The Visible and the Invisible*, ed. Claude Lefort, trans. Alphonso Lingis (Evanston: Northwestern University Press, 1968) pp 142–43. Also see his *Phenomenology of Perception*, especially part II, "The World as Perceived," p. 203–368, and "Eye and Mind," in *The Primacy of Perception*, ed. James M. Edie (Evanston: Northwestern University Press, 1964).
26 For critiques of and warnings about comparative endeavors, see Gerald James Larson, "Introduction: the 'Age-Old Distinction Between Same and Other'," in Gerald James Larson and Elliot Deutsch, eds., *Interpreting Across Boundaries: New Essays in Comparative Philosophy* (Princeton: Princeton University Press, 1988) and Donald Lopez, *Elaborations on Emptiness: Uses of the Heart Sūtra* (Princeton: Princeton University Press, 1996), p. 239–60.
27 Liz Wilson, *Charming Cadavers: Horrific Figurations of the Feminine in Indian Buddhist Hagiographic Literature* (Chicago: University of Chicago Press, 1996).
28 For some interesting, if controversial, examples, see Joanne C. Watkins, *Spirited Women: Gender, Religion and Cultural Identity in the Nepal Himalaya* (New York: Columbia University Press, 1996); Rita M. Gross, *Buddhism After Patriarchy: a Feminist History, Analysis, and Reconstruction of Buddhism* (Albany: State University of New York Press, 1993); Miranda Shaw, *Passionate Enlightenment: Women in Tantric Buddhism* (Princeton: Princeton University Press, 1994).
29 Bernard Faure, *Chan Insights and Oversights: An Epistemological Critique of the Chan Tradition* (Princeton: Princeton University Press, 1993), p. 159–166.

30 See, Jonathan Z. Smith, *Map is Not Territory: Studies in the History of Religions* (Leiden: E. J. Brill, 1978).
31 Faure, *Chan Insights*, p. 164.
32 Ibid., p. 160.
33 See, for instance, David Kalupahana, *A History of Buddhist Philosophy: Continuities and Discontinuities* (Honolulu: University of Hawai'i Press, 1992).

Bibliography

Anacker, Stefan. *Seven Works of Vasubhandu: the Buddhist Psychological Doctor.* Delhi: Motilal Banarsidas, 1986.

Anguttara Nikaya: Numerical Discourses of the Buddha: An Anthology of Suttas from the Anguttara Nikaya. Translated by Nyanaponika and Bhikkhu Bodhi. Walnut Creek, CA : Altamira Press, 1999.

Aṣṭasāhasrikā Prajñāpāramitā. Edited by P. L. Vaidya. Buddhist Sanskrit Texts No. 4. Darbhanga: Mithila Institute, 1960.

Austin, James H. *Zen and the Brain: Toward an Understanding of Meditation and Consciousness.* Cambridge: MIT Press, 1998.

Advayasiddhi. Edited by Malati J. Shendge. Baroda: Oriental Institute, 1964.

Babb, Lawrence A. "Glancing: Visual Interaction in Hinduism." *Journal of Anthropological Research* 37 (1981): 387–401.

Barasch, Moshe. *Icon: Studies in the History of an Idea.* New York: New York University Press, 1992.

Basham, A. L. *The Wonder That Was India.* New York: Grove Press, 1959.

Bergson, Henri. *Time and Free Will: An Essay on the Immediate Data of Consciousness.* Translated by F. L. Pogson. New York, 1960.

Bhagavad Gītā. Translated by Franklin Edgerton. Cambridge: Harvard University Press, 1972.

Bhattacharyya, Benoytosh. *An Introduction to Buddhist Esotericism.* London: Oxford, 1932, 2nd ed., 1964.

Bhattacharyya, Dipak C. *Studies in Buddhist Iconography.* 2 vols. New Delhi: Mahonar Book Service, 1978.

Boisselier, Jean and David L. Snellgrove. *The Image of the Buddha.* London: Serinda Publications/UNESCO, 1978.

Boman, Thorlieff. *Hebrew Thought Compared with Greek.* Translated by Jules L. Moreau. Philadelphia: Westminster Press, 1960.

Boyd, Richard. "Metaphor and Theory Change." In *Metaphor and Thought,* Andrew Ortony, ed. 2nd edition. Cambridge: Cambridge University Press, 1993.

Brown, C. Mackenzie. "Purāṇa as Scripture: From Sound to Image of the Holy Word in the Hindu Tradition." *History of Religions,* 26, 1 (1986), 68–86.

Buddhaghoṣa. *Path of Purification (Visuddhamagga)*. Translated by Bhikkhu Ñyāṇamoli. Colombo: A. Semage, 1964.

Campbell, Joseph. *Hero with a Thousand Faces*. New Jersey: Princeton University Press, 1968.

Candrakirti. *Mūlamadhyamakakārikās de Nāgārjuna avec la Commentaire di Candrakirti*. Edited by Louis de La Vallée Poussin. Osnabrück: Biblio Verlag, 1970.

——. *Lucid Exposition of the Middle Way: The Essential Chapters from the Prassanapada of Candrakirti*. Translated by Mervyn Sprung. Boulder: Prajna Press, 1979.

Chang, Garma C. C. *The Buddhist Teaching of Totality: The Philosophy of Hwa Yen Buddhism*. University Park: Pennsylvania State University Press, 1971.

Chidester, David. *Word and Light: Seeing, Hearing, and Religious Discourse*. Urbana and Chicago: University of Illinois Press, 1992.

Cleary, Thomas F. *Entry Into the Inconceivable*. University of Hawaii Press, 1983.

——. *Entry into the Realm of Reality: the Text*. Boston & Shaftesbury: Shambala, 1989.

Collins, Steven. "Notes on Some Oral Aspects of Pāli Literature." *Indo-Iranian Journal* 35 (1992): 121–135.

Conze, Edward. *Buddhism: Its Essence and Development*. New York: Harper, 1959.

——. *Buddhist Thought in India*. Ann Arbor: University of Michigan Press, 1967.

——. *The Prajñāpāramitā Literature*. London: Mouton & Co., 1960.

——. "The Development of Prajñāpāramitā Thought." In *Thirty Years of Buddhist Studies*. Oxford: Bruno Cassirer, 1967.

——. *The Large Sūtra on Perfection Wisdom (Pañcavimśatisāhasrikā)*. Berkeley: University of California Press, 1975.

——. *The Perfection of Wisdom in Eight Thousand Lines and its Verse Summary*. San Francisco: Four Seasons Foundation, 1973.

——. *Perfect Wisdom: The Short Prajñāpāramitā Texts*. London: Luzac & Co Ltd., 1973; reprint, Devon, England: Buddhist Publishing Group, 1993.

Cook, Francis H. *Hua-yen Buddhism: the Jewel Net of Indra*. University Park: Pennsylvania State University Press, 1977.

Coomaraswamy, Ananda. *History of Indian and Indonesian Art*. New York: E. Weyhe, 1927.

Cozort, Daniel. *Highest Yoga Tantra: An Introduction to the Esoteric Buddhism of Tibet*. Ithica: Snow Lion Publications, 1987.

Dalia Lama, Tsong-ka-pa, and Jeffrey Hopkins. *Deity Yoga: In Action and Performance Tantra*. Ithica: Snow Lion Publications, 1981.

Dalai Lama. *The Kalachakra Tantra: Rite of Initiation*. Translated and edited by Jeffrey Hopkins. London: Wisdom Publications, 1985.

Dasgupta, Sh. B. *An Introduction to Tantric Buddhism*. Berkeley: University of California Press, 1974.

Dasgupta, Surendradnath. *History of Indian Philosophy*. 5 vols. Delhi: Motilal Banarsidass, 1922, 1992.

Descartes, René. *Discourse on Method, Optics, Geometry, and Meteorology*. Indianapolis: Bobbs-Merrill, 1965.

——. *Meditations on First Philosophy*. New York: Cambridge University Press, 1986.

Eck, Diana. *Darśan: Seeing the Divine Image in India*. Chambersburg, Pa.: Anima Books, 1981.

Eckel, Malcolm David. *To See the Buddha: A Philosopher's Quest for the Meaning of Emptiness*. Princeton: Princeton University Press, 1992.

Edgerton, Franklin. *Buddhist Hybrid Sanskrit Grammar and Dictionary*. Delhi: Motilal Banarsidass, 1993.

Ellul, Jaques. *The Humiliation of the Word*. Translated by Joyce Main Hanks. Grand Rapids, Mich.: Eerdmans, 1985.

Emerick, R. E., ed. *The Sūtra of Golden Light: Being a Translation of the Suvarṇabhāsottamasūtra*. London: Luzac & Co., 1970.

Fabian, Johannes. *Time and the Other: How Anthropology Makes Its Object*. New York: Columbia University Press, 1983.

Falk, Nancy. "Buddhist Pūja." *Encyclopedia of Religions*, ed. Mircea Eliade. New York, 1987.

Faure, Bernard. *Chan Insights and Oversights: An Epistemological Critique of the Chan Tradition*. Princeton: Princeton University Press, 1993.

Foster, Hal, ed. *Vision and Visuality*. Seattle: Bay Press, 1988.

Foucault, Michel. *The Birth of the Clinic: An Archaeology of Medical Perception*. Translated by Alan Sheridan. New York: Vintage, 1973.

——. *The Order of Things: An Archeology of the Human Sciences*. New York: Random House, 1973.

——. *Discipline and Punish: The Birth of the Prison*. Translated by Alan Sheridan. New York: Vintage, 1979.

Foucher, A. *The Beginning of Buddhist Art and Other Essays in Indian and Central Asian Archeology*. Paris: P. Geuthner, 1917.

Frauwallner, Eric. *Studies in Abhidharma Literature and the Origins of Buddhist Philosophical Systems*. Translated by Sophie Francis Kidd. State University of New York Press, 1995.

Freud, Sigmund. *Civilization and Its Discontents*. Translated by James Strachey. New York, 1961.

Edgerton, Franklin. *Buddhist Hybrid Sanskrit Grammar and Dictionary*. 2 vols. New Haven: Yale University Press, 1953. Reprint ed. Delhi: Motilal Banarsidass, 1993.

Gaṇḍavyūha Sūtra. Edited by P. L. Vaidya. Buddhist Sanskrit Texts, No. 5. Darbhanga: Mithila Institute, 1960.

Garfield, Jay L. *The Fundamental Wisdom of the Middle Way: Nāgārjuna's Mūlamadhyamakakārikā*. New York: Oxford University Press, 1995.

Gombrich, Richard. "How the Mahāyāna Began." In *The Buddhist Forum*, vol. 1, Tadeusz Skorupski, ed. London: School of Oriental and African Studies, 1990.

Gómez, Luis O. *Selected Verses from the Gaṇḍavyūha: Text, Critical Apparatus and Translation*. Unpublished doctoral dissertation, Yale, 1967.

——. "The Bodhisattva as Wonder-worker." In *Prajñāpāramitā and Related Systems: Studies in Honor of Edward Conze*, Lewis Lancaster, ed. Berkeley: Berkeley Buddhist Studies Series, 1977.

——, ed. *Barabuḍur: History and Significance of a Buddhist Monument.*. Berkeley Buddhist Studies Series 2. Berkeley: Asian Humanities Press, 1981.

—— and Jonathan Silk, eds. *Studies in the Literature of the Great Vehicle: Three Mahāyāna Texts*. Ann Arbor: Collegiat Institute for the Study of Buddhist Literature and Center for South and Southeast Asian Studies, University of Michigan, 1989.

——. "Two Tantric Meditations: Visualizing the Deity." In *Buddhism in Practice*, ed. Donald S. Lopez, Jr., 318–327. Princeton: Princeton University Press, 1995.

——. *The Land of Bliss: The Paradise of the Buddha of Measureless Light.* Honolulu: University of Hawai'i Press, 1996.

Gonda, Jan. *Eye and Gaze in the Veda.* Amsterdam-London: North Holland Publishing Company, 1969.

Goodall, Dominic, ed. *Hindu Scriptures.* Berkeley: University of California Press, 1996.

Goody, Jack, ed. *Literacy in Traditional Societies.* Cambridge: Cambridge University Press, 1968.

Griffiths, Paul J. *On Being Mindless: Buddhist Meditation and the Mind-Body Problem.* La Salle, Illinois: Open Court, 1986.

Griffiths, Paul J. and John Keenan, et al. *The Realm of Awakening: Chapter Ten of Asaṅga's Mahāyānasaṅgraha.* New York: Oxford University Press, 1989.

Gross, Rita M. *Buddhism After Patriarchy: A Feminist History, Analysis, and Reconstruction of Buddhism.* Albany: State University of New York Press, 1993.

Guenther, Herbert V. *Philosophy and Psychology in the Abhidharma.* Berkeley: Shambala Press, 1976.

Handelman, Susan A. *The Slayers of Moses: The Emergence of Rabbinic Interpretation in Modern Literary Theory.* Albany: State University of New York Press, 1987.

Harrison, P. M. "Buddhānusmṛti in the Pratyutpanna-buddha-saṃmukhāvasthita-samādhi-sūtra." *Journal of Indian Philosophy* 9 (1978): 35–57.

Hattori, Masaki. *Dignāga, On Perception, Being the Pratyakṣapariccheda of Dignāga's Pramāṇasamuccaya.* Cambridge: Harvard University Press, 1968.

Hirakawa, Akira. "The Rise of Mahāyāna Buddhism and Its Relationship to the Worship of Stūpas." In *Memoires of the Research Department of the Toyo Bunkyo* 22 (1963): 57–106.

——. *A History of Indian Buddhism From Śākyamuni to Early Mahāyāna.* Translated and Edited by Paul Groner. Honolulu: University of Hawaii Press, 1990.

Hisao, Inagaki, trans. *The Three Pure Land Sūtras.* Berkeley: Numata Center for Buddhist Translation and Research, 1995.

Hodge, Stephen. "Considerations on the Dating and Geographical Origins of the *Mahāvairocanābhisaṃbodhi-sūtra.*" In *The Buddhist Forum III*, ed. Tadeusz Skorupski and Ulrich Pagel. London: School of Oriental and African Studies, University of London, 1994.

Hopkins, Jeffrey, trans. and ed. *Tantra in Tibet: The Great Exposition of Secret Mantra.* George Allen & Unwin, 1977.

Huntington, C. W., Jr. and Geshé Namgyal Wangchen. *The Emptiness of Emptiness: An Introduction to Early Indian Mādhyamika.* Honolulu: University of Hawaii Press, 1989.

Husserl, Edmund. *Phenomenology and the Crisis of Philosophy.* Translated by Quentin Lauer. New York: Harper & Row, 1962.

Irigaray, Luce. *Speculum of the Other Woman.* Translated by Gillian G. Gill. Ithica: Cornell University Press, 1985.

Ives, Waldo. "Nagarjuna and Analytic Philosophy, II." *Philosophy East and West* 28, 3 (July 1978): 287–98.

Jackson, Roger R. "Matching Concepts: Deconstructive and Foundationalist Tendencies in Buddhist Thought." *Journal of the American Academy of Religion* 57, 3 (1989): 561–589.

Jaini, Padmanabh S. "On the *Sarvajñatvā* (Omniscience) of Mahāvira and the Buddha." In *Buddhist Studies in Honour of I. B. Horner*, ed. L. Cousins, A. Kunst, and K. R. Norman. Boston: D. Reidel, 1974.

Jay, Martin. *Downcast Eyes: The Denigration of Vision in Twentieth-Century French Thought*. Berkeley: University of California Press, 1994.

Jayatilleke, K. N. *Early Buddhist Theory of Knowledge*. London: George Allen & Unwin Ltd., 1963.

Johnson, E. H., trans. *The Buddhacarita or Acts of the Buddha*. 2 vols. Delhi: Oriental Books Reprint Corporation, 1972.

Jonas, Hans. *The Phenomenon of Life: Toward a Philosophical Biology*. New York: Harper & Row, 1966.

Kalupahana, David J. *Nagarjuna: The Philosophy of the Middle Way*. Albany: State University of New York Press, 1986.

——. *A History of Buddhist Philosophy: Continuities and Discontinuities*. Honolulu: University of Hawaii Press, 1992.

Kinnard, Jacob. *Imaging Wisdom: Seeing and Knowing in the Art of Indian Buddhism*. Surrey: Curzon Press, 1999.

Klimkeit, Hans-Joachim. *Gnosis on the Silk Road: Gnostic Texts from Central Asia*. San Francisco: Harper Collins, 1993.

Lakoff, George. "Contemporary Theory of Metaphor." In *Metaphor and Thought*, Andrew Ortony, ed. 2nd edition. Cambridge: Cambridge University Press, 1993.

Lakoff, George and Mark Johnson. *Metaphors We Live By*. Chicago: University of Chicago Press, 1980.

Lamotte, Étienne. "The Assessment of Textual Interpretation in Buddhism." Translated by Sara Boin-Webb in *Buddhist Hermeneutics*, ed. Donald Lopez. Honolulu: University of Hawaii Press, 1988.

——. *History of Indian Buddhism: From the Origins to the Śaka Era*. Translated by Sara Webb-Boin. Lauvin: Institut Orientaliste, 1988.

Lancaster, Lewis, ed. *Prajñāpāramitā and Related Systems: Studies in Honor of Edward Conze*. Berkeley Studies Series 1. Berkeley: University of California Press, 1977.

Larson, Gerald James. "Introduction: the 'Age-Old Distinction Between Same and Other'." In *Interpreting Across Boundaries: New Essays in Comparative Philosophy*, eds. Gerald James Larson and Elliot Deutsch. Princeton: Princeton University Press, 1988.

——. "Contra Pluralism." *Soundings* 73.2–3 (Summer/Fall 1990): 303–326.

Levin, David Michael. *The Opening of Vision: Nihilism and the Postmodern Situation*. New York: Routledge, 1988.

——, ed. *Sites of Vision: The Discursive Construction of Sight in the History of Philosophy*. Cambridge: MIT Press, 1997.

Lopez, Donald S., Jr. "Interpretation of Mahāyāna Sūtras." In *Buddhist Hermeneutics*, ed. Donald S. Lopez, Jr. Honolulu: University of Hawaii Press, 1988.

——. "Authority and Orality in the Mahāyāna." *Numen* 42 (1995): 21–47.

——. *Elaborations on Emptiness: Uses of the Heart Sūtra*. Princeton: Princeton University Press, 1996.

Luk, Charles, trans. *The Vimalakirti Nirdeśa Sūtra*. Boston: Shambala, 1990.

Das Mahāparinirvāṇasūtra. Edited by Ernst Walschmidt. Abhandlungen der deutchen Akademie der Wissenschaften zu Berlin, Philologish-historische Klasse, 1949–50. Berlin: Akademie Verlage, 1950–51.

Majjhima-Nikāya. Edited by Robert Charles. London: Luzac, for the Pali Text Society, 1960.

Matilal, Bimal Krishna. *Epistemology, Logic, and Grammar in Indian Philosophical Analysis*. Paris: Mouton, 1971.

MacLuhan, Marshall *The Gutenberg Galaxy*. Toronto: University of Toronto Press, 1962.

McMahan, David L. "Orality, Writing and Authority in South Asian Buddhism: Visionary Literature and the Struggle for Legitimacy in the Mahāyāna." *History of Religions*. 37, 3 (1998), 249–274.

Merleau-Ponty, Maurice. *The Phenomenology of Perception*. Translated by Colin Smith. London: Routledge & Kegan Paul, 1962.

——. *The Primacy of Perception*. Edited by James M. Edie. Evanston, Ill: Northwestern University Press, 1964.

——. *The Visible and the Invisible*. Edited by Claude Lefort, translated by Alphonso Lingis. Evanston: Northwestern University Press, 1964.

Miles, Margaret R. "Image." In *Critical Terms for Religious Studies*, ed. Mark C. Taylor, 160–72. Chicago: University of Chicago Press, 1998.

Mohanty, Jitendra Nath. *Reason and Tradition in Indian Thought: An Essay on the Nature of Indian Philosophical Thinking*. Oxford: Clarendon Press, 1992.

Monier-Williams, Monier. *A Sanskrit-English Dictionary*. New Delhi: Marwah, 1899.

Murti, T. R. V. *The Central Philosophy of Buddhism: A Study of the Mādhyamika System*. London: George Allen and Unwin Ltd., 2nd ed., 1960.

——. "*Saṃvṛti* and *Paramārtha* in the Mādhyamika and Advaita Vedānta." In *The Problem of the Two Truths in Buddhism and Vedanta*, ed. Mervyn Sprung, 9–26. Boston: Reidel, 1973.

Nagao, Gadjin M. *Mādhymamika and Yogacāra: A Study of Mahāyāna Philosophies*. Translated by Leslie Kawamura. Albany: State University of New York Press, 1991.

Nāgārjuna. *Root Verses on the Middle Way* (*Mūlamadhyamakakarikas*). Edited by J. W. de Jong. Madras: Adyar Library and Research Center, 1977.

Nakamura, Hajime. *Indian Buddhism: A Survey with Bibliographical Notes*. Japan: Kufs Publication, 1980.

Ñānananda, Bhikkhu. *Concept and Reality in Early Buddhist Thought: an Essay on Papañca and Papañca-saññā-sankha*. Ceylon: Buddhist Publication Society, 1971.

Ñāṇamoli, Bhikkhu and Bhikkhu Bodhi, eds. and trans. *The Middle Length Discourses of the Buddha: A New Translation of the Majjhima Nikāya*. Boston: Wisdom Publications, 1995.

Ong, Walter J. *Orality and Literacy: The Technologizing of the Word*. New York: Methuen, 1982.

Ortony, Andrew, ed. *Metaphor and Thought*. 2nd edition. Cambridge: Cambridge University Press, 1993.

——. "Metaphor, Language, and Thought." In *Metaphor and Thought*, ed. Andrew Ortony, 1–21. 2nd edition. Cambridge: Cambridge University Press, 1993.

Prajñā-pāramitā-ratna-guṇa-saṃcaya-gāthā. Edited by Akira Yuyama. Cambridge: Cambridge University Press, 1976.

Radman, Zdravko. *Metaphors: Figures of the Mind*. Dordrecht, The Netherlands: Kluwer Academic Publishers, 1997.

Rawlinson, Andrew. "The Position of the *Aṣṭasāhasrikā Prajñāpāramitā* in the Development of Early Mahāyāna." In *Prajñāpāramitā and Related Systems: Studies in Honor of Edward Conze*, ed. Lewis Lancaster, 3–34. Berkeley Studies Series 1. Berkeley: University of California Press, 1977.

Ray, Reginald A. *Buddhist Staints in India: A Study in Buddhist Values and Orientations*. New York: Oxford University Press, 1994.

Rhie, Marylin M. *Wisdom and Compassion: the Sacred Art of Tibet*. New York: Abrams, 1991.

Richard Rorty, ed. *The Linguistic Turn: Recent Essays in Philosophical Method*. Chicago: University of Chicago Press, 1967.

——. *Philosophy and the Mirror of Nature*. Princeton: Princeton University Press, 1979.

Saddharmapuṇḍarīkasūtra. Edited by P. L. Vaidya. Budhist Sanskrit Texts, No. 6. Darbhanga: Mithila Institute, 1960.

Sādhanamāla. Edited by Benoytosh Bhattacharya. Baroda: Oriental Institute, 1968.

Sagal, Paul T. "Nagarjuna's Paradox (That All Views Are Absurd)." *American Philosophical Quarterly* 29, 1 (Jan 1992): 79–86.

Said, Edward W. *Orientalism*. New York: Vintage, 1979.

Saṃyutta-Nikāya of the Sutta-Pitaka. Edited by Leon Feer. London: Published for the Pali Text Society by Luzac, 1960–70.

Śankara. *Dṛg-dṛśya-vivek: An Inquiry into the Nature of the 'Seer' and the 'Seen.'* Translated by Swami Nikhilananda. Mysore: Sri Ramakrishna Ashrama, 1970.

Schopen, Gregory. *Bones, Stones, and Buddhist Monks: Collected Papers on Archeology, Epigraphy, and Texts in Monastic Buddhism in India*. Honolulu: University of Hawai'i Press, 1997.

——. "Monks and the Relic Cult in the Mahāparinibbāna Sutta: An Old Misunderstanding in Regard to Monastic Buddhism." In *From Benaras to Beijing: Essays on Buddhism and Chinese Religion in Honour of Jan Yün-Hua*, ed. Gregory Schopen and K. Shinohara, 187–201. Okville, Ontario: Mosaic Press, 1991.

——. "An Old Inscription from Amarāvatī and the Cult of the Local Monastic Dead in Indian Buddhist Monasteries." *Journal of the International Association of Buddhist Studies* 14, 2 (1991): 281–329.

——. "The Phrase '*sa pṛthivīpradeśaā caityabhūto bhavet* in the *Vajracchedikā*: Notes on the Cult of the Book in the Mahāyāna." *Indo-Iranian Journal* 17 (1975): 147–181.

Shaw, Miranda. *Passionate Enlightenment: Women in Tantric Buddhism*. Princeton: Princeton University Press, 1994.

Smart, Ninian. *Doctrine and Argument in Indian Philosophy*. London, Allen and Unwin, 1964.

Smith, Jonathan Z. *Map is Not Territory: Studies in the History of Religions*. Leiden: E. J. Brill, 1978.

Snellgrove, David L. *The Hevajra Tantra*. Oxford: Oxford University Press, 1959.

——. *Indo-Tibetan Buddhism: Indian Buddhists and Their Tibetan Successors*. Boston: Shambhala, 1987.

Stcherbatsky, Th. *The Central Conception of Buddhism and the Meaning of the Word "Dharma."* Delhi: Motilal Banarsidas, 1922, 1970.

Streng, Frederick Jr. *Emptiness: A Study in Religious Meaning*. Nashville: Abingdon Press, 1967.

The Sutta Nipāta. Translated by Dines Anderson and Helmer Smith. London: Pali Text Society, 1913.

Suvarṇaprabhāsa Sūtra. Edited by S. Bagchi. Buddhist Sanskrit Texts No. 8. Darbhanga: Mithila Institute, 1967.

Suvikrāntavikrāmīparipṛcchā Prajñāpāramitā Sūtra. Edited by Ryusho Hikata. Fukuoka: Kyushu University, 1958.

Suzuki, Daisetz Teitaro. *On Indian Mahayana Buddhism*. Edited by Edward Conze. New York, Harper & Row, 1968.

——. *Zen Buddhism: Selected Writings of D. T. Suzuki*. Edited by William Barret. Garden City, N.Y.: Anchor Books, 1956.

Sweetser, Eve. *From Etymology to Pragmatics: Metaphorical and Cultural Aspects of Semantic Culture*. Cambridge: Cambridge University Press, 1990.

Tanabe, George J., Jr. *Myōe the Dreamkeeper: Fantasy and Knowledge in Early Kamakura Buddhism*. Cambridge: Harvard University Press, 1992.

Tāranātha. *Taranatha's Geschichte des Buddhismus in Indien*. Translated by Anton Schiefner. Tokyo: Suzuki Gakujutsu Zaidan, 1965.

Tucci, Guiseppe. *The Religions of Tibet*. Berkeley: University of California Press, 1970.

——. *Minor Buddhist Texts*. 2 vols. Delhi: Motilal Banarsidass, 1986.

Tuck, Andrew P. *Comparative Philosophy and the Philosophy of Scholarship: On Western Interpretation of Nagarjuna*. New York: Oxford University Press, 1990.

Trainor, Kevin. *Relics, Ritual, and Representation in Buddhism: Rematerializing The Sri Lankan Theravāda Tradition*. Cambridge: Cambridge University Press, 1997.

Tyler, Stephen A. "The Vision Quest or What the Mind's Eye Sees." *Journal of Anthropological Research*, 40, 1 (1984): 23–39.

Vajracchedikā Prajñāpāramitā. Edited by Edward Conze. Rome: Serie Orientale Roma XIII, 1957.

Varela, Francisco, Evan Thompson, and Eleanor Rosch. *The Embodied Mind: Cognitive Science and Human Experience*. Cambridge: MIT Press, 1991.

Vasubhandu. *Abhidharmakośabhāṣyam*. Edited by Louis de La Vallée Poussin, Eng trans. Leo M. Pruden. Berkeley: Asian Humanities Press, 1990.

Walshe, Maurice. *Thus Have I Heard: The Long Discourses of the Buddha*. London: Wisdom Publications, 1987.

Warder, A. K. "The Concept of a Concept." *Journal of Indian Philosophy* 1, 2 (1970): 181–196.

——. *Indian Buddhism*. Delhi: Motilal Banarsidas, 1970.

Warren, Henry Clarke. *Buddhism in Translations*. Cambridge: Harvard University Press, 1896; reprint, New York: Athuneum, 1984.

Watkins, Joanne C. *Spirited Women: Gender, Religion and Cultural Identity in the Nepal Himalaya*. New York: Columbia University Press, 1996.

Wayman, Alex. *The Buddhist Tantras: Light on Indo-Tibetan Esotericism*. New York: Samuel Weiser, 1973.

——. *The Yoga of the Guhyasamāja Tantra: The Arcane Lore of Forty Verses*. Delhi: Motilal Banarsidass, 1977.

——. "The Buddhist Theory of Vision." In *Buddhist Insight: Essays by Alex Wayman*, ed. George Elder. Delhi: Motilal Banarsidas, 1984, p. 153–61.

Williams, Paul. *Mahāyāna Buddhism: the Doctrinal Foundations*. London and New York: Routledge, 1989.

——. "Some Aspects of Language and Construction in the Madhyamaka." *Journal of Indian Philosophy* 8 (1980): 1–45.

Willson, Martin. *In Praise of Tārā: Songs of the Saviouress*. Boston: Wisdom Publications, 1986.

Wilson, Liz. *Charming Cadavers: Horrific Figurations of the Feminine in Indian Buddhist Hagiographic Literature*. Chicago: University of Chicago Press, 1996.

Wolfson, Elliot R. *Through a Speculum That Shines: Vision and Imagination in Medieval Jewish Mysticism*. Princeton: Princeton University Press, 1994.

Yūichi, Kajiyana. "Prajñāpāramitā and the Rise of Mahāyāna." In *Buddhist Spirituality*, ed. Takeuchi Yoshinori. New York: Crossroad, 1993.

Index

Abhidharma 23–4, 31, 49, 97–8
all-knowledge (*sarvajñatā*) 78–9, 189–90
Amitābha 117, 149–52
Asaṇga 48, 115–6, 159–61
Avalokiteśvara 1, 124

Babb, Lawrence 153–54, 170–1
Bacon, Francis 184–5
Barach, Moshe 212
Bergson, Henri 184
Bhagavad Gītā 99, 114
Bhartṛhari 47–8
Bhāvaviveka 50, 68, 70–1, 113
bodhisattva 29–31, 105, 115–6, 121–30
Bodhnath 1
bodies of the Buddha 159–61, 211
Boyd, Richard 64–5
buddha-fields (*buddhakṣetra*) 116–21, 148
Buddhavacana 16, 86–9, 98–104

Chidester, David 74–5, 126–7, 181, 185
Chih-i 102–3
Collins, Steven 87–8
Conze, Edward 77, 152
Cousins, Lance 88
cults of the book 93–5, 108

darśan 114, 152–8, 170–1, 194
devotional practices 114, 147–77
Descartes, René 183–6, 190
dharmas 19, 23–9, 80, 115
Dharmakāya (Dharma-body) 92–3, 147–8, 206, 209–10, 211
dialectic (see *paradoxical dialectic)*
Dignaga 48–50
Dravidian languages 59–62

Eck, Diana 153
Eckel, Malcolm David 41, 50
enjoyment body (*sāṃbhogikakāya*) 120
emptiness 26–39, 70–1, 116, 120, 133–7, 174, 190

Faur, José 61, 203
Faure, Bernard 193–4
Foucault, Michel 184–5

Gómez, Luis 115–6
Gombrich, Richard 89–90
Griffiths, Paul J. 145

Hirakawa, Akira 91–2, 148, 206
Hodge, Stephen 162–3
Hua-yen 134, 141

image worship 152–8
insight (*vipaśyana, vipassanā*) 23, 69, 73
interpenetration 134–7, 141
ineffability 21–2, 25–6, 33–4

Irigaray, Luce 186–7

Jay, Martin 7, 181–3
Jayatilleke, K. N. 21, 52
Johnson, Mark 3, 63–5
Jonas, Hans 58–9, 74–6, 181–2

Kalupahana, David 200, 214
Kamalaśīla 70–1, 73, 113
kingship 116–21
kūṭāgāra 84, 118, 170

Levin, David 7, 182, 188
Lakoff, George 3, 63–5, 203
language and concepts 43–7
  devaluation of 3–4, 15–53
  early Buddhism 17–23
  Mahāyāna 25–33
Lopez, Donald S., Jr. 15, 89

maṇḍala 6, 162, 164–77
Maitreya's tower 127–8, 136–8, 170, 189
meditation 143–77
Merleau-Ponty, Maurice 55, 96, 111, 181, 191–2
metaphor 55–82
  concretization of 131–2, 137–42, 174–7
  contemporary theories 3, 62–5
  cutting 72–3, 82
  entering a realm 72–3, 82, 137–8, 209
  for knowledge 56–62, 71–82
  light 72–3, 82, 131–2, 137
  penetration 72–3, 82, 137–8
  spatial 74–82, 137–40
  tactile 67–8
  visual 56–82, 137–42
Murti, T. R. V. 20, 195
Mus, Paul 210

Nāgārjuna 33, 42, 50
Nagao, Gadjin 41
Nakamura, Hajime 113, 152
nirvāṇa 22, 29, 77

ocularcentrism 180–96
  in ancient Greece 7
  in Buddhist traditions 13–4, 187–96
  in modern Western thought 13–4, 180–8
Ong, Walter 96–7, 206–7
orality 85–9, 108–9
Ortony, Andrew 63

paradoxical dialectic 33–43, 133–7, 195
perception 46–53
Perfection of Wisdom literature 10, 27–43, 92–4, 133–7, 152
*pramāṇa*s 18, 47–53
prapañca 19, 45, 199
pratyakṣa 47–51

Ray, Reginald A. 148, 156–7
Rorty, Richard 181–2, 185–6
Ruciraketu 169
recollection of the Buddha (*Buddhānusmṛti*) 149–52

sādhana 161–77, 191
Said, Edward 186
Samantabhadra 127–30
Samuel, Geoffry 163
saṃjñā 44–6
Sautrāntikas 19, 31
Sartre, Jean Paul 191
Sarvāstvāda 19, 23–4, 26, 31
Schopen, Gregory 9, 93, 148, 209
skilful means (*upāya*) 102, 105–6, 115, 159
Smith, Jonathan Z. 193–4, 207
somaticization of doctrine 174–7
space (ākāśa) 74–82, 108, 139–40, 188
spatialization of time 79–81, 139–40, 188–89
*śravaka*s (hearers) 11, 87, 101–2, 104–5, 107
strategies of legitimation 99–110
stūpas 1, 91, 118, 148
stūpa cults 91–3, 148
Sweetser, Eve 57, 59
symbolic fantasy 131

Tanabe, George J. 130

Tantra 161–77, 191
Tārā 165–8
thaumaturgy 114–6
Trainor, Kevin 155
Tylor, Stephen 58–62, 186
Two truths 33

unanswered questions 20–2
Upaniṣads 51–3, 62

Varela, Francisco 191
Vasubhandu 48
Veda 18, 52
vikalpa 45–6
vipaśyanā (*see insight*)
vision
  in ancient Greece 57–9, 75
  and doctrine 130–42
  and hearing 8, 74–6, 105–10
  in Indo-European history 56–62
  and writing 95–9
visionary literature 83–110, 111–42, 168–72
visuality 55
visualization practices 106, 114, 117, 143–77, 191
Voltaire 183

Warder 121
Williams, Paul 44, 106
Wilson 193
writing 9, 89–9, 194

Zen 43